formatio
TRADITION. EXPERIENCE.
TRANSFORMATION.

Formatio books from InterVarsity Press follow the rich tradition of the church in the journey of spiritual formation. These books are not merely about being informed, but about being transformed by Christ and conformed to his image. Formatio stands in IVP's evangelical publishing tradition by integrating God's Word with spiritual practice and by prompting readers to move from inward change to outward witness. IVP uses the chambered nautilus for Formatio, a symbol of spiritual formation because of its continual spiral journey outward as it moves from its center. We believe that each of us is made with a deep desire to be in God's presence. Formatio books help us to fulfill our deepest desires and to become our true selves in light of God's grace.

Developing a Conversational
Relationship with God

HEARING GOD

DALLAS WILLARD

IVP Books

An imprint of InterVarsity Press
Downers Grove, Illinois

InterVarsity Press
P.O. Box 1400, Downers Grove, IL 60515-1426
World Wide Web: www.ivpress.com
E-mail: email@ivpress.com

InterVarsity Press® *is the book-publishing division of InterVarsity Christian Fellowship/USA*®*, a student movement active on campus at hundreds of universities, colleges and schools of nursing in the United States of America, and a member movement of the International Fellowship of Evangelical Students. For information about local and regional activities, write Public Relations Dept., InterVarsity Christian Fellowship/USA, 6400 Schroeder Rd., P.O. Box 7895, Madison, WI 53707-7895, or visit the IVCF website at* <www.intervarsity.org>.

Scripture quotations, unless otherwise noted, are from the New Revised Standard Version of the Bible, *copyright 1989 by the Division of Christian Education of the National Council of the Churches of Christ in the USA. Used by permission. All rights reserved.*

Cover design: Cindy Kiple
Cover photograph: Jeffrey Conley/Getty Images

ISBN-10: 0-8308-2226-7
ISBN-13: 978-0-8308-2226-3

Printed in the United States of America ♾

Library of Congress Cataloging-in-Publication Data

Willard, Dallas, 1935-
   [In search of guidance]
   Hearing God : developing a conversational relationship wtih God /
Dallas Willard.
     p. cm.
   Originally published: In search of guidance. Ventura, CA : Regal
Books, c 1983.
   Includes bibliographical references.
   ISBN 0-8308-2226-7 (pbk. : alk. paper)
   1. Spiritual life—Chrisitianity. 2. God—Will. I. Title.
[BV4501.2.W5327 1999]
231.7—dc21   *99-36482*
                                                                 CIP

P	32	31	30	29	28	27	26	25	24	23	22	21	20	19	18	17	16
Y	21	20	19	18	17	16	15	14	13	12	11	10	09	08	07	06	

To Jane Lakes Willard
Sweet lady,
Good soldier,
Faithful companion on the way

CONTENTS

Preface

Hearing God? A daring idea, some would say—presumptuous and even dangerous. But what if we are made for it? What if the human system simply will not function properly without it? There are good reasons to think it will not. The fine texture as well as the grand movements of life show the need. Is it not, in fact, more presumptuous and dangerous to undertake human existence *without* hearing God?

Among our loneliest moments, no doubt, is the time of decision. There the weight of our future life clamps down upon our hearts. Whatever comes from our choice will be our responsibility, our fault. Good things we have set our hearts on become real only as we choose them. But those things, or those as yet undreamed of, may also be irretrievably lost if our choices are misguided. We may find ourselves stuck with failures and dreadful consequences that must be endured for a lifetime.

Then quickly there follows the time of second thoughts—and third, and fourth: Did I do the good and wise thing? Is it what God wanted? Is it even what *I* wanted? Can I live with the consequences? Will others think I am a fool? Is God still with me? Will he be with me even if it becomes clear that I made the wrong choice?

While we are young, desire, impulse and personal associations may blithely carry us through choices that would paralyze us ten years later. In the bloom of youth we just do what we have to do or whatever turns us on. How simple it is! Often we are not even conscious of having chosen. After collecting a few disasters, however, and learning that actions are forever, that opportunities seldom return and that consequences are relentless, we hungrily cry, "Thy will be done on earth as it is in heaven!" More than reflecting a mere general concern for world affairs to conform to his will, our prayer expresses the burning need for God to be a constant guiding presence in our individual lives.

God has created us for intimate friendship with himself—both now and forever. This is the Christian viewpoint. It is made clear throughout the Bible, especially in such passages as Exodus 29:43-46 and 33:11, Psalm 23, Isaiah 41:8, John 15:14 and Hebrews 13:5-6. As with all close personal relationships, we can surely count on God to speak to each of us when and as it is appropriate. But what does this really mean? And how does it work in practice? I hope in the following pages to give a clear and workable answer to these questions.

There is no avoiding the fact that we live at the mercy of our ideas. This is never more true than with our ideas about God. Meaning well is not enough. Those who operate on the wrong information are likely never to know the reality of God's presence in the decisions which shape their lives and will miss the constant divine companionship for which their souls were made.

My strategy has been to take as a model the highest and best type of communication that I know of from human affairs and then place this model in the even brighter light of the person and teaching of Jesus Christ. In this way it has been possible to arrive at an ideal picture of what an intimate relationship with God is meant to be and also come to a clear vision of the kind of life where hearing God is not an uncommon occurrence.

To take this ideal picture seriously is to exclude all tricks, mechanical formulas and gimmickry for finding out what God wants one to do. We cannot reduce it to a device that we use to make sure we are always right. Indeed I hope to make it clear that the subject of hearing God cannot be successfully treated by thinking only in terms of what God wants us to do if that automatically excludes—as is usually assumed—what *we* want to do and even what *we* want *God* to do. *Hearing God is but one dimension of a richly interactive relationship, and obtaining guidance is but one facet of hearing God.*

It may seem strange, but being in the will of God is very far removed from just doing what God wants us to do—so far removed, in fact, that we can be solidly in the will of God, and be aware that we are, without knowing God's preference with regard to various details of our lives. We can be in his will as we do certain things without our knowing that he prefers these actions to certain other possibilities. Hearing God makes sense only in the framework of living in the will of God.

When our children, John and Becky, were small, they were often completely in my will as they played happily in the back yard, though I had no preference that they should do the particular things they were doing there or even that they should be in the back yard instead of playing in their rooms or having a snack in the kitchen. Generally speaking we are in God's will whenever we are leading the kind of life he wants for us. And that leaves a lot of room for initiative on our part, which is essential: our individual initiatives are central to his will for us.

Of course, we cannot fail to do what he directs us to do and yet still be in his will. And quite apart from any specific directions he may give us, there are many ways of living and being that are clearly not in his will. The Ten Commandments given to Moses are so deep and powerful on these matters that if humanity followed them, daily life would be transformed beyond recognition, and large segments of the public media would collapse for lack of material. Consider a daily newspaper or television newscast and eliminate from it every report that presupposes a breaking of one of the Ten Commandments. Very little will be left.

But one who inquires seriously after God's guidance must never forget that even if one was to do all the particular things God wants and explicitly commands us to do, one might still not be the person God would have one be. It is always true that "the letter kills, but the Spirit gives life" (2 Cor 3:6). An obsession merely with *doing* all God commands may be the very thing that rules out *being* the kind of person that he calls us to be.

Jesus told a parable to make clear what God treasures in those who intend to serve him:

> Who among you would say to your slave who has just come in from plowing or tending sheep in the field, "Come here at once and take your place at the table?" Would you not rather say to him, "Prepare supper for me, put on your apron and serve me while I eat and drink; later you may eat and drink"? Do you thank the slave for doing what was commanded? So you also, when you

have done all that you were ordered to do, say, "We are worthless slaves; we
have done only what we ought to have done!" (Lk 17:7-10; cf. Mt 5:20)

The watchword of the worthy servant is not mere obedience but love, from
which appropriate obedience naturally flows.

Much of what you will read here is only elaboration on this parable.
Certainly I hope to be of some service to those who continue to think just in
terms of *doing* what they are told to do. But for all the good that is in that
attitude, it remains the attitude of the unprofitable servant. And it severely
limits spiritual growth, unlike the possibilities of a life of free-hearted
collaboration with Jesus and his friends in the kingdom of the heavens.

Moreover if we are firmly gripped by a true picture of life with Jesus and
are moving by experience deeper and deeper into its reality, we will be able,
strongly but calmly, to resist the mistakes and abuses of religious authority.
From the local congregation up to the highest levels of national and international influence, we hear people and groups claiming that they have been
divinely guided as to what *we* are to do. This is sometimes benign and correct,
both in intention and outcome. But this is not always the case.

An appropriate response to misuse of religious authority will be available
to those who have an understanding of how individualized divine guidance,
on the one hand, and individual or corporate authority, on the other, meld
together in Jesus' community of transforming love. Today there is a desperate
need for large numbers of people throughout our various social groupings
who are competent and confident in their own practice of life in Christ and
in hearing his voice. Such people would have the effect of concretely
redefining Christian spirituality for our times. They would show us an
individual and corporate human existence freely and intelligently lived from
a hand-in-hand, conversational walk with God. That is the biblical ideal for
human life.

In the pages that follow, therefore, I deal with hearing God as it bears upon
a *whole life* in the will of God—upon the question of *who* God wants us to
be as well as (where appropriate) of what he wants us to do. What he wants
us to do is very important, of course, and we must be careful to learn how to

know it and do it, but it is never enough by itself to allow us to understand and enter the radiant life before the shining face of God that is offered to us in the grace of the gospel—a life pleasing to him, in view of which he can say, "This is my beloved child, in whom I am well pleased."

Chapter one clarifies the tension in which Christians live, believing that hearing God is very important to our walk with him but at the same time lacking a confident understanding of how it works for the individual in practice. Chapter two removes some common misunderstandings about God's communications with us. Chapter three explains the various ways in which he is with us. Chapter four examines some objections to the very idea of God's communicating with individuals. Chapter five deals with the various ways in which he communicates and explains and defends the centrality of the "still small voice." Chapters six and seven discuss the centrality of God's speaking—God's Word—to his creation and to the process of redemption. The Word of God is not foreign to routine reality; it is at the very heart of it. Chapter eight clarifies how we can be sure that we are hearing God. Finally, chapter nine deals with what to do on those occasions, sure to come, when God is not speaking—or at least when we are not hearing him.

To deal effectively with hearing God as part of a life within his will, it is necessary to consider many deeper issues about his intentions for us and about the nature of the world in which he has placed us. From time to time difficult subjects must be discussed. But my hope is to leave you with a clear sense of how to live confidently in a personal walk that is complemented by an ongoing conversational relationship with God.

For a presentation of the larger picture of life with Jesus Christ in the kingdom of God, of which hearing God is only one part, I would refer readers to my books *The Spirit of the Disciplines* and *The Divine Conspiracy*.

Thanks to Raymond Neal, Beth Webber, Lynda Graybeal and Tom Morrissey for their indispensable assistance with this book at various points in its development.

One

A Paradox About Hearing God

There is not in the world a kind of life more sweet and delightful
than that of a continual conversation with God.
Those only can comprehend it who practice and experience it;
yet I do not advise you to do it from that motive.
It is not pleasure which we ought to seek in this exercise;
but let us do it from a principle of love,
and because God would have us.
BROTHER LAWRENCE, *THE PRACTICE OF
THE PRESENCE OF GOD*

SUNDAY DINNER WAS FINISHED, BUT WE LINGERED ROUND THE TABLE savoring the good food and reflecting on the morning's service at church. The congregation—where I then served as a very young (and very green) assistant pastor—was excited about its plans for a new sanctuary to replace its old building, which was much loved but long overused and outgrown.

The morning message had focused on the plans for the new building. Our pastor spoke of his vision for the church's increased ministry. He indicated how strongly he felt God's guidance in the way the congregation was going, and he testified that God had *spoken* to him about things that should be done.

My wife's grandmother, Mrs. Lucy Latimer ("Mema" to us all), seemed deep in thought as we continued to chatter along. Finally she said quietly, "I wonder why God never speaks to me like that."

This simple comment, which came like a bolt out of the blue from the heart of this woman of unshakable faith and complete devotion, forever changed my attitude toward glib talk about God's speaking to us or about divine guidance. Through her words—in a way I came to understand only later—God spoke to me.

I was given a vivid realization, which has never left me, of the extent to which such talk places many sincere Christians on the outside, looking in. It is not necessarily that their experience is lacking, but they do not understand the language or how their experience works. This leaves them feeling confused and deficient and may lead them to play a game that they do not really understand and that rightly makes them very uncomfortable. It undermines their confidence that they are fully acceptable to God.

Mema, in fact, had a richly interactive life with God, as we all knew. But for whatever reasons, she had not been able to relate her experience of God's presence in her life—of which she was completely certain—to the idea of God's speaking with her. This left her at a loss for how to deal with the *conversational* side of her friendship with God.

Up to that point in my own experience I had rashly assumed that if you were really a Christian, then God spoke to you as a matter of course and you knew it. I was sure that he spoke individually and specifically about what he wanted each believer to do and that he also taught and made real on an individual basis the general truths all must believe in order to enter into life with him.

The Moving of God

Later I came to realize that this confidence was not based on genuine understanding. It came from my experiences of a series of revival meetings in which I was immersed as a young man. During those meetings I became accustomed to interacting with a characteristic type of thought and impulse, which was to me the moving of God upon my mind and heart. It was an experience clearly marked out for me and one that guided my actions, though I held no theory or doctrine about it.

Then as I subsequently grew into the Christian ministry, I learned to wait upon "the word of God" to come to me. In the most primary of senses the word of God is simply *God's speaking*. I also learned to expect his speaking to come through me to others. Experience taught me the remarkable difference between when it was "just me" talking, or even "just me" quoting and discussing Scripture, and when a certain something more was taking place.

Through their writings great Christians of the past such as John Calvin and William Law offered what we might call "the ministry of Eli" to me.[1] (See the story in 1 Sam 3:8-9.) They gave me further insight into what was happening in my experiences and why it was happening. They helped me to identify and respond to experiences of God's speaking, just as Eli helped Samuel in the biblical story.

They also assured me that the same Spirit who delivered the Scriptures to holy men of old speaks today in the hearts of those who gather around the written Word to minister and be ministered to. And they warned me that *only if* this happened could I avoid being just another more or less clever letter-learned scribe—trying to nourish the souls of my hearers out of the contents of my own brain, giving them only what *I* was able to work up through my own efforts from the Bible or elsewhere.

It was not easy, however, for me to see that our most sacred experiences often blind us. The very light that makes it possible for us to see may also dazzle our eyes to the clearest of realities and make it impossible for us to see what lies in a shadow. Caught up in my own experiences of the workings of God's voice, I really did not understand it at all. I only knew its reality, and I thoughtlessly assumed it was a functioning, intelligible fact in every believer's life. Obviously I had a lot to learn.

So for a long while I was unable to appreciate the huge problems that the very idea of God's speaking to us created for some of the most faithful adherents of the church—not to mention those entirely outside it. When someone seemed to have difficulty with hearing God, I simply passed it off as a sign of weakness of faith or even rebellion on their part. Yet I could not entirely avoid an awareness that many of the most faithful and devout Christians can make no sense of what is called "divine guidance"—except possibly as it comes in the form of outright necessities imposed by force of circumstances.

I saw them driven to turn all guidance into blind force and to treat God's will as nothing but fate. And I was distressed at how often people identified some brutal event as God's will—even when it clearly came from a decision made by human beings. They then easily moved on to the faith-destroying, even blasphemous idea that everything that happens in this world is caused by God.

The Ongoing Conversation

Today I continue to believe that people are meant to live in an ongoing conversation with God, speaking and being spoken to. Rightly understood I believe that this can be abundantly verified in experience. God's visits to Adam and Eve in the Garden, Enoch's walks with God and the face-to-face conversations between Moses and Jehovah are all commonly regarded as highly exceptional moments in the religious history of humankind. Aside from their obviously unique historical role, however, they are not meant to be exceptional at all. Rather they are examples of the normal human life God intended for us: God's indwelling his people through personal presence and fellowship. Given who we are by basic nature, we live—really live—only through God's regular speaking in our souls and thus "by every word that comes from of the mouth of God."

During the time spent writing this book, I made a special point of drawing others out in conversation concerning their experiences of hearing God. When a spirit of acceptance is established, and it is clear that the topic is to be dealt with seriously, then the stories begin to flow. And as understanding and confidence grow, other cases come to mind that are seen to be or to contain a word from God to the individual. Many might be surprised to discover what a high percentage of serious Christians—and even non-Christians—can tell of specific experiences in which they are sure God spoke to them.

Of course talking *to* God is an almost universal practice. The words "Talking to God: An Intimate Look at the Way We Pray" covered the front of *Newsweek*'s issue for January 6, 1992. The main article was devoted to some sociological studies of the practice of prayer recently undertaken in the United States. "This week," the article said, ". . . more of us will pray than will go to work, or exercise, or have sexual relations. . . . 78 percent of all Americans pray at least once a week; more than half (57 percent) report praying at least once a day. . . . Even among the 13 percent of Americans who are atheists or agnostics, nearly one in five still prays daily."

As these studies also found, it is widely recognized that a major part of prayer is listening to God and letting God direct us. But those who experience a directing word from God rarely speak about it. Often they have never spoken of it at all, even to their closest friends.

The UFO Syndrome

Is it not with good reason that we hesitate to speak about experiences we regard as God's speaking to us? Similarly those who think they have sighted a UFO or those who have had the near-death experiences much discussed in recent years soon learn to keep their mouths shut. They know that they may single themselves out for unwanted attention if they are not very careful.

Perhaps they will be regarded as eccentric or even crazy. And since *those* experiences really are strange and very hard to interpret, these people genuinely fear being misguided. They do not wish to go public with something that might just be a mistake on their part. They also fear being thought of as arrogant, as taking themselves to be special or, to borrow language the apostle Paul used about his own experiences, as being "too elated by the abundance of revelations" (2 Cor 12:7 RSV).

Similar doubts and hesitations justifiably trouble those who feel they are spoken to by God. "Why is it," comedian Lily Tomlin asks, "that when we speak to God we are said to be praying but when God speaks to us we are said to be schizophrenic?" Such a response, from ourselves or others, to someone's claim to have heard from God is especially likely today just because of the lack of specific teaching and pastoral guidance on such matters. Indeed like the Sadducees of old, many church leaders discourage the very thought that God *would* speak to the individual. And some leaders obviously prefer that he speak only to them and not to their flock. After all, it is well known that people go off into all sorts of errors and become quite unmanageable once God starts "talking" to them.

Our Leaders Hear from God

Faced with such inner fears and such a lack of teaching—or even with explicit denial or discouragement—disciples of Christ today may be somewhat encouraged by another message that emanates from their fellowships. For we are also constantly confronted with suggestions or implications that ideally we *should* be engaged in communications with God just like our leaders.

Certainly our Christian leaders commonly indicate that God has spoken to them. And precisely because they are our leaders, there is a strong suggestion that we should strive to be like them. Here are a few random cases.

In a television interview on January 31, 1983, Dr. Ken Taylor, who produced the widely used version of the Scriptures known as *The Living Bible,* told how he had been concerned about children having a Bible that they could easily understand. According to his statement, one afternoon "God revealed" to him "the idea of a thought-for-thought translation instead of word-for-word." This idea worked so well that such versions have now been published in many languages around the world.

Very commonly it is in times of great inward distress that we hear the voice of God directed specifically to us. In the 1640s George Fox, founder of the Friends or Quaker movement, wandered the fields and byways of the English countryside, seeking someone who could show him the way to peace with God. He finally became convinced that

> there was none among them all that could speak to my condition. And when all my hopes in them and in all men were gone, so that I had nothing outwardly to help me, nor could I tell what to do; then, oh! then I heard a voice which said, "there is one, even Jesus Christ, that can speak to thy condition"; and when I heard it, my heart did leap for joy. Then the Lord did let me see why there was none upon the earth that could speak to my condition, namely, that I might give him all the glory.[2]

In book eight of his *Confessions* St. Augustine, who lived from A.D. 354-430, tells how in a similarly distraught condition he "heard from a neighboring house a voice, as of boy or girl, I know not, chanting, and oft repeating, 'Take up and read. Take up and read.'" He could remember no child's game with these words. "So, checking the torrent of my tears, I arose; interpreting it to be no other than a command from God, to open the book, and read the first chapter I should find." Thus he came upon Romans 13:13-14. His condition was immediately transformed, as was Fox's centuries later, and one of the greatest and most influential of all Christians entered the kingdom of the heavens.

Quite characteristically a weekly publication from a large local church states that the minister "has been given a bold vision by our Lord." The vision is that every person in the entire geographical area where the church is located should be called to Christ in a one-year period by a telephone call from some person in the church. Notice this is not described as a bright idea that struck the minister but as a vision communicated to him by God. And of course that makes all the difference in the world in its meaning for the congregation that the minister leads.

I cite these cases here not because they are exceptional, but precisely because they are so common. There is a practically endless supply of such stories. They vary in detail as we move from one denominational tradition to another, but to some significant degree they are present in all Christian communions, except those that have moved beyond theological liberalism into simple humanism.

Should we expect anything else, given the words of the scriptural record and the heritage of the Christian church? As Christians we stand in a millennia-long tradition of humans who have been addressed by God. The ancient Israelites heard the voice of their God speaking to them out of the midst of fire (Deut 4:33). A regular place of communion and conversational interchange between the high priest and God was established in the mercy seat over the ark of God (Ex 25:22; see also Lk 1:11-21).

But the *individual* with faith among the Israelites also cried out expectantly to be taught by God: "Teach me to do your will, for you are my God. Let your good spirit lead me on a level path" (Ps 143:10). Israel's experience led the prophet Isaiah—who also had firsthand experience of conversing with God (Is 6)—to describe conditions of the faithful this way: "Then you shall call, and the LORD will answer; you shall cry for help, and he will say, Here I am. . . . The LORD will guide you continually" (Is 58:9, 11).

Abiding Includes Conversing

On the evening before his crucifixion Jesus assured his little band of followers that although he was leaving them, he would continue to manifest himself to all who loved him. Judas who was also called Thaddaeus (not Judas Iscariot) then asked just the right question: *How* would this manifesting take place (Jn 14:22)? Jesus' reply was that he and his Father would "come to them and make our home with them" (14:23).

Certainly this abiding of the Son and the Father in the faithful heart involves more than conscious communication or conversation, but it surely does involve these too, in a manner and a measure our Lord himself considers to be appropriate. It is simply beyond belief that two persons so intimately related as indicated in Jesus' answer to Thaddaeus would not explicitly speak to one another. The Spirit who inhabits us is not mute, restricting himself to an occasional nudge, a hot flash, a brilliant image or a case of goosebumps.

Such simple reasonings add further weight to the examples set by well-known Christians that confirm the thought that ideally we should be engaged in personal communion with God. We might well ask, "How could there be a personal relationship, a personal walk with God—or with anyone else—*without* individualized communication?"

Sometimes today it seems that our personal relationship with God is treated as no more than a mere arrangement or understanding that Jesus and his Father have about us. Our personal relationship then only means that each believer has his or her own unique account in heaven, which allows them to draw on the merits of Christ to pay their sin bills. Or possibly it means that God's general providence for his creation is adequate to provide for each person.

But who does not think there should be much more to a personal relationship than that? A mere benefactor, however powerful, kind and thoughtful, is not the same thing as a *friend.* Jesus says, "I have called you friends" (Jn 15:15) and "Look, I am with you every minute, even to the end of the age" (Mt 28:20, paraphrase; cf. Heb 13:5-6).

One-to-One with God

In the last analysis nothing is more central to the practical life of the Christian than confidence in God's individual dealings with each person. The individual care of the shepherd for his sheep, of the parent for the child and of the lover for the beloved are all biblical images that have passed into the fundamental consciousness of Western humanity. They pervasively and essentially mark our art and general culture as well as our religion. Not only conservative and liberal Christians, high-church and Pentecostal but also Christian and Jew, and even Jew and Muslim, come together in saying, "The Lord is *my* shepherd, *I* lack for nothing. *He* makes *me* lie down in green pastures, *he* leads *me* beside still waters" (Ps 23:1-2, paraphrase).

The biblical record always presents the relationship between God and the believer as more like a friendship or family tie than like merely one person's arranging to take care of the needs of another. If we pass before our minds that startling array of biblical personalities from Adam to the apostles Paul and John, we behold the millennia-long saga of God's invading human personality and history on a one-to-one basis. There is nothing general or secondhand about the divine encounters with Abraham, Moses, Isaiah, Nehemiah, Mary or Peter.

The saga continues up to our own day in the lives of those recognized as leaders in the spiritual life. When, coming through the ages, we consider St. Augustine, Theresa of Ávila, St. Francis of Assisi, Martin Luther, George Fox, John Wesley, C. H. Spurgeon, Phoebe Palmer, D. L. Moody, Frank Laubach, A. W. Tozer or Henri Nouwen, we see in each case a person who regards personal communion *and* communication with God both as life-changing episodes and as daily bread. Untold thousands of humble Christians whose names will never appear in print—who will never preach a sermon or lead a crusade—can testify equally well to exactly the same kinds of encounters with God as are manifested by the great ones in the Way.

Robert C. McFarlane was a well-known businessman in the Los Angeles area. He had moved to California from Oklahoma in 1970, and within just a few days of his arrival—due to a disastrous misunderstanding with a close friend—he had to take control of an insurance agency. He did not want it, but he had to make it succeed in order to save the large amount of money he had invested in it.

By the spring of 1973 he was in the third straight year of constant strain and stress in the operation of the business. He had recently been converted through the ministry of the Rolling Hills Covenant Church in Southern California in answer to the prayers of his wife, Betty, and her many Christian friends.

One day that spring the continual danger of defeat, the daylight and dark hours of effort, the frustration at every turn and the hardened memories of the cause of his financial difficulties came upon him with special force. Robert drove toward his office, facing yet another day of futility and failure but having to accomplish the absolute necessities to keep the business afloat.

Suddenly he was filled with a frantic urge to turn left onto the road out of town—and just disappear. Afterward he always felt he was going to make that turn. How far he would have gone is of course unknown. But into the midst of his inner turmoil there came a command: "Pull over to the curb."

As he relates it, it was as if the words were written on the windshield. After he pulled over there came to him, as though from someone with him in the car, these words: "My Son had strains that you will never know, and when he had those strains, he turned to me, and that's what *you* should do."

After hearing these words Robert sat at the wheel for a long time, sobbing aloud. He then drove on to his Long Beach office, where he faced twenty-two major, outstanding problems. All the most significant problems—whether they concerned company disagreements; clients' deciding to remain with his agency; payments by clients of sizable, late premiums or whatever—were substantially resolved by that day's end.

Wilhelm Hermann, a great theologian of the late nineteenth century, goes so far as to mark the Christian out in terms of a personal communion with God. "We hold a man to be really a Christian when we believe we have ample evidence that God has revealed himself to him in Jesus Christ, and that now the man's inner life is taking on a new character through his communion with the God who is thus manifest."[3]

More recently the English philosopher and theologian John Baillie wrote, "Our knowledge of God rests on the revelation of his personal presence. . . . Of such a presence it must be true that to those who have never been confronted with it argument is useless, while to those who have, it is superfluous."[4]

The faith in a God who speaks personally to the soul is nowhere recorded more plainly than in the hymns of the church from all ages, sung week by week by the church as it congregates and day by day by Christians as they go about their lives at work, at home, at play: "Savior, Like a Shepherd Lead Us," "All the Way My Savior Leads Me," "Lead On, O King Eternal," "Where He Leads Me," "Lead, Kindly Light," "He Leadeth Me," "Holy Spirit,

Faithful Guide," "Jesus, Savior, Pilot Me," "If Thou But Suffer God to Guide Thee," "Guide Me, O Thou Great Jehovah" and "Jesus, Still Lead On." This brief list hardly begins to mention all the hymns devoted to personal divine guidance and the conversational communion of the soul with God. The words of these hymns follow a familiar pattern:

> He walks with me, and He talks with me,
> And He tells me I am His own,
> And the joy we share as we tarry there,
> None other has ever known.[5]

The Paradox

In the light of all this it is not an exaggeration to speak of a *paradox* in the contemporary experience and understanding of hearing God. It is a paradox that seriously hinders our practical faith.

On the one hand we have massive testimony to and widespread faith in God's personal, guiding communication with us—far more than mere providential and blindly controlling guidance. This is not only recorded in Scripture and emblazoned upon the history of the church; it also lies at the heart of our worship services and our individualized relationships with God, and it actually serves as the basis of authority for our teachers and leaders. Only very rarely will someone profess to teach and lead the people of God on the basis of his or her education, natural talents and denominational connections alone. Authority in spiritual leadership derives from a life in the Spirit, from the minister's personal encounter and ongoing relationship with God.

On the other hand we also find a pervasive and often painful uncertainty about how hearing God's voice actually works today and what its place is in the church and in the Christian's life. Even those who firmly believe that they have been addressed or directly spoken to by God may be at a loss to know what is happening or what to do about it. In the Bible, poor flustered Gideon said to the Lord, who in some fashion stood before him, "Do something to prove that you are the one who is speaking to me!" (Judg 6:17, paraphrase).

Even if we were to beg for a word from God, we may have so little clarity on what it should be like and so little competence in dealing with it that when it comes it will only add to our confusion. I believe that this is one reason why such a word may be withheld from us by God when it would otherwise be entirely appropriate and helpful.

Our need for understanding is clearly very great. We are all too familiar with the painful confusion of individuals who make big efforts to determine God's will for them—people who are frequently very sincere and devout. We see them make dreadful errors following a whim or chance event that because of their desperation, they force to serve as a sign from God. We see them sink into despair, skepticism, even cynicism, often accompanied by a continuation of religious routine now utterly mechanical and dead. They "know" on the basis of what has happened to them, that for all practical purposes they are simply on their own.

We are also all too familiar, even if only though newspaper accounts, with the tragic domination of groups by those who lay claim to a special sign or word from God. Religious dictators are in unceasing supply and show up in surprising guises and places. Often they are not effectively resisted precisely because the other members of the group have no clear idea, tested and proven in experience, of how such a word from God really works. They are vulnerable to madness in the name of God.

First Steps Toward a Solution

I believe we, as disciples of Jesus Christ, cannot abandon faith in our ability to hear from God. To abandon this is to abandon the reality of a personal relationship with God, and that we must not do. Our hearts and minds, as well as the realities of the Christian tradition, stand against it.

The paradox about hearing God's voice must, then, be resolved and removed by providing believers with a *clear understanding* and a *confident, practical orientation toward God's way of guiding us and communicating with us,* which is the aim of the chapters that follow. But before we can even begin working on this task, there are three general problem areas that must be briefly addressed.

First, what we know about guidance and the divine-human encounter from the Bible and the lives of those who have gone before us shows that *God's communications come to us in many forms.* We should expect nothing else, for this variety is appropriate to the complexity of human personality and cultural history. And God in redemption is willing to reach out to humanity in whatever ways are suitable to its fallen and weakened condition. We should look carefully at these many forms to see which ones are most suited to the kind of relationship God intends to have with his people. If we give primacy to forms of communication that God does not on the whole prefer in relation to his children, that will hinder our understanding of and cooperation with his voice—perhaps even totally frustrating his will for us. One of the main tasks of the chapters that follow is to prevent this.

Second, *we may have the wrong motives for seeking to hear from God.* We all in some measure share in the general human anxiety about the future. By nature we live in the future, constantly hurled into it whether we like it or not. Knowing what we will meet there is a condition of our being prepared to deal with it—or so it would seem from the human point of view. Francis Bacon's saying that knowledge is power is never more vividly realized than in our concern about our own future. So we ceaselessly inquire about events to come. The great businesses and the halls of government are filled today with experts and technocrats, our modern-day magicians and soothsayers. A new discipline of "futurology" has recently emerged within the universities. The age-old trades of palm reading and fortune telling flourish.[6]

Within the Christian community, teaching on the will of God and how to know it continues to be one of the most popular subjects. Russ Johnston draws upon his own wide experience to remark,

> A certain church I know has elective Sunday School classes for their adults. Every three months they choose a new topic to study. The pastor tells me that if they can have someone teach on knowing God's will, they can run that class over and over, and still people sign up for it in droves.
>
> I've spoken at many conferences where part of the afternoons are set aside for workshops on various topics. If you make one of the workshops "Knowing the Will of God," half the people sign up for it even if there are twenty other choices.[7]

But is not a self-defeating motive at work here—one that causes people to take these classes and workshops over and over without coming to peace about their place in the will of God?

I fear that many people seek to hear God solely as a device for securing their own safety, comfort and righteousness. For those who busy themselves to know the will of God, however, it is still true that "those who want to save their life will lose it" (Mt 16:25). My extreme preoccupation with knowing God's will for me may only indicate, contrary to what is often thought, that I am overconcerned with myself, not a Christlike interest in the well-being of others or in the glory of God.

Frederick B. Meyer writes, "So long as there is some thought of personal advantage, some idea of acquiring the praise and commendation of men, some aim of self-aggrandizement, it will be simply impossible to find out God's purpose concerning us."[8] Nothing will go right in our effort to hear God if this false motivation is its foundation. God will not cooperate. We must discover a different motivation for knowing God's will and listening to his voice.

Third, our understanding of God's communication with us is blocked when *we misconceive the very nature of our heavenly Father and of his intent for us* as his redeemed children and friends. From this then comes a further misunderstanding of what the church, his redemptive community, is to be like and especially of how authority works in the kingdom of the heavens.

God certainly is not a jolly good fellow, nor is he our buddy. But then neither are we intended by him to be robots wired into his instrument panel, puppets on his string or slaves dancing at the end of the whiplash of his command. Such ideas must not serve as the basis for our view of hearing God. As E. Stanley Jones observed,

> Obviously God must guide us in a way that will develop spontaneity in us. The development of character, rather than direction in this, that, and the other matter, must be the primary purpose of the Father. He will guide us, but he won't override us. That fact should make us use with caution the method of sitting down with a pencil and a blank sheet of paper to write down the instructions dictated by God for the day. Suppose a parent would dictate to the child minutely everything he is to do during the day. The child would be stunted under that regime. The parent must guide in such a manner, and to the degree, that autonomous character, capable of making right decisions for itself, is produced. God does the same.[9]

A Conversational Relationship

The ideal for hearing from God is finally determined by who God is, what kind of beings we are and what a personal relationship between ourselves and God should be like. Our failure to hear God has its deepest roots in a failure to understand, accept and grow into a conversational relationship with God, the sort of relationship suited to friends who are mature personalities in a shared enterprise, no matter how different they may be in other respects.

It is within such a relationship that our Lord surely intends us to have and to recognize his voice speaking in our hearts as occasion demands. He has made ample provision for this in order to fulfill his mission as the Good Shepherd: to bring us life and life more abundantly. The abundance of life comes in following him, and "the sheep follow him because they know his voice" (Jn 10:4).

The next chapter begins to deal with these problems that confront our search for God's voice by looking at some general but essential guidelines.

Some Topics for Reflection

1. Could you be sure that God has not spoken to you? What events in your past life *could* have been messages from God? Reflect on the details of some of these events.

2. What is the paradox about hearing God discussed in this chapter? Do you find that the tension it sets up is present in your life and the lives of religious people around you?

3. What might be the drawbacks of having a conversational relationship with God? What kind of person would you expect to be less than enthusiastic about living in such a relationship?

4. Can you make any sense at all of an intimate personal relationship where there are no specific communications?

5. Should a leader who claims to have been spoken to by God ever be questioned about it? How might one intelligently go about this in a spirit of love?

6. Everything considered, would you *really* like to be spoken to by God?

Two

Guidelines for Hearing from God

He brought me to the banqueting house,
and his banner over me was love. . . .
Eat, O friends; drink, yea, drink abundantly, O beloved.
SONG OF SOLOMON 2:4; 5:1 (KJV)

Those possessed of genuine love have God's life in them
and are well acquainted with him.
Those who are not have no knowledge of him,
for God is love.
1 JOHN 4:7-8 (PARAPHRASE)

YOU MAY HAVE SEEN THE FILM *THE STEPFORD WIVES*. IT IS THE STORY of a couple, probably in their early or mid-thirties, who move into the upper-middle-class community of Stepford, where the men are mostly workers in high-tech industries and businesses and the women are housewives.

The wife of the couple soon notices that most of the other Stepford wives uniformly exhibit very strange behavior patterns. They are continually ecstatic about sewing, cleaning their houses, manicuring their lawns and baking. When they get together they mainly trade recipes or coo over their clean floors and their latest triumphs in making their husbands' lives more comfortable. They never fight, nor are they unpleasant to anyone—especially not to their husbands—and they have no opinions or interests that reach beyond their family, home and club.

Just a few of the wives remain on the feisty, individualistic side. But these women eventually leave for a "vacation" with their husbands, and upon their return they dwell on baking and clean floors just like the rest.

When this happens to the best friend of our most recent Stepford wife— who is already very suspicious about what is going on—she becomes desperate and stabs her old friend with a knife to see if she will bleed. She does not! She merely repeats pathetic little maneuvers around her kitchen, mouthing the same inane niceties over and over, while her frightened friend backs away and runs out of the door.

By this time, however, her own robot replacement is almost ready. In the end we see her (or it) with the placid robot look on her face, ready to wear frilly blouses and aprons, bake cakes, grow ecstatic over clean floors and be sweet, sweet, *sweet*—a totally controlled wife!

Leaving its social agenda aside, the message of *The Stepford Wives* is obvious and important. But it is one that is too often forgotten. In close personal relationships conformity to another's wishes is not desirable, be it ever so perfect, if it is mindless or purchased at the expense of freedom and the destruction of personality. This is a point that must be grasped firmly as we come to think about God's relationship with his human creation and about what his love for us means.

In our attempts to understand how God speaks to us and guides us, we must above all hold on to the fact that this is to be sought *only as a part of a certain kind of life,* a life of loving fellowship with the King and his other subjects within the kingdom of the heavens. We must never forget that God's speaking to us, however we experience it in our initial encounter, is intended to develop into an intelligent, freely cooperative relationship between mature people who love each other with the richness of genuine *agape* love. We must therefore make it our primary goal not just to hear the voice of God but to be mature people in a loving relationship with him. Only in this way will we hear him rightly. This is our *first* general guideline.

Love: A Way of Being With

When we love someone, of course we want to please them. We don't want this only in order to avoid trouble or gain favor; it is our way of being with them, of sharing their life and their person. The gushing pleasure of a small child who is helping her or his parent comes from the expansion of the child's little self through immersion in the life of a larger self to which the child is lovingly abandoned. *With* its parent the child does big things that he or she could not undertake alone. But the child would not even be interested in doing these things apart from the parent's interest, attention and affection.

Adults also get a sense of this larger power and larger life when they enjoy requited love. When in the manner appropriate to the people involved, two become one, they identify with one another, expanding their selves and their world. The beloved, who both loves and is loved, does not want to order the lover about; instead the beloved desires that the lover understand what is needed so that no orders are necessary.

In this union of souls—in the conscious delight and rest in one another that is the highest and most exalted relationship possible between two persons—it is not right for one person to always tell the other what to do. And so it is in our union with God, a person both loving and beloved. He does not delight in having to always explain what his will is; he enjoys it when we understand and act upon his will. Our highest calling and opportunity in life is to love him with all our being.

God as Taskmaster

Far too commonly, no doubt, we think of God as did the man in the parable of the talents who regarded his lord as "a harsh man." He was, accordingly, afraid of his master and in his blindness proudly gave him back exactly what "belonged" to him (Mt 25:14-30). Such a person could not "enter into the joy of [his] master" because—misconceiving their relationship as he did—he could neither enter into his lord's mind and life nor open his own life to his lord. He actually abused his lord by taking him to be interested only in getting his own back, while the lord for his part was really interested in sharing his life and goods with others.

In the same way we demean God immeasurably by casting him in the role of the cosmic boss, foreman or autocrat, whose chief joy in relation to humans is ordering them around, taking pleasure in seeing them jump at his command and painstakingly noting down any failures. Instead we are to be God's friends (2 Chron 20:7; Jn 15:13-15) and fellow workers (1 Cor 3:9).

The role of taskmaster, whether a pleased one *or* an angry one, is a role that God accepts only when appointed to it by our own limited understanding. He thus often condescends to us because our consciousness cannot rise any higher (clouded as it is by our experiences in a fallen world with our superiors, whether they be parents, bosses, kings or those who stand over us in manipulative "love"). And the rule then, as always, is: "Let it be done for you according to your faith" (Mt 8:13). Well, no doubt it is better that we have *some* relation to God than no relation at all!

When we come to learn how we can hear God and what divine guidance *really* is, we must be sure to come in such a way that we do justice to the revelation of God in Christ. Hearing God and seeking guidance, as I showed in chapter one, are an almost universal human preoccupation. It is hard, however, to cleanse our minds of those motives, images and concepts that would brutalize the very God whom we hope to approach.

In the primitive rituals and the "Bible roulette" (picking verses at random for guidance) frequently practiced by present-day believers, we see both the desperate urgency and the superstitious character of human efforts to get a word from God, especially a word on what is going to happen and what we should do about it. If necessary some people are prepared to *force* such a word from him or someone else. Like King Saul many of us have our own versions of a witch of Endor (1 Sam 28).

Hearing God cannot be a reliable and intelligible fact of life *except* when we see his speaking as one aspect of his presence with us, of his life in us. Only our *communion* with God provides the appropriate context for *communications* between us and him. And within those communications, guidance will be given in a manner suitable to our particular lives and circumstances. It will fit into our life together with God in his earthly and heavenly family. Again, this is our *first* preliminary insight to help us in learning to discern God's voice.

Merely Human?

When the crowds saw what Paul had done, they shouted, . . . "The gods have come down to us in human form!" . . . And the crowds wanted to offer sacrifice. . . . [But] when the apostles Barnabas and Paul heard of it, they . . . rushed out into the crowd, shouting, "Friends, why are you doing this? We are mortals just like you." (Acts 14:11-15)

A *second* truth that is preliminary to any successful attempt on our part to hear God's voice concerns the relationship of our personal experience to the contents of the Bible and, by extension, to the lives of the saints and heroes of the faith throughout the ages.

The above scene from the book of Acts portrays the common human response to people who are living in such a close relationship with God that special manifestations of his presence stand out in their lives. We immediately think, "They just aren't human!" By this we mean that their experience—including their experience of God—is not like ours and perhaps that they are even some special kind of people, so our experience of God could never be like theirs.

It is, no doubt, hard to believe that someone clearly manifesting a transcendent life could still be human. One of the most serious and severe doctrinal struggles in the early church was over the question of whether Jesus was authentically human. A primary function of the doctrine of the virgin birth, when first introduced, was to secure the fact that Jesus really did have a human body, since he was literally born of a woman. His body came forth from a womb.[1] Still earlier, in "the days of his flesh" when his humanity was quite visible through his literal bodily presence and processes, his closest friends and associates apparently could not see his divinity. Philip, as the end drew near, said, "Lord, show us the Father, and we will be satisfied." Jesus could only reply, "Have I been with you all this time, Philip, and you still do not know me? Whoever has seen me has seen the Father" (Jn 14:8-9).

Jesus was human, yet divine; divine, yet human. We must understand this precarious balance if we are to do justice to the realities of Jesus' redemptive presence in history. It is fairly easy to state, but only the gracious inward assistance of God will enable us to base our lives upon it.

This problem of uniting the life of God with the life of humanity continued to bother the early believers. Elijah was cited by James, the Lord's brother, as a case well known in this respect, which could help the believers understand their own experience and its possibilities. The story of Elijah's terror before Jezebel, his running for his life and his dissolving into a mass of righteous self-pity (1 Kings 19) shows clearly that he really was human. He was, after all, "a human being like us" (Jas 5:17), regardless of his occasional fantastic feats in the power of God.

The humanity of Moses, David and Elijah, of Paul, Peter and Jesus Christ himself—of all that wonderful company of riotously human women and men whose experience is recorded in the Bible and in the history of the church— teaches us a vital lesson: *Our humanity will not by itself prevent us from knowing and interacting with God just as they did.*

How to Believe the Bible Stories

Conversely if we are really to understand the Bible record, we must enter into our study of it on the assumption that the experiences recorded there are basically of the same type as ours would have been if we had been there. Those who lived through those experiences felt very much as we would have if we had been in their place. Unless this comes home to us, the things that happened to the people in the Bible will remain unreal to us. We will not genuinely be able to believe the Bible or find its contents to be real, because it will have no experiential substance for us.

Failure to read the Bible in this realistic manner accounts for two common problems in Christian groups that hold the Bible central to their faith. One is that it becomes simply a book of doctrine, of abstract truth about God, which one can search endlessly without encountering God himself or hearing his voice. This same attitude led the religious authorities of Jesus' own day to use the Scriptures for the very purpose of avoiding him. They searched the Scriptures fervently, yet Jesus said of them, "you do not have his word abiding in you" (Jn 5:38). A. W. Tozer has pointedly remarked in this connection that

it is altogether possible to be instructed in the rudiments of the faith and still have no real understanding of the whole thing. And it is possible to go on to become expert in Bible doctrine and not have spiritual illumination, with the result that a veil remains over the mind, preventing it from apprehending the truth in its spiritual essence.[2]

The other problem that arises when we do not understand the experience of biblical characters in terms of our own experience is that we simply stop reading the Bible altogether. Or else we take it in regular doses, choking it down like medicine because someone told us that it would be good for us—though we really do not find it to be so.

The open secret of many "Bible-believing" churches is that only a very small percentage of their members study the Bible with even the degree of interest, intelligence or joy that they bring to bear upon their favorite newspaper or magazine. In my opinion, based upon considerable experience, this is primarily because they do not know and are not taught how to understand the experience of biblical characters in terms of their own experience.

Perhaps they are even warned *not* to understand it in this way, told that it is dangerous to do so. But the Bible itself teaches that we are to understand it in terms of our own experience when it says that Paul, Barnabas and Elijah were human beings like us and that Jesus knows how we feel in our weaknesses because he himself "in every respect has been tested as we are" (Heb 4:15). It means that their experience was substantially like our own.

If we are to hear God's voice ourselves and on an individual basis, we must above all else observe how his word came to those people described in the Scriptures. How did they experience God's communication? What was it like for them to hear God? We must prayerfully but boldly use our God-given imaginations as we read the stories of people who encountered God. We must ask ourselves what it would be like if *we* were Moses standing by the bush (Ex 3:2), little Samuel lying in his darkened room (1 Sam 3:3-7), Elisha under inspiration from the minstrel (2 Kings 3:15), Ananias receiving his vision about Paul (Acts 9:11) or Peter on his rooftop (Acts 10:10). We must pray for the faith and for the experiences that would enable us to believe that *such things could happen to us*. Only then will we be able to recognize, accept and dwell in them when they come. This is our *second* general guideline.

Humble Arrogance: Who, Me, Lord?

> Nevertheless, do not rejoice at this, that the spirits submit to you, but rejoice that your names are written in heaven. (Lk 10:20)

Richard Attenborough's movie *Gandhi* has a scene set in South Africa where the young Indian lawyer and a white clergyman are walking together on a boardwalk, contrary to South African law at the time. They are accosted by some brutish-looking young white men who seem about to harm them. But the mother of the ringleader calls from an upstairs window and commands him to go about his business.

As they walk on, the clergyman exclaims over their good *luck.* Gandhi comments, "I thought you were a man of God."

The clergyman replies, "I am, but I don't believe he plans his day around me!"

The audience laughs, of course. A cute point indeed! But beneath it lie an attitude and a set of beliefs that may make it impossible for us to take seriously the possibility of divine guidance. And if we do not take it seriously, then of course we shall not be able to enter into it.

To the statement made above—that we must think of ourselves as capable of having the same kinds of experiences as did Elijah or Paul—many will spontaneously reply, "But who am I to put myself in the place of these great ones? Who am I even to suppose that God might guide me or speak to me, much less that my experience should be like that of a Moses or Elisha?"

One who has such a reaction often presumes that it honors the greatness of God. In fact it contradicts what God has taught about himself in the Bible and in the person of Christ. *His greatness is precisely what allows him to "plan his day" around me or anyone and everyone else as he chooses.*

Within the scriptural record those spoken to by God, such as Moses or Gideon, often tried to plead unworthiness or inadequacy. While such responses are in a sense fitting, they are also beside the point. They are irrelevant, as God makes perfectly clear in the stories concerned.

We might even find it hard to believe if we were told that a high government official or some other important, though merely human, dignitary had called to talk to us. We might think, on the one hand, that we are not that important and, on the other hand, that such a communication might seem to *make* us important. Similar thoughts may be stirred up at the suggestion of God's talking to us. But these thoughts are simply irrelevant to his purposes in dealing with us. Moreover they contain tragic misconceptions that have the power to shut us off from the individualized word of God.

In the first place, we *are* that important. We were important enough for God to give his Son's life for us and to choose to inhabit us as a living temple. Obviously then we are important enough for him to guide us and speak to us whenever that is appropriate.

In the second place, *his speaking to us does not in itself* make *us important.* Just as when he spoke to the ancient people of Israel, his speaking to us only gives us greater opportunity to be and to do good and greater responsibility for the care and guidance of others. But if we allow God's conversational walk with us (or anything else, for that matter) to make us think we are people of great importance, his guidance will pretty certainly be withdrawn. For we cannot be trusted with it. Under the kingdom of the heavens, those who exalt themselves will be abased as Jesus taught, and pride is the condition that comes right before a fall.

In seeking and receiving God's word to us, therefore, we must at the same time seek and receive the *grace of humility.* God will gladly give it to us if, trusting and waiting on him to act, we refrain from *pretending* we are what we know we are not, from *presuming* a favorable position for ourselves in any respect and from *pushing* or trying to override the will of others in our context. (This is a fail-safe recipe for humility. Try it for one month. Money-back guarantee if it doesn't work!)

Moses may well be the all-time record holder for lengthy conversations with God. If there were such a category in the *Guinness Book of Records,* Moses would certainly head the list. But he was also one of the least presumptuous human beings who ever walked the earth: "Moses was very humble, more so than anyone else on the face of the earth" (Num 12:3). Certainly a connection existed between his meekness and his close working and talking relationship with God. Psalm 25:9 says of God, "He leads the humble in what is right, and teaches the humble his way."

The Strength of True Meekness

In his book *George Mueller of Bristol,* A. T. Pierson comments on this verse from the Psalms in a way that both elaborates the present point and will prove highly useful later in this book:

> Here is a double emphasis upon *meekness* as a condition of such guidance and teaching. *Meekness is a real preference for God's will.* Where this holy habit of mind exists, the whole being becomes so open to impression that, without any *outward* sign or token, there is an *inward* recognition and choice of the will of God. God guides, not by a visible sign, but by *swaying the judgment.* To wait before him, weighing candidly in the scales every consideration for or against a proposed course, and in readiness to see which way the preponderance lies, is a frame of mind and heart in which one is fitted to be guided; and God touches the scales and makes the balance to sway as he will. *But our hands must be off the scales,* otherwise we need expect no interposition of his in our favor.[3]

This brings us to the *third* preliminary truth that we must keep constantly before us in our search for a word from God: When God speaks to us, *it does not prove that we are righteous or even right.* It does not even prove that we have correctly understood what he said. The infallibility of the messenger and the message does not guarantee the infallibility of our reception. Humility is always in order.

This is an especially important point to make since the appeals "God told me" or "the Lord led me" are commonly used by the speaker to prove that "I am right," that *"you* should follow *me"* or even that *"I* should get *my* way." Once for all let us say that no such claim is automatically justified.

This is such a common misunderstanding for seeking divine instruction that some may say, "What is the use of it then? Why should God speak to me, or I listen, if it will not give me unquestionable authority and absolutely ensure that I am on the right track?"

In the chapters that follow I hope to offer a fully satisfactory response to this question. We shall, in due order, have to examine the entire issue of authority and of being "right" in relation to hearing God's voice. But in our efforts to comprehend what an individual word from God is and how it works, we must never lose sight of the fact that God's purposes are *not* merely to secure and support us in our various roles or to make sure that we are right.

Indeed, being right is one of the hardest burdens humans beings have to bear, and few succeed in bearing up under it gracefully. There is a little placard I have seen that reads, "Lord, when we are wrong, make us willing to change, and when we are right, make us easy to live with!" A very wise prayer.

Paul the apostle has warned us that knowledge puffs up, whereas love builds up, and that no one knows anything as well as they ought to know it (1 Cor 8:1-2). This is so, it seems, even if we are hearing God. The voice of God we seek to hear in the Way of Christ is only *one* part of a life of humility, power, faith and hopeful love, whose final overall character is life with God in the embrace of "the everlasting arms" (Deut 33:27 KJV).

The next chapter will offer a clearer picture of what the experience of that life is like—of how it is that we are to be with God and God with us.

Some Topics for Reflection

1. Why does the *Stepford Wives* model of human relationships seem attractive to some people? What are its strengths and weaknesses?

2. Does the picture of love as a way of "being with" fit into what you have experienced in your life? Think of all the types of relationships in which love plays a role.

3. Discuss or reflect privately on the idea that one of God's main tasks is to see to it that no one gets away with anything.

4. What is the relationship between communion, communication and guidance in human affairs—say between a mother and daughter or between friends? To what extent would this carry over or not carry over to God and his children?

5. Do you see inherent conflicts between being spoken to by God and meekness or humility? What must be understood in order to resolve these?

6. Identify the three general guidelines for hearing from God that are presented in this chapter.

Three

Never Alone

Then the LORD God said,
"It is not good that the man should be alone."
GENESIS 2:18

Look, the young woman is with child and shall bear a son,
and shall name him Immanuel.
ISAIAH 7:14

I am with you always, to the end of the age.
MATTHEW 28:20

A LITTLE GROUP FROM A COLLEGE THAT I ATTENDED AS A YOUNG man used to hold religious services on Thursday evenings for the inmates at a county jail located about thirty miles east of Chattanooga, Tennessee. The people imprisoned there were not hardened criminals but were quite ordinary men who were serving short sentences of several months to a year for minor offenses. Isolation from their friends and families caused them to suffer acutely.

They seemed for the most part really to look forward to our weekly visits, perhaps more for the singing than anything else. In our group was a young lady who was a beautiful Christian as well as a fine musician. She would play the accordion and the men would join in enthusiastically with the songs and hymns. There was one song in particular that they rarely if ever failed to request:

I've seen the lightning flashing,
I've heard the thunder roll;
I've felt sin's breakers dashing,
Trying to conquer my soul.
I've heard the voice of Jesus,
Telling me still to fight on.
He promised never to leave me,
Never to leave me alone.

Then they would swing into the chorus with all the pathos of desperate men contemplating their last hope on earth:

No, never alone; no, never alone!
He promised never to leave me,
Never to leave me alone.[1]

There is so much loneliness all around us. I once found myself in London with several days on my hands while waiting for a charter flight back to the United States. A great deal of my time was spent in Westminster Cathedral (not Westminster *Abbey*) in meditation and prayer. In the abbey one senses the great past—the majestic history of the English people and of God's dealings with them. In the cathedral, by contrast, which is some distance up from the abbey toward Victoria Station, there is a divine presence beyond all national histories. Something about the vast, obscure interior of that building impresses me with the nearness of God.

In front of the cathedral is a square with benches, some tables, and off to one side a religious bookstore and a McDonald's—golden McArches and all. Here street people of London come to sleep safely in the morning sun, if it is shining, and to glean scraps of *haute cuisine* left by those who dine with McDonald.

I recall watching one woman on a number of occasions as she slept—with children and pigeons flocking around her. She was blond, a little heavyset and about middle-aged. While she showed the marks of street life, she looked very much like many a wife at the center of a happy family. And I thought, *Whose daughter is she? Whose sister, or mother, or neighbor or classmate?*

And here she is—alone, alone, alone!"

A similar but even more profound feeling had come over me when our first child was born. I realized painfully that this incredibly beautiful little creature we had brought into the world was utterly separate from me and that nothing I could do would shelter him from his aloneness in the face of time, brutal events, the meanness of other human beings, his own wrong choices, the decay of his own body and, finally, death.

It is simply not within human capacity to care effectively for others in the depths of their life and being or even to be *with* them in finality—no matter how much we may care about them. If we could only *really* be with them, that would almost be enough, we think. But we cannot, at least not in a way that would satisfy us. For all of us the words of the old song are true: "You must go there by yourself."

That would be the last word on the subject but for God. He is able to penetrate and intertwine himself within the fibers of the human self in such a way that those who are enveloped in his loving companionship will never be alone. This surely is the meaning of the great affirmation at the end of Romans 8:

> Who will separate us from the love of Christ? Will hardship, or distress, or persecution, or famine, or nakedness, or peril, or sword? . . . No, in all these things we are more than conquerors through him who loved us. For I am convinced that neither death, nor life, nor angels, nor rulers, nor things present, not things to come, nor powers, nor height, nor depth, nor anything else in all creation, will be able to separate us from the love of God in Christ Jesus our Lord. (vv. 35, 37-39)

Even our anguish over those dear to us can be completely put to rest when we see they are living in the presence from which nothing can separate them. The final and complete blessing and ultimate good, the *summum bonum* of humankind, comes to those with lives absorbed in the Way of Christ—life in the presence of God. The completely adequate word of faith in all our sorrows and all our joys is "Immanuel, God with us!" Thus we sing:

Where'er Thou art may we remain;
Where'er Thou goest may we go;
With Thee, O Lord, no grief is pain,
Away from Thee all joy is woe.

Oh, may we in each holy tide,
Each solemn season, dwell with Thee!
Content if only by Thy side
In life or death we still may be.[2]

"In your presence," the psalmist says, "there is fullness of joy; in your right hand are pleasures forevermore" (Ps 16:11). Even in the valley of the shadow of death there is nothing to fear. Why? Because "you are with me" (Ps 23:4).

On the other hand the fact that only God can take away our aloneness by his presence explains why the ultimate suffering and punishment is separation from the presence of God. The psalmist cries out in terror, "Do not cast me away from your presence, and do not take your holy spirit from me" (Ps 51:11).

The Giver and His Gifts

It is, of course, true that the person and presence of God with us is sought in part for its external effects. In many of this world's religions the favor of the gods is mainly or totally sought simply because of the advantage it brings. The psalmist, once again, describes the presence of God as a place to hide from the pride of man (Ps 31:20; see also 27:5; 32:7). After refusing to enrich and fortify himself with plunder from his victory over the kings (Gen 14:22-24), Abraham, father of the faithful, is given a vision of God saying to him, "Do not be afraid. . . . I am your shield; your reward shall be very great" (15:1).

When Jehovah was angered by the sins of the Israelites on their journey to Canaan and seemed about to desert them, Moses prevailed upon him by saying, "For how shall it be known that I have found favor in your sight, I and your people, unless you go with us? In this way, we shall be distinct, I and your people, from every people on the face of the earth" (Ex 33:16).

Yet trying to control our circumstances by means of the presence of God is not, finally, what we rest in as disciples of Jesus. We are told to "be content with what you have; for he has said, 'I will never leave you or forsake you.' So we can say with confidence, 'The Lord is my helper; I will not be afraid. What can anyone do to me?' " (Heb 13:5-6). The promise here is not that God will never allow any evil to come to us but that no matter what befalls us, we are *still* beyond genuine harm due to the fact that he remains with us and his presence is utterly enough by itself.

Our contentment lies not in his *presents* but in the *presence* of the One whose presents they are. In all our trials we are more than conquerors because, as we have seen, nothing shall be able to "separate us from the love of God in Christ Jesus our Lord" (Rom 8:39).

Thomas à Kempis speaks for all the ages when he represents Jesus as saying to him, "A wise lover regards not so much the gift of him who loves, as the love of him who gives. He esteems affection rather than valuables, and sets all gifts below the Beloved. A noble-minded lover rests not in the gift, but in Me above every gift."[3] The sustaining power of the Beloved Presence has through the ages made the sickbed sweet and the graveside triumphant; transformed broken hearts and relations; brought glory to drudgery, poverty and old age; and turned the martyr's stake or noose into a place of coronation.

As St. Augustine has written, when we come to our final home, "there we shall rest and see, see and love, love and praise. This is what shall be in the end without end."[4] It is this for which the human soul was made. It is our temporal and eternal calling: "Man's chief end is to glorify God and enjoy him forever."[5]

But now loneliness is loose upon the landscape. It haunts the penthouse and the rectory, the executive suite and the millionaire's mansion, as well as the barren apartment, the assembly line, the cocktail bar and the city streets. It is, as Mother Teresa of Calcutta once said, the leprosy of the modern world. A popular song of some years back deplored the fate of Eleanor Rigby and exclaimed over "all the lonely people! Where do they all come from?"

There is a simple and correct answer to this question: the lonely people live apart from God. They live "without hope and without God in the world" (Eph 2:12 NIV). Their many experiences of alienation are rooted in their alienation from God.

Is it actually possible to make clear what a life *with* God is like, a life in which one is never alone? Is it at least feasible to explain it in terms that would enable an honest and open-minded person to approach the possibility of entering into it? Let us look at various forms that God's presence with us may take.

We will be looking at concrete ways of understanding our "with" relationship to God, in which we are forever done with isolation and loneliness. The following words from Scripture provide some intriguing suggestions:

> You shall be for me a priestly kingdom and a holy nation. (Ex 19:6)

> To him who loves us and freed us from our sins by his blood, and made us to be a kingdom, priests serving his God and Father, to him be glory and dominion forever and ever. (Rev 1:5-6)

The basic idea here is that God calls us to a direct and fully self-conscious personal relationship with him (as priests) in which we share responsibility with him (as kings) in the exercise of his authority. Exactly what does this involve, and how do we experience it? There are a number of phases involved, as I've described below.

"Blind" Faith

First of all, what we may call "blind" faith is a valid, though very minimal, way of God's being with us. Here we find ourselves really believing in God and believing that he is with us. Perhaps we believe because of past experiences or because we have faith in the faith of others or even because of abstract reasonings that tell us he simply *must* be here. But our conviction—almost a mere will that it shall be so—is the only way that he is present in our lives. We have no awareness of his being here with us at all and no evidence of his action in or around us. Still we believe. Still we are faith-full.

Although this kind of faith is not to be despised—far from it—the human heart can never be content to treat God's being with us merely as a matter of blind faith with nothing else to go on. Abstract reasoning from the doctrine of God's omnipresence, mental assent to the dogma that God must be with the believer, faith in the faith of others, even remembrance of past experiences of God—none of these can be an adequate foundation for sustained spiritual growth.

Those who understand God's presence only in these ways must be encouraged to believe that there is much more for them to know and receive. Otherwise they will never enter into their capacities as kings and priests, never "reign in life through the one man, Jesus Christ" (Rom 5:17 NIV).

Sensing God's Presence

Perhaps the first step beyond mere faith that God must be here is an indeterminate but often very powerful sense, feeling or impression of God's presence. As is the case in our discerning the *voice* of God (to be discussed later), we need considerable experience in order to learn how to accurately recognize and assess the meanings of such impressions. Yet a sense of God's presence is frequently verified through the judgment of the worshiping community and serves as a basis for intelligent appraisal and cooperation by and among individual members of the group. Different people simultaneously sense that certain things are to be done—that God is here and is moving in *that* direction.

This corporate sensing is a well-known phenomenon. Experienced ministers and laypeople frequently find they have synchronized their activities unerringly in a meeting or other form of service through their sense of God's presence and intent for the particular occasion. It is something they come to expect and to rely upon. And those who sense God's presence while alone in prayer, service, meditation or study find easy communication with multitudes of others who have had similar—or even, it often seems, identical—experiences. They talk a common language, based upon the sameness of their individual experiences.

Such a strong sense of the presence of another also occurs at a purely secular level, where the "other" is a human being. We may have the distinct impression that someone is looking at us or listening to us, only to later learn that in fact a certain person *was* looking intently at us or listening to us at that time. It is not an uncommon occurrence.

There are those who are able to attract the attention of another person (across a large hall, for example) merely by staring intently at the back of that person's head. Some "smart" weapons of warfare are able to detect when they are being "watched" by radar, and perhaps we are not altogether unlike them. Some people seem more sensitive than others to such things, just as some have better eyesight or more acute hearing than others have.

It is clear enough that one person's conscious concentration upon another frequently evokes a reciprocal awareness. Since this is known to be true among human beings, we should not be surprised that God's attention to us should result in our reciprocal awareness of *his* presence.

Sometimes, of course, the sense of God with us becomes much more distinct. My oldest brother, J. I. Willard, served for over thirty years as a minister under the blessing of God. But his entry into the ministry came through long and intense struggles with personal and financial issues.

One evening he faced a major decision that had to be made the next day, a decision that would commit him for years into the future. He prayed long into the night, falling asleep at around 1:30 a.m. But, he relates, at 2:00 a.m. "that room lit up with the glory of God. I saw a figure. I did not see a face, but I recognized it to be the person of Christ. I felt a hand on my shoulder, and I heard a voice that said, 'Feed my sheep.'"

As has been the case for many others who have been given such experiences, the presence of God almost overwhelmed his consciousness, and it also transformed various aspects of his personality. He was suddenly living in the study of the Bible, memorizing much of it without trying to do so, even though his days were spent in hard physical labor. He had been painfully addicted to tobacco all of his adult life; desire for it was removed without his asking. According to him, the "aroma" of that room full of the presence of God has stayed with him ever since. Many others would testify that it is so.

The God Who Acts

The sense of God's presence is sometimes accompanied in Christian experience by extraordinary events or powerful effects not easily attributable, if attributable at all, to merely natural causes. This range of effects is a third form taken by God's presence with us, and the sense of his presence is by no means essential to it. The mark of the working of God's Spirit with us is the *incommensurability* of the effects with our merely human powers. The outcome is beyond natural powers to accomplish. Such humanly unaccountable effects fit into and even certify the principles and purposes of the rule of God in human history, as manifested in the works of Christ and the Scriptures generally.

It Couldn't Be You

After many years of highly successful ministry, Dwight Lyman Moody had an experience of which he himself said,

> I cannot describe it, I seldom refer to it, it is almost too sacred an experience to name. . . . I can only say God revealed Himself to me, and I had such an experience of His love that I had to ask Him to stay His hand. I went to preaching again. The sermons were not different; I did not present any new truths; and yet hundreds were converted. I would not now be placed back where I was before that blessed experience if you should give me all the world; it would be as small dust in the balance.[6]

In his day Moody was a constant source of wonder precisely because the effects of his ministry were so totally incommensurable, even incongruent, with his obvious personal qualities. He was a man of very ordinary appearance, unordained by any ecclesiastical group and quite uncultured and uneducated—even uncouth and crude to many.

At the height of Moody's effectiveness, between 1874 and 1875, Dr. R. W. Dale, one of the leading nonconformist clergymen in England, observed his work in Birmingham for three or four days. He wished to discover the secret of Moody's power. After his observations were completed he told Moody that the work was most plainly the work of God, for he could see no relation between him personally and what he was accomplishing. A smaller person might well have been offended at this, but Moody only laughed and replied that he would be very sorry if things were otherwise.[7]

In the Bible Abraham fathered Isaac—the son of promise and spirit—with Sarah, *contrary* to nature. It was achieved through the energy of the Spirit, altogether beyond Abraham and Sarah alike. But at an earlier point in time Abraham and Hagar were quite competent to beget Ishmael through the mere energies of their bodies (Gal 4:22-28). Life with effects beyond the natural *always* depends upon intimate interactions between us and God, who is therefore present.

When Paul and Barnabas set out on their first missionary journey (Acts 13—14), they moved at every turn in a power that was far beyond themselves. The result was an astonishing series of events, establishing communities of believers in Christ throughout central Asia Minor. When they returned to their home in Syrian Antioch, they brought the community of believers together and matter-of-factly "reported everything that God had done *with them,* and how *he* had opened the door of faith to the Gentiles" (14:27, paraphrase). There was no doubt of God's presence with them because it was he who energized their activities with a power beyond their own. The fulfillment of Jesus' words concerning the divine helper—"he abides with you, and he will be in you" (Jn 14:17)—was to them the most obvious fact of their lives. "If the Spirit of him who raised Jesus from the dead dwells in you, he who raised Christ from the dead will give life to your mortal bodies through his Spirit that dwells in you" (Rom 8:11; also Eph 1:19-20).

Is That All?

Brother Lawrence tells us:

> I make it my business to persevere in his Holy presence, wherein I keep myself by a simple attention and a general fond regard to God, which I may call an ACTUAL PRESENCE of God; or, to speak better, an habitual, silent, and secret conversation of the soul with God, which often causes me joys and raptures inwardly, and sometimes also outwardly, so great that I am forced to use means to moderate them and prevent their appearance to others.[8]

So far we have considered three forms or aspects of God's presence with us: (1) when he is indeed close to us, but we are not aware of him or his effects, having only blind faith or abstract reasoning to turn us toward him; (2) when he is sensed, or there is a strong impression of his presence; and (3) when he acts in conjunction with our actions to change our surroundings in ways beyond our own powers.

Many who would agree with these three points might wish to accept what has been said so far as a complete account of the forms of God's presence with us. But Brother Lawrence has something more in mind, and I believe he is right. To stop now would be to omit what is most important in the ongoing relationship between human beings and God and to rob of its substance the biblical idea of the *priesthood* and the *royalty* of the believer. It would leave our interaction with God too close to the level of vague feelings, the Ouija board and even superstitious conjecture.

How can we be friends of God if this is all there is to it? How is the rich conceptual content and knowledge found in the Bible to be understood as something communicated to us in revelation if the three forms of presence so far discussed are the totality of human interaction with God? Why, if God is personal, would he not also *talk* with us?

So we must add to the above that God is also with us in a conversational relationship: he speaks with us individually as it is appropriate—which is only to be expected between persons who know one another, care about each other and are engaged in common enterprises.

It is just such a conversational manner of presence that is suited to the personal relationship with God so often spoken of in the Christian community. It is this that turns Paul's statement that "all who are led by the Spirit of God are children of God" (Rom 8:14) into a *framework for personal development* as distinct from an incitement to play the robot or be a mere interpreter of vague impressions and signs.

Two Types of Guidance

Before going any further we should note that there are, as is generally understood, two types of guidance commonly found in life. One is the *mechanical* variety that is involved in driving a car or in the remote electronic control of a model airplane or space probe. We guide something in this sense whenever, by consciously employed means, we cause it to proceed in a certain way preferred by us. The simplest and clearest cases of this fall within the area of mechanical guidance.

But there is also *personal* guidance. Here too we wish to bring events to proceed in a certain way, but now we are dealing with people. They have a mind with which to consider matters on their own and a will concerning what is to be done. The ideal then for personal guidance is to bring things to the desired outcome, but at the same time to allow the mind being guided its fullest scope and the will its uncoerced initiative.

Thus the outcome is really also the work of the individual being guided, not merely of the one who is guiding. The individual's uniqueness counts before God and must not be overridden. It remains the individual's life after all since we have guided only through her or his own understanding, deliberation and decisions.

For this purpose we must *communicate* with the one who is to be guided. This is the only means by which we can have an impact on the individual and yet leave him or her the mental and spiritual space to retain integrity as a free personality, to live as our friend and to govern his or her own life.

God generally deals with his nonhuman or nonpersonal creation as one guides a car: by a causal influence mediated through the general system of physical reality that he has ordained in his creation. But God's *personal* creatures, whether angelic or human, are also guided by communication of his intentions and thoughts. They are *addressed* by him. In Psalm 32:9 we are admonished, "Do not be like a horse or a mule, without understanding, whose temper must be curbed with bit and bridle." We are to be led by—guided by—reasonable, intelligible communication, not by blind impulse, force or sensation alone.

Discerning God's Words

Such a communication may occur in one of two ways. First, God communicates through what we will recognize as a voice or as words addressed to—or even through—us. The primary manner of communication from God to humankind is the Word of God, or God's speaking. The Bible itself is God's speaking preserved in written form. God spoke directly to Moses, to Ezekiel, to Paul and to many others. Through them he spoke indirectly to the people of Israel and to the church, and now—in the Bible—he speaks to world history.

In Acts 9:10-16, for example, we have the story of a man named Ananias. The events here immediately follow Paul's being struck down as the risen Christ addressed him on the road to Damascus. Paul went into seclusion in Damascus, where he fasted and prayed for three days. Apparently around the end of that time the Lord appeared to Paul's fellow believer Ananias, of the same city, and told him that he should go and speak to Paul (then called Saul). Thus Paul was put in touch with and ministered to by the believers in Damascus.

What we see here is not a matter of abstract argumentation, of strong impressions or of naturally unaccountable events. The same is true for Peter's experience on the rooftop in Joppa (Acts 10), before he was called to preach the gospel in the house of Cornelius, the Roman.

According to the records we have, such things happened to Paul over and over. He was about to go into Bithynia on his second missionary journey. Somehow, as we are told in Acts 16:6-9, the Holy Spirit would not let him go. Then as he waited at Troas, he had a dream that instead of staying on his home territory in Asia Minor, he should take a radically new direction and enter Europe. In the dream a man from Macedonia called to him, saying, "Come over . . . and help us."

These purposeful and conscious communications by words seem to have been quite normal experiences for the early Christians. If we look at the advice on how the meetings of the church were supposed to proceed, as given in 1 Corinthians 14, we see it is assumed that numerous people in the congregation are going to have some kind of communication from God which they will be sharing with the others in the group: "When you come together, each one has a hymn, a lesson, a revelation, a tongue, or an interpretation. Let all things be done for building up" (1 Cor 14:26).

The ancient prophecy of Joel was fulfilled in the early church: "Your sons and your daughters shall prophesy, and your young men shall see visions, and your old men shall dream dreams" (Acts 2:17; Joel 2:28-32). The wish of Moses "that all the LORD's people were prophets, and that the LORD would put his spirit on them" (Num 11:29) is substantially granted in the church of Jesus Christ when it functions as its Lord intended.

Discerning God's Voice in Shared Activity

There is a second way in which the intentions and thoughts of God are communicated to those who are with him. It is one that involves a much more active role on the part of the recipient and is very common among those who are most mature in his family or kingdom. Here we come to understand what God wants us to understand through immersion with him in his work. We understand what he is doing so well that we often know exactly what he is thinking and intending to do.

I believe that this is a great part of the condition described by the apostle Paul as *having the mind of Christ:* "Those who are spiritual discern all things, and they are themselves subject to no one else's scrutiny. 'For who has known the mind of the Lord so as to instruct him?' But we have the mind of Christ" (1 Cor 2:15-16).

Psalm 32 has an interesting statement in relation to this way of being with God. The psalmist here says, "I will instruct thee and teach thee in the way which thou shalt go: I will guide thee with mine eye" (v. 8 KJV). Newer versions generally say something like, "I will guide you with my eye upon you."

In two very distinct types of experience one person is guided by the eye of another. First, very few husbands, wives or children have not occasionally been forcibly guided by the stare of their partner or parent. The fatherly or motherly eye on the child speaks silent volumes of profound instruction at a moment's notice.

There is, however, a second and even more important way in which we are guided by the eye of another. This happens when we are working or playing closely with another and know the intentions and thoughts of the other's mind *by our awareness of what they are focused upon.* Someone else can work with me effectively only if they can see what I am doing without having to be told what I am thinking and what they should do to help. Model employees, for example, are by no means those who stand waiting, no matter how solicitously, for someone to tell them what to do. Everyone breathes more easily when the new person on the job no longer has to be told what to do at every stage.

A similar distinction can be drawn with respect to levels of friendship. In *The Transforming Friendship,* Leslie Weatherhead describes a kind of friendship interaction that is cognitive but occurs beyond words:

> If my friend's mother in a distant town falls ill and he urgently desires to visit her, which would reveal deeper friendship—my lending him my motor-bike in response to his request for it, or my taking it to his door for him as soon as I heard of the need, without waiting to be asked? In the first case there has to be a request made with a voice. But in the second the fact of the friendship creates in me a longing to help. The first illustrates the communion between two persons on what we might call the level of the seen; but the second illustrates the communion, at a deeper level, of two persons on what we may call the level of the unseen.[9]

In many cases our need to wonder about or be told what God wants in a certain situation is nothing short of a clear indication of how little we are engaged in his work.

On one sabbath Jesus came upon a man with a withered hand in the synagogue (Mk 3:1-5). He called him out and asked the people gathered around whether one should do good on the sabbath (heal the man) or do evil (leave him in distress). The whole condition of these people was loudly and eloquently declared by their silence. They did not know what to do! "They were silent" (3:4).

After he had healed the man, however, they thought it right to make plans to kill Jesus. This was only another fruit of the same heart that *could* wonder whether or not the man should be healed. But Jesus knew what God wanted done in this case because *he knew the mind of God generally.* On another occasion when he was denounced for healing on the sabbath he calmly replied, "My Father is still working, and I also am working" (Jn 5:17).

So our union with God—his presence with us, in which our aloneness is banished and the meaning and full purpose of human existence is realized—*consists chiefly in a conversational relationship with God while we are each consistently and deeply engaged as his friend and colaborer in the affairs of the kingdom of the heavens.*

I want to emphasize that there is an important place for blind faith in God's presence, as we have described it, as well as for the feeling or sense that he is near and for a display of the supernatural effects of his presence. But no amount of these can take the place of intelligible communication through word and shared activity.

When all of these types of presence are in place, it is then that the royal priesthood of the believer (Ex 19:6) is realized as it should be. It is then that having a personal relationship with God becomes a concrete and common-sense reality rather than a nervous whistling in the spiritual dark.

God does indeed guide us in many ways, by special acts of intervention in our lives as well as by general providential ordering of the world. But his direct communication with us, by word and by shared activity, is the most important part. This is because we are to become the temple of God, one that actively understands and cooperates with God's purposes; one that is inhabited through a willing, clear-eyed identification of ourselves with Jesus Christ.

Hence it is Christ *in us* that is our hope of glory (Col 1:27). Paul attempts to capture this paradoxical reality in the following well-known statement: "I have been crucified with Christ; and it is no longer I who live, but it is Christ who lives in me. And the life I now live in the flesh I live by faith in the Son of God, who loved me and gave himself for me" (Gal 2:19-20).

The interpretation of these and similar passages from Scripture given above is not something that has only recently come to light. Such an understanding is not a solitary brainstorm on my part. In fact it represents the mainstream of Christianity throughout the ages, though this understanding must be renewed constantly. You may wish to compare what you have just read to the section on "Several Manners of Divine Presence" in Jeremy Taylor's *The Rule and Exercise of Holy Living*,[10] which will give a sense of the solidarity of what I have said here with what has been taught in past times.

Mistaken Interpretations

To conclude this chapter it will be useful as further clarification to single out three interpretations of how God speaks to us, including how he gives us guidance, that are commonly accepted but that are surely mistaken and certainly are very harmful to our efforts to live a life in which God is heard and his guidance received.

The message-a-minute view. According to this first view, either God is telling you what to do at every turn of the road *or* he is at least willing and available to tell you if you would only ask him.

I do not believe that either the Bible or our shared experience in the Way of Christ will substantiate this picture. There is no evidence in the life of Peter or Paul, for example, that they were *constantly* receiving communication from God.

The union Christ had with the Father was the greatest that we can conceive of in this life—if indeed we can conceive of it. Yet we have no indication that even Jesus was constantly awash with revelations as to what he should do. His union with the Father was so great that he was at all times obedient. This obedience was something that rested in his mature will and understanding of his life before God, not on always being told "Now do this" and "Now do that" with regard to every detail of his life or work.

Putting it this way returns us to the idea that *God speaks ultimately to the mature Christian.* This is not to say that people at the time of conversion—or as they first enter the church or begin to come alive in their experience of God—do not receive words from him. God meets us where we are. Yet God's working through the Holy Spirit and the indwelling Christ to speak to us is not to keep us constantly under his dictation. Too much intrusion on a seed that has been planted, as on the life of a plant or a child, simply makes normal, healthy growth impossible.

Thus E. Stanley Jones helpfully observes,

I believe in miracle, but not too much miracle, for too much miracle would weaken us, make us dependent on miracle instead of our obedience to natural law. Just enough miracle to let us know He is there, but not too much, lest we depend on it when we should depend on our own initiative and on His orderly processes for our development.[11]

A redemptive community consists not of robots but of mature people who know how to live together and who know how to live with God. For that reason I think this model of a message a minute is mistaken and very harmful in our efforts to hear God. Extensive observations of individuals who *try* to live with this model, or at least profess to, show that they simply cannot do it and that any sustained effort to do so leads quickly to disaster.

Of course the question is not whether God *could* give a message every minute. Surely he could do that. He could give ten or a thousand messages a nanosecond—even more if that would suit his purpose of bringing forth the cosmic family of God. But it does not. Sometimes we get caught up in trying to glorify God by praising what he can do, and we lose sight of the practical point of what he actually does do.

All of this must be kept in mind as we develop our educational programs, hold our evangelistic meetings, run teaching missions and carry on with all the other activities of the church. In our services and in our models both of the ministry and of ministers, we must remember that we are not making robots who sing, clap, pray, give and show up for meetings when they are supposed to. We are bringing forth the sons and daughters of God to live their unique lives in this world to his glory. We must do all we can to suit the means we employ to that end.

The it's-all-in-the-Bible view. I believe this second view is seriously misguided and very harmful. It intends to honor the Bible, but it does so with a zeal that is not according to knowledge.

The Bible gives direct instructions about many situations in our lives. We do not need to make long inquiries into God's will in order to know whether we should worship an idol, take something that is not ours, engage in illicit sex or mistreat our parents. But many other questions force us to realize that many of the specific circumstances of our lives are simply not dealt with in the Bible.

The Bible will not tell which song you are supposed to sing next Sunday or which verse you should take as a text for a talk or a sermon. Yet it is very likely that God's special leading is claimed for nothing more frequently than for the selection of texts and sermon topics.

Neither will the Bible tell you what to do with most of the details of your life. Suppose you want to know how to raise your children. It will tell you some very important things but not everything you need and want to know on that subject. Your family, your work and your community will present you with many, many choices and issues about which the Bible simply says nothing.

The *principles* are all there, however. I happily insist that so far as principles are concerned, the Bible says all that needs to be said or can be said. But the principles have to be applied before they can be lived out, and it is largely at the point of application that almost everything imaginable has been "proven" from the Bible. In order to get the applications so desperately desired, however, the principles of proof have to be scandalously loosened.

Our reverence for and faith in the Bible must not be allowed to blind us to the need for personal divine instruction *within* the principles of the Bible yet *beyond* the details of what it explicitly says. A distinguished minister once said on television that if we would only accept the Bible as the Word of God, all differences between Christians would be resolved. But in fact it is Bible-believing Christians who disagree with each other most often and most heatedly.

Nearly every faction in Christendom claims the Bible as its basis but then goes on to disagree as to what the Bible says. An exalted view of the Bible does not free us from the responsibility of learning to talk with God and to hear him in the many ways he speaks to humankind.

A misguided expectation of the Bible's ability to speak specifically to an individual or a situation leads some people to play the Bible roulette mentioned earlier. They allow the Bible to fall open where it will and then stab their finger at random on the page to see which verse it lands on. Then they read the selected verse to see what they should do.

Despite the fact that some great Christians have used this technique, it is certainly not a procedure recommended *by* the Bible, and there is no biblical reason why one might not just as well use a dictionary, the *Encyclopaedia*

Britannica or the morning newspaper or simply open the Bible and wait for a fly to land on a verse.

A novel approach was recently suggested by a minister who stated in all seriousness that we should look up the year of our birth to cast light on what we should do. Unless you were born in the first half of the twentieth century (the earlier the better) this method will do you no good, since there are few verses numbered beyond 20 or 30. I was born in 1935, so I thought I would see what direction I could get from Genesis 19:35. I will leave it to your curiosity to see what that verse says, but I shudder to think what instruction might be derived from this method.

Of course God is so great that he sometimes does use almost anything you can imagine for his purposes in the life of a person who is sincerely seeking him. Even truly superstitious methods are not beyond his forbearance and use. But that does not certify them as methods chosen by him for the spiritual life.

In the upper room (Acts 1:26) lots were cast—akin to flipping a coin or drawing straws—to determine who would replace Judas among the twelve apostles. This method was often used in biblical times, and Proverbs 16:33 assures us that while the lot is cast into the lap, "the decision is the LORD's alone." Even the most biblically oriented churches of today would not think of rolling dice or flipping a coin to determine a policy for the church or to settle an issue in some individual member's life. This is true even though all might agree that God *could* determine the coin or the dice to come out as he wished.

So we have made some progress. Nevertheless you still hear people tell of opening the Bible at random and reading a verse to decide whether to undertake some enterprise or move or to marry a certain person. Many devout people will do such things to hear God—so great is their need and anxiety—though they may later try to hide it or laugh at it when revealed. Worse still, many actually act upon the fruit of this "guidance" to the great harm of themselves and others around them. They are the losers at Bible roulette. What a stark contrast to this unhappy condition is the simple word of Jesus: "My sheep hear my voice. I know them, and they follow me" (Jn 10:27).

The whatever-comes view. This third mistaken view of how God speaks is commonly adopted and has much to recommend it in terms of the peace of mind and freedom from struggle that it provides. But in fact it amounts to giving up any possibility of a *conscious* interchange between God and his children.

The view even shows up in some of our most loved hymns. There is a well-known hymn entitled "If Thou but Suffer God to Guide Thee." This may seem to be exactly what we are talking about: allowing God to guide us. But when we study the hymn closely we find it counsels us to accept *everything* that happens as the guidance of God.

If you wish to know what God would have you do, it is no help at all to be told that whatever comes is his will. For you are, precisely, in the position of having to decide in some measure what *is* to come. Does it mean that whatever you do will be God's will? I certainly hope not.

We can at least say that if Moses had accepted this view, there would have been no nation of Israel. Perhaps there would have been a nation of "Mosesites" instead. When the people made and worshiped the golden calf while Moses was on Sinai receiving God's commandments, God said to him, "Now let me alone, so that my wrath may burn hot against them and I may consume them; and of you I will make a great nation" (Ex 32:10). Not only did Moses not accept whatever came, he actually and successfully withstood God's own declared intent in the matter, appealing to God's reputation before the surrounding nations and to his friendship with Abraham. "And the LORD changed his mind about the disaster that he had planned to bring on his people" (32:14).

Many things that happen are not the will of God, although obviously he does not act to stop them. For example, "the Lord is . . . not wanting any to perish, but all to come to repentance" (2 Pet 3:9). Nevertheless countless people do perish and fail to come to repentance.

God's world is an arena in which we have an indispensable role to play. The issue is not simply what God wants but also what we want and will. When we accept whatever comes, we are not receiving guidance. The fact that something happens does not indicate that it is God's will.

With respect to many events in our future, God's will is that *we* should determine what will happen. What a child does when *not* told what to do is the final indicator of what and who that child is. And so it is for us and our heavenly Father. (We shall return to this point in the final chapter.)

In opposition to these three mistaken views of discerning God's voice, we have the *conversational* view, where—in a manner to be explored further—there is appropriate, clear, specific communication through conscious experience from God to the individual believer within the context of a life immersed in God's kingdom.

> Then you shall call, and the LORD will answer;
> you shall cry for help, and he will say, Here I am. . . .
> The LORD will guide you continually,
> and satisfy your needs in parched places,
> and make your bones strong;
> and you shall be like a watered garden,
> like a spring of water, whose waters never fail. (Is 58:9, 11)

Many may still wonder whether we really do live in a universe where this could happen. Does the human and physical reality of our universe call for it? Does it even allow it? This is the issue to which we must now turn.

Some Topics for Reflection

1. Have you known people who were so close to God that they were never lonely? What do you think of the prospects of such a relationship for you? For others in the contemporary world?

2. Do the four basic forms of our being with God and God's being with us adequately cover that relationship? What would you add? Or take away?

3. How important do you think blind faith is to the stability of the Christian's walk?

4. Discuss or reflect on some instances where you are sure God *acted* with you. How can you learn more about this from experience?

5. Can you explain to someone else the two main types of guidance (mechanical and personal) and the two aspects of personal guidance?

6. Do you think that the critiques of the three views of hearing God said to be erroneous are sound? What would you disagree with in these critiques?

Four

Our
Communicating
Cosmos

Earth's crammed with Heaven,
and every common bush afire with God;
but only he who sees takes off his shoes.
ELIZABETH BARRETT BROWNING

In him we live and move and have our being.
ACTS 17:28

ONE CAN FIND A PRACTICALLY ENDLESS SUPPLY OF STORIES ABOUT people hearing God, and each is of considerable interest in its own right. I love to dwell on them myself, and I have noticed that other people rarely tire of hearing them, even when they do not entirely believe them. Although none of these stories is to be treated as "canonical," taken together they serve as an essential point of reference for research into divine guidance and hearing God.

One remarkable illustration concerns Peter Marshall, the Scot who in the middle of the twentieth century became one of America's most widely acclaimed ministers. Through his outstanding qualities as a man and a minister, he brought the office of the chaplain of the United States Senate to a new level of prominence.

Back in Britain, on one foggy, pitch-black Northumberland night, he was taking a shortcut across the moors in an area where there was a deep, deserted limestone quarry. As he plodded blindly forward, an urgent voice called out, "Peter!" He stopped and answered: "Yes, who is it? What do you want?" But there was no response.

Thinking he was mistaken, he took a few more steps. The voice came again, even more urgently, "Peter!" At this he stopped again and, trying to peer into the darkness, stumbled forward and fell to his knees. Putting down his hand to brace himself, he found nothing there. As he felt around in a semicircle he discovered that he was right on the brink of the abandoned quarry, where one step more would certainly have killed him.[1]

Many widely read religious papers and magazines, from almost every denomination and theological persuasion, provide us with a constant stream of such stories. In his book *Does God Speak Today?* David Pytches compiled "real-life accounts" of "words" given to disciples of Jesus in modern times. He adds fourteen cases of what are pretty clearly *mistaken* claims of hearing from God.[2] It is useful to study these latter cases when it comes to understanding how God speaks. We need to know both what it is and what it is not.

The Limits of Signs

It is, however, important to recognize that there is a limit to how much our faith can grow by contemplating such stories—no matter how well attested they may be, no matter how reliable the minds and characters of the people involved. And this limit is not neglected in the teachings of the Bible itself.

Jesus tells of father Abraham's words to the rich man in hell, that if the rich man's brothers still on earth "do not listen to Moses and the prophets neither will they be convinced even if someone rises from the dead" (Lk 16:31). This fits in with Jesus' refusal to do religious stunts or signs for those who demanded them (Mt 12:39-40; Mk 8:11-12; Lk 23:8-9; Jn 2:18; 6:30). I believe he refused because he knew that such deeds, no matter how wondrous, would be fruitless against the false ideas and mindsets of the observers. I cannot imagine that he would have withheld signs if they truly could have helped people to have genuine faith in him.

The signs, however, could not help. Our preexisting ideas and assumptions are precisely what determine what we can see, hear or otherwise observe. These general ideas—which so often we hold because they express how we want things to be—determine what stories can mean to us. They cannot, therefore, be changed by stories and miraculous events alone, since they prevent a correct perception of those very stories and events.

Agnes Sanford relates how, as the young wife of an Episcopal minister, her child came down with a serious ear infection. It lasted for six weeks, while she prayed fearfully and fruitlessly. Then a neighboring minister called to see her husband and learned that the child was sick. Quite casually, though intently and in a businesslike manner, he prayed for the little boy, who immediately shut his eyes, lost his fever flush and went to sleep. When the boy awoke, his fever was gone and his ears were well. Sanford remarks,

> The strange thing is that this did not immediately show me a new world. Instead, it perplexed me greatly. Why did God answer the minister's prayers when He had not answered mine? I did not know that I myself blocked my own prayers, because of my lack of faith. Nor did I know that this [successful] prayer could not come from resentment and darkness and unhappiness, as a pipeline can be clogged with roots and dirt. This doubt and confusion remained in my mind, even though the child himself, whenever he subsequently had a bit of an earache, demanded that I pray for him.[3]

Necessity of a General Understanding of God

We find such a failure to see a new world strange only because we do not pay attention to how our minds work. It only illustrates the fact that looking at or being told of God's specific interventions in our lives—whether to guide us, speak to us or perform saving deeds in our behalf—does not automatically clear up our confusions or straighten out the entanglements of our hearts. Such events may in fact only entertain or confuse us. They *may* stimulate us to seek understanding; but they do not of themselves *give* us faith and understanding.

Our understanding must grow *before* we can have any significant appreciation of what we are experiencing on occasions when God intervenes in our lives. We must have a correct general understanding of God and his ways.

That is why the rich man was told, "Let them hear Moses and the prophets."

The role of the Scriptures and of scriptural interpretation is to provide us with a general understanding of God and to inspire and cultivate a corresponding faith. The power of stories alone to generate life-changing faith is overestimated today. Lack of general understanding may also limit the effects of a word truly given by God to the individual. Very often in my experience the word given *to* me is actually spoken *by* me. In a way I have come to recognize through repeated occurrence, it simply comes out, with no preliminaries. I do not, however, always understand its true significance at the time. Many others have the same experience

This is exactly what happened t⸱ Peter on the occasion of his great confession: "You are the Messiah, the Son of the living God" (Mt 16:16-17). Notice what followed in Peter's case. First, Jesus authenticated that this word given to Peter was indeed from his Father in the heavens. Then he began to explain further what was going to happen to him—persecution, death, resurrection. Immediately Peter showed that he did not understand what he himself had just said. God had enabled Peter to recognize Jesus as the Christ, but Peter still did not know what the Christ would be. Consequently he tried to cast Christ in a strictly human role. Jesus had to tell Peter to get out of his way because he had his mind in the wrong place and was actually playing the role of adversary (Satan).

God is always trying in many ways to teach us about himself. He will certainly meet us with inward illumination as we study and strive to understand:

> If you indeed cry out for insight,
>   and raise your voice to understanding;
> if you seek it like silver,
>   and search for it as for hidden treasures—
> then you will understand the fear of the LORD
>   and find the knowledge of God. (Prov 2:3-5)

All of this must be kept clearly in view as we go on now to consider the basic questions: *"What kind of world do we live in?"* and *"How does God relate to us, confined as we are within it?"* Admittedly we are entering an intellectual and spiritual hardhat area, where many have received injuries to their practical faith in God. We must deal with a number of difficult problems that trouble many thoughtful Christians and non-Christians alike: problems about the *very idea* of our being in a conversational relationship with God. The Bible has been given to us to help us with these problems, but we still have to work hard to resolve them.

If you are one who has no difficulty in this respect, perhaps you should just count your blessings and immediately skip to chapter five, which deals with the various ways God communicates personally with us. But if you find that you do not have any real confidence that God *would* or *could* speak to you and guide you, this chapter is designed to help. Put on your hardhat, your hard nose and your best brains, and prayerfully dig in.

Four Negative Responses

Many people's honest response to what has been said in the previous chapters will be (1) that God *would not* communicate with run-of-the-mill human beings by surrounding them with his presence and speaking to them, or (2) that he *does not* communicate with *them* in that way or even (3) that he *cannot* do so. Perhaps yet others, motivated by the need to control the divine presence and word for what they sincerely regard as proper ends, will even think (4) that God *should not* communicate with individuals as I have indicated he does. I would offer the following replies to these negative responses.

Truth #1: God Would

When considering whether God would be with ordinary human beings in a conversational relationship, we must remember not to think of him in the likeness of any human dignitaries we know. The famous, the rich and the great among humanity are still severely limited in their powers of communication by the fact that they are merely human. They are narrowly limited in their ability to interact personally with others. So it is possible for them to be in intimate contact only with a small number of other people—even with all the wonders of modern communications technology. Their span of consciousness, their capacity to pay attention and the scope of their willpower permit nothing more.

Beyond such factual limitations, human greatness is often taken to mean, and essentially to *require,* having nothing to do with those who are just ordinary people. This greatness is seen as involving a certain exclusiveness, insularity or snobbishness. If we are unable to clear our minds of such associations with greatness, we will be unable to imagine that the great God would talk to *us.* We will think of him as a dignitary who is too busy, too conscious of his status or too high up to communicate with us.

How hard it is for us to come to an adequate conception of the *lowliness* of God—of how his greatness is precisely what makes him able, available and ready to hear and speak personally with his creatures!

This lowliness was, of course, at the very center of Jesus' teaching about God. In his actions and words he made clear how totally accessible God is to the weak, to the downtrodden and castaway, to little children. "Let the little children come to me, and do not stop them; for it is to such as these that the kingdom of heaven belongs" (Mt 19:14). Our Lord's phrase "such as these" includes many characteristics of children, but here I want to stress the element of unimportance. The humanly unimportant ones are important to God. God being who he is and now revealed in the person of Jesus Christ, *we should be surprised if he does* not *speak to us.*

E. Stanley Jones has asked,

> Does God guide? Strange if he didn't. The Psalmist asks: "He that planted the ear, shall he not hear? He that formed the eyes, shall he not see?" (Ps. 94:9) And I ask: "He that made the tongue and gave us power to communicate with one another, shall he not speak and communicate with us?" I do not believe that God our Father is a dumb, non-communicative impersonality.[4]

Truth #2: God Does

What about those who believe that God just simply does not speak to *them?* Here we must consider, I believe, two separate lines along which the cause of their difficulty may be found.

Are we "in tune"? First of all, *the fact that we do not hear does not mean that God is not speaking to us.* It is common even at our human level for us not to hear those who speak to us. It has probably happened to most of us this very day. Someone spoke to us, but we did not know it, did not hear it. Moreover we know that messages from radio and television programs are passing through our bodies and brains at all hours of the day: messages that an appropriately tuned receiver could pluck from the very air we breathe.

What an apt picture this is, it seems to me, of human beings in relation to God: we are showered with messages that simply go right through or past us. We are not *attuned* to God's voice. We have not been taught how to hear it sounding out in nature—for as we read in Psalm 19, "The heavens announce the glory of God"—or in a special communication directed by God to the individual.

Some of Jesus' deepest teachings are about hearing. He taught in parables so those who did not really want to hear the truth could avoid it. He realized that not everyone has ears for the straightforward purpose of hearing but that some use their ears to sift out only what they want to hear, leaving the rest aside. One of his most repeated sayings was, "If anyone has ears to hear, let him hear." But he also urged his hearers to make a great effort to hear, assuring them that what they received would be proportional to their desire and effort (Mk 4:23-24).

Are we ready vessels? This brings us to the second source of difficulty for those who say, "God just doesn't speak to me." Here a bit of honest soul-searching may be required. Possibly they are being spoken to and do not hear. It may also be that *they could make no good use of a word from God because of how they are living.*

Do they stand ready to obey and change, should that be what God directs? Do they *want* to know if they are on a wrong path? In general it is a good thing for God to speak to us, but there may be reasons in individual cases why it would be best for God to speak very little or even not at all. If it is true that God does not speak to me, then I must inquire whether or not I am such a case.

The question must be asked, "To what use would I try to put a word from God?" God is not a snob, and he is not far away: "See, the LORD's hand is not too short to save, nor his ear too dull to hear" (Is 59:1). But when he speaks it is to accomplish his good purposes in our lives and through his creation.

God's guidance is not a gimmick that we can keep on tap for our gain. It is not there to enable us to beat our competitors. We cannot invoke it to help us win bets on football matches or horse races or to prove that something is theologically correct. While it is available to every person who walks with God, it is not *at our disposal as we see fit* without regard to the purposes of God's government. Nor should it be, for that would be very dangerous.

We pray, "Our Father which art in heaven, hallowed be thy name; thy kingdom come, thy will be done on earth as it is in heaven." This preamble to the Lord's Prayer beautifully expresses the purpose of all God's activities in us: "Hallowed be *thy* name. *Thy* kingdom come. *Thy* will be done." Hearing God—as a reliable, day-to-day reality for people with good sense—is for those who are devoted to the glory of God and the advancement of his kingdom. It is for the disciple of Jesus Christ who has no higher preference than to be like him.

Are we ready to be in business with God? If you find yourself in a position where you can honestly say, "God has never spoken to me," then you well might ask, "Why *should* God speak to me? What am *I* doing in life that would make speaking to me a reasonable thing for him to do? Are we in business together in life? Or am I in business just for myself, trying to 'use a little God' to advance my projects?"

When our lives are devoted to the will of God, he has reason to speak to us. If our lives are not devoted to his purposes, he still may speak to us, even use us for his ends if we are strategically placed. After all we are his creatures no matter how misguided or rebellious. But for a willing walk in conscious, loving cooperation with God, we must come to grips with the issue *What are we living for?* We must face it clearly.

It may well be that I have never come to the place where I can truly say, "I am living for one thing and one thing only—to be like Christ, to do his work and live among his people and serve them and him in this world. My life is to bless others in the name of God." If we have not come to that place,

then the question that normally arises as "How do we hear the word of God?"
is replaced for us by the prior question "What would we do if we heard the
word of God?"

G. Campbell Morgan has a few incisive words to say on this point. Having
mentioned that when God speaks to us his word comes as a disturbing
element into our lives, he continues,

> You have never heard the voice of God, and you say: "The day of miracles is
> past. I am never disturbed. I make my own plans and live where I please and
> do as I like. What do you mean by a disturbing element?" . . . Beloved, you are
> living still among the fleshpots and garlic of Egypt. You are still in slavery. . . .
> You know no disturbing voice? God never points out for you a pathway
> altogether different from the one you had planned? Then, my brother, you are
> living still in the land of slavery, in the land of darkness.[5]

Perhaps we do not hear the voice because we do not expect to hear it. Then
again, perhaps we do not expect it because we know that we fully intend to
run our lives on our own and have never seriously considered anything else.
The voice of God would therefore be an unwelcome intrusion into our plans.
By contrast, we expect great spiritual leaders to hear that voice just because
we see their lives wholly given up to doing what God wants.

Frank Laubach tells of the immense change that came over his life at the
point when he resolved to do the will of God:

> As for me, I never lived, I was half dead, I was a rotting tree, until I reached
> the place where I wholly, with utter honesty, resolved and then re-resolved that
> I *would* find God's will, and I *would* do that will though every fiber in me said
> no, and I *would* win the battle in my thoughts. It was as though some deep
> artesian well had been struck in my soul. . . . You and I shall soon blow away
> from our bodies. Money, praise, poverty, opposition, these make no difference,
> for they will all alike be forgotten in a thousand years, but this spirit which
> comes to a mind set upon continuous surrender, this spirit is timeless.[6]

Truth #3: God Certainly Can
Many fear that the physical universe, being what it is, makes communication

with God impossible. It puts him too far away. Even some who understand both the lowliness of God's greatness and the greatness of God's lowliness and who really live to do the will of God are still troubled by the thought that brutal nature interposes itself as a barrier between us and him.

The poet Alfred, Lord Tennyson, after the death of his close friend A. H. Hallam, writes as if he were addressed by the personage of Sorrow:

"The stars," she whispers, "blindly run";
A web is woven across the sky;
From out waste places comes a cry
And murmurs from a dying sun.[7]

The very face of nature—especially in times when the word of God does not come and we are not at peace with him—becomes cold, hard and forbidding: "I will break your proud glory, and I will make your sky like iron and your earth like copper. Your strength shall be spent to no purpose: Your land shall not yield its produce, and the trees of the land shall not yield their fruit" (Lev 26:19-20). "The sky over your head shall be bronze, and the earth under you iron. The Lord will change the rain of your land into powder, and only dust shall come down upon you from the sky until you are destroyed" (Deut 28:23-24).

The "warfare" between science and theology. Even beyond such experiences of nature's seemingly godless course (common through all generations of humanity), there is a special burden of unbelief that has been borne by Western civilization for the last several hundred years—the idea that it is *unscientific* to believe that God could speak to us or guide us. Today it is simply assumed that scientific knowledge excludes the presence of God from the material universe of which we human beings are supposed to be a pitifully small and insignificant part. This is called "naturalism."

The discoveries of the immensity of space and of the forces of nature—which appear to determine everything that happens and *seem* to run their course with no assistance from the hand of a personal God—can be quite overwhelming. When the great French mathematician and astronomer Pierre Simon de Laplace presented Emperor Napoleon with a copy of his book on celestial mechanics, the emperor asked him where God fit into his system. Laplace indignantly drew himself up and replied, "Sir, I have no need of any such hypothesis!"

According to the current model of the natural sciences, nature proceeds without invoking God. You will not find any laboratory manual, any statistical analysis of social processes—even in a Christian school or college!—that introduces God *as a factor* in its calculations.

The social institution of higher education, the university system, stands in world culture as the source of unquestioned authority so far as *knowledge* is concerned. Without going into detail we must acknowledge that it currently throws its weight behind a picture of reality without God, a picture in which human beings are entirely on their own. Regardless of what the recognized system of education might say of itself for public relations purposes, it presumes in its processes that *you can have the best education possible and be ignorant of God.*

Thus we may seem to have a picture imposed upon us of reality in which humanity is encapsulated within a material world. God, if he really exists, is pictured as being wholly *beyond* that material world, which for its part seems to run without God. Given such a view of things, one of the most difficult issues we face in trying to think about hearing God concerns the "how" of it all.

For example, if you want to talk to someone in another country, you will have to put into action a chain of events in the physical substance, the inorganic matter, between here and there. You will perhaps begin by dialing a number on your telephone. This will cause electrical impulses to propagate themselves by various means across the intervening space. A physical apparatus located at the other end will be sensitive to those impulses and will convert them into a form that your faraway friend can hear or see and understand.

The point is that to communicate across such a distance, *we must go through an intervening physical reality.* Even if I wish to speak directly to you as you stand here with me, I must do the same thing. I make some sort of noise with my vocal cords that strikes your eardrum, which somehow—in a way no one fully understands—causes you to think of specific things or events. I *bring about* your thinking, and that is what my communication with you comprises.

Given such a picture of communication, the questions we must now face are as clear as they are compelling: Is this the *only way* in which God can communicate with us? Does God always have to go *through* physical substance? Does the entire realm of organic and inorganic matter stand *between* us and God? *Where* is God in relation to that realm? How does God relate to us if he is far off from us?

Not all of reality involves space. For many these will be the most difficult questions in this chapter, perhaps even in the whole book. So I shall hasten to remind you that God does *not* have to go through physical intermediaries of any sort to reach us—though on some occasions he obviously chooses to do so. The material world in which we are placed by him permits him to be nearer to us even than our own eyes, ears and brain are near. It is "in him" that we "live and move and have our being" (Acts 17:28).

Our faith may all too easily fall victim to our mind's tendency to *spatialize* everything. If we think of God as being literally outside the physical realm, then it will seem as if he is utterly out of reach for us and we out of reach for him. The edge of the known universe is now thought to be something like thirteen or fourteen million light-years away. Beyond that, even light waves, traveling at the speed of 186,284 miles per second, can never reach us! How then can we reach God or he us if he is out there?

The great scientist and Christian Blaise Pascal wrote,

> When I see the blind and wretched state of man, when I survey the whole universe in its dumbness and man left to himself with no light, as though lost in this corner of the universe, without knowing who put him there, what he has come to do, what will become of him when he dies, incapable of knowing anything, I am moved to terror, like a man transported in his sleep to some terrifying desert island, who wakes up quite lost and with no means of escape. Then I marvel that so wretched a state does not drive people to despair.
>
> I see other people around me, made like myself. I ask them if they are any better informed than I, and they say they are not. Then these lost and wretched

creatures look around and find some attractive objects to which they become addicted and attached. For my part I have never been able to form such attachments, and considering how very likely it is that there exists something besides what I can see, I have tried to find out whether God has left any traces of himself.[8]

The traces of God that have always been obvious to the earnest seeker (Rom 1:19) are found in the purposeful order that appears within nature and history as well as in the purposeful interventions that seem to show up in history and in our individual lives. It is impossible to develop this point fully here, but the *order* of events large and small throughout our world strongly suggests to an unbiased observer that there is a providential and personal oversight of our world and our lives.

This is what the apostle Paul has in mind when he says in his sermon on Mars Hill in Athens that God has so arranged our world that we should seek the Lord and—as the Jerusalem Bible nicely translates it—"by feeling [our] way toward him, succeed in finding him. Yet in fact he is not far from any of us, since it is in him that we live, and move, and exist" (Acts 17:27-28).

The New Testament presents Christ the Son as continuously "sustaining all things by his powerful word" (Heb 1:3) and as the very glue of the universe. "In him all things hold together" (*sunistemi*, Col 1:17). A. H. Strong spells this out:

> Christ is the originator and the upholder of the universe. . . . In him, the power of God, the universe became an actual, real thing, perceptible to others; and in him it consists, or holds together, from hour to hour. The steady will of Christ constitutes the law of the universe and makes it a cosmos instead of a chaos, just as his will brought it into being in the beginning.[9]

Hints from current physics. Now we come to a most important point for our present concerns. The current state of the physical sciences, in opposition to the crudely mechanical view that was dominant in some previous centuries, is very congenial to the view of God's presence in his world that we find in the New Testament. Sir James Jean interpreted the result of developments in physics during the first part of the twentieth century as follows:

Today there is a wide measure of agreement, which on the side of Physics approaches almost to unanimity, that the stream of knowledge is heading towards a non-mechanical reality; the universe begins to look more like a great thought than like a great machine. Mind no longer appears as an accidental intruder into the realm of matter; we are beginning to suspect that we ought rather to hail it as the creator and governor of the realm of matter.[10]

More recently, in his essay "Remarks on the Mind-Body Question" Nobel laureate Eugene Wigner has pointed to a general recognition among physicists that thought or the mind is primary to physical reality: "It is not possible to formulate the laws of quantum mechanics in a fully consistent way without reference to consciousness." Princeton physicist John A. Wheeler even goes so far as to hold that subjective and objective realities, consciousness and matter, mutually create each other. Another leading physicist, Jack Sarfatti, remarks that "an idea of the utmost significance for the development of psycho-energetic systems . . . is that the structure of matter may not be independent of consciousness."[11]

I do not wish to make more of these recent interpretations of physics than is strictly warranted. In particular, no suggestion is offered here that physics proves any theological position or even that it proves matter to be dependent on mind, as the New Testament teaches. My sole point is that according to some influential contemporary views of physical reality, there is, so to speak, an inside—or better, a *nonside* or an unside—to matter that allows for a nonspatial and yet causal dimension to be in action within the physical world. This dimension accommodates very well the biblical view of God's omnipresent relation to his world in its creation and continued sustenance. The mental or spiritual side of reality does not traverse space to have its effects, any more than one of our own thoughts has to traverse space to influence another person or to influence our emotions or actions.

The crucial point in all this is that there is no reason in the established truths of science to suppose that God cannot reach us and be with us in order to guide and communicate with us. There is plenty of room left for God in the picture of the world presented to us by contemporary science. We can be comfortable, then, with the view that we live in the kind of material universe in which hearing directly from God is possible. This view is expressed in the Bible—in John 1, Hebrews 1 and so on. Since it is the nature of mind, always and everywhere, to guide, is it not therefore reasonable to *expect* guidance and communication from God?

This could never be learned from examining matter itself or the material universe by merely human abilities. The possibilities of physical matter are to be fully revealed only from the mind of its Maker. Archbishop William Temple has written with insight on this subject:

> We do not know what Matter is when we look at Matter alone; only when Spirit dwells in Matter and uses it as a tool do we learn the capacities of Matter. The sensitiveness of eye and ear, the delicacy of the artist's touch, are achievements which we could never anticipate from the study of the lifeless. So, too, we do not know what Humanity really is, or of what achievements it is capable, until Divinity indwells in it. . . . We must not form a conception of Humanity and either ask if Christ is Human or insist on reducing Him to the limits of our conception; we must ask, "What is Humanity?" and look at Christ to find the answer. We only know what Matter is when Spirit dwells in it; we only know what Man is when God dwells in him.[12]

Perhaps the most profound revelation of the nature of physical matter to appear so far in human history is the body of Jesus Christ in his transfiguration and resurrection.

Such explorations clarify faith. It would be a great mistake to think that the discussions above are irrelevant to the question of having confidence in hearing God's voice. There is a lyric that says, "If you believe in things you don't understand you will suffer!" Over and over humanity has proven this true. Perhaps the song oversimplifies things, but the human heart *is* largely dependent on the head. A lack of understanding *does* weaken faith and misdirect life—sometimes disastrously.

Even though it surely is not possible to understand everything, our faith will be strengthened by such understanding as we are able to acquire. Science, vaguely understood, is a power in our age, a weighty authority, whether we like it or not. If you really do believe that the idea of hearing from

God is *unscientific* in the world in which you live, you are going to have great difficulty in making enough sense of it to deal with it in practice or even to be open and intelligent concerning it. This is precisely where many people now stand, in bewilderment between their education and their faith. To the degree that you come to understand that the whole of reality is something penetrated by God, you can begin to open yourself up to the possibility of receiving a direct communication from him.[13]

A comparison may help. God's relation to the world is similar—though not identical—to your relation to your body. You inhabit your body, yet it is not possible to locate or physically identify you—or any act of your consciousness or any element of your character—at any point in your body. God inhabits space, though he infinitely exceeds it as well (1 Kings 8:27). "The whole earth is full of his glory" (Is 6:3). The heavens are the throne of God, and the earth is his footstool (Is 66:1; Mt 5:34; 23:22). Your whole body is accessible to you, and you are accessible through it. As your consciousness plays over and through your whole body, so in a similar—though of course not identical—fashion, "the eyes of the LORD range throughout the entire earth, to strengthen those whose heart is true to him" (2 Chron 16:9).

Chariots of fire. We live in a world much too obsessed by practical concerns and governed by a fallen ideology—in part the ideology of the scientific—and it shapes our minds away from God. We need to have done for our understanding what Elisha did for his young assistant on one occasion when they were in great danger.

The king of Syria was at war with Israel, but every time he laid his battle plans, Elisha would tell them to the king of Israel. The king of Syria naturally supposed that there was an Israelite spy among his confidants, but his aides all denied it, explaining that "it is Elisha, the prophet in Israel, who tells the king of Israel the very words that you speak in your bedchamber" (2 Kings 6:12).

This sort of thing is a part of the very life of the Bible. If we cannot make sense of such things in terms of what experiencing them would be like for us, then—to reemphasize an earlier theme—we will not be able to believe it, *really* believe it. Our very reading of the Bible may force us into skepticism about what is most important: a genuine, living relationship with God.

The king of Syria, for his part, went right to the heart of the problem: "Get Elisha!" he said. When Elisha's young helper stepped outside one morning he found they were completely surrounded by Syrian troops. The scriptural account of what happened then is so good I must quote it directly:

> When an attendant of the man of God rose early in the morning and went out, an army with horses and chariots was all around the city. His servant said, "Alas, master! What shall we do?" He replied, "Do not be afraid, for there are more with us than there are with them." Then Elisha prayed: "O LORD, please open his eyes that he may see." So the LORD opened the eyes of the servant, and he saw; the mountain was full of horses and chariots of fire all around Elisha. (2 Kings 6:15-17)

What did the young man see? Spiritual or personal reality is a type of reality that does not necessarily reveal itself to good eyesight. This is also true in some measure of the spiritual side of you and me. God enabled the young man to see the powers of his realm that totally interpenetrated and upheld all the normal, visible reality around him (even the Syrian army itself). Every working of visible reality is a movement within the encompassing *Logos,* the sustaining Word of God, and it rests on nothing else but God through his Son (Heb 1:1-3).

How we need our Elishas today who, by life and teaching as well as by prayer, might open our eyes to see the reality of God's presence all around us, in every bit of matter as well as beyond!

In our "existence as usual" we are like Jacob, wearily asleep on a rock in a desert ravine. He went to sleep in his sorrow, alienation and loneliness, seeing only the physical landscape. In his dream—or was he only then truly awake?—he beheld God's interaction with the place he was in. Awakening, he cried out, "Surely the LORD is in this place—and I did not know it! . . . How awesome is this place! This is none other than the house of God, and this is the gate of heaven" (Gen 28:16-17).

The angels keep their ancient places;
Turn but a stone, and start a wing!
'Tis ye, 'tis your estranged faces,
That miss the many-splendoured thing.[14]

Truth #4: And God Should!

From the humility and generosity of his great heart, Moses said, "Would that all the LORD's people were prophets, and that the LORD would put his spirit on them!" (Num 11:29). But this might be a mixed blessing, for one further serious objection to individual believers' living in a conversational relationship with God comes from a feeling that *this would lead to chaos in the church,* the community of believers, and that therefore it should not happen.

Many beleaguered ministers will understand what this means. Perhaps the last thing they would hope for in their congregations is that people should be able to contradict and criticize their leaders—or one another—on the basis of their own private "conversations" with God.

Leaders with thoughts like these will feel the weight of a logic that objects to the very essence of the Protestant (as in "protest") movement—a movement that continues apace today in an ever-increasing number of sects emerging within and upon the fringes of Christendom. Such a logic, driving as it does towards a hierarchy of authority and subordination, naturally results in *one person's speaking for God and thus enforcing conformity.*

What is in question here is nothing less than the model of leadership and authority that is suitable for the redeemed community, which is living out the good news of God's reign in the context of human life. "Living stones" (1 Pet 2:5) in conversation with God himself begin to look much better, despite all their problems, once we compare them to the alternative—dead stones.

Sheepdogs or shepherds? In our examples and training for Christian leadership, we too often emphasize getting others merely to do as they are told. In this way the church largely conforms to the leadership structures of the world. Indeed, "leadership" is normally an empty euphemism when applied to our standard communal efforts, whether in a church or outside it.

To manipulate, drive or manage people is not the same thing as to *lead* them. The sheepdog forcibly maneuvers the sheep, whereas the biblical shepherd simply calls as he calmly walks ahead of the sheep. This distinction between the sheepdog and the shepherd is profoundly significant for how we think of our work as leaders of Christ's people. We must ask ourselves frequently which role we are fulfilling and constantly return ourselves, if necessary, to the practice of the shepherd.

When we lead as shepherds, our confidence is in only one thing: the word of the Great Shepherd, coming through us or, otherwise, to his sheep. We know that they know his voice and will not follow another (Jn 10:1-16). We do not *want* them to follow another, even if we ourselves are that "other." Only this supreme confidence frees us to be true ministers of Christ. We are then sure that "every plant that my heavenly Father has not planted will be uprooted" (Mt 15:13). And we have heard the Master say, "Everything that the Father gives me will come to me, and anyone who comes to me I will never drive away" (Jn 6:37).

Following the practice of the shepherd, we would never stoop to drive, manipulate or manage, relying only on the powers inherent in unassisted human nature (see 1 Pet 4:11). Not only that, but the undershepherds (ministers under God) count on their flock to minister the word of God—along with "all good things" (Gal 6:6)—to *them*. Ministry of the word is never a one-way street when it is functioning rightly in any group. "A redemptive teaching relationship," as Henri Nouwen has said, "is bilateral. . . . The teacher has to learn from his student. . . . Teachers and students are fellowmen who together are searching for what is true, meaningful, and valid, and who give each other the chance to play each other's roles."[15]

It is at this point, however, that we must abandon the metaphor of sheep, lest they become sheep for slaughter. We are to lead "willingly," not "for sordid gain. . . . Do not lord it over those in your charge, but be examples to the flock" (1 Pet 5:2-3). We are indeed to be "the servant of all" (Mk 9:35); redemptive mutual submission (Eph 5:21) is achieved in this way.

So much current religious work is desperately out of line with these scriptural injunctions! This is bound to be so if those who lead do not rely intelligently on Christ's power and readiness to govern and guide his people effectively. They will invariably turn to controlling the flock through their own abilities to organize and drive, all suitably clothed in a spiritual terminology and manner. As their faith is, so shall it be. It will be in fact "my church" and "my ministry"—this is often explicitly said—and the flock will never experience how completely and in what manner *God* is Lord of *his* church.

Leadership: Cultic or Christlike? Spokespeople for the Christian community as well as the general public are frequently heard to lament the way in which cults turn their adherents into mindless robots. In our highly fragmented society, which is dominated by gadgetry and technology, lonely and alienated people are ready prey for any person who comes along and speaks with confidence about life and death—especially when that person has some degree of glamour and professes to speak for God.

There are now more than two and a half thousand distinct cults active in the United States alone, most based on the premise that God speaks to one or several central people in the group in a way that he does not speak to the ordinary members. These members are taught not to trust their own minds or their own communications with God except within the context of the group, with all its pressures toward conformity to the word from on high. Frequently adherents are taught to accept pronouncements that are self-contradictory and fly in the face of all common sense if the leader says they must.

These are common factors among many of the cults, even the more extreme groups that form around personalities such as Jim Jones and Charles Manson. But the more "mainline" religious groups, if they would be honest, might find that their *own* models of leadership actually prepare the way for cult phenomena because they too use these methods to some extent. I must ask *myself,* as a Christian minister, to what extent *I,* in order to secure enough conformity and support to maintain and enlarge *my* plans, might be prepared to have people put away their minds and their own individual experiences of guidance and communication with their Lord.

A great minister speaks. In contrast to the cultish mentality, consider the immense spiritual healthiness of that good man Charles Haddon Spurgeon:

For my part I should loathe to be the pastor of a people who have nothing to say, or who, if they do say anything, might as well be quiet, for the pastor is Lord Paramount, and they are mere laymen and nobodies. I would sooner be the leader of six free men, whose enthusiastic love is my only power over them, than play the director to a score of enslaved nations.

What position is nobler than that of a spiritual father who claims no authority and yet is universally esteemed, whose word is given only as tender advice, but is allowed to operate with the force of law? Consulting the wishes of others he finds that they are glad to defer to him. Lovingly firm and graciously gentle, he is the chief of all because he is the servant of all. Does not this need wisdom from above? What can require it more? David when established on the throne said, "[It is the Lord] who subdueth my people under me," and so may every happy pastor say when he sees so many brethren of differing temperaments all happily willing to be under discipline, and to accept his leadership in the work of the Lord. . . . Brethren, our system will not work without the Spirit of God, and I am glad it will not, for its stoppages and breakages call our attention to the fact of His absence. Our system was never intended to promote the glory of priests and pastors, but it is calculated to educate manly Christians, who will not take their faith at second-hand.[16]

What then are we to say? Without doubt, having everyone personally confer with God does risk disagreements and uncooperativeness. If the spirit of the prophets is subject to the prophets, individual prophets may from time to time find themselves earnestly questioned and examined—perhaps overturned—by those they are appointed to lead. These leaders will then require a real security before other human beings, as well as a genuine authority from the Lord, for them to succeed in leading; they will also need a true humility—everyone thinking others better than themselves (Phil 2:3)—for them to carry on with their work.

Leading as Jesus led. How, though, could we ever have thought that anything other than this was required of a minister of the kingdom of God? For my part I can only say this is exactly what we want to see in our leaders of the church of the Lord Jesus Christ. It is exactly the spirit in which *he* led. The spirit and the manner of the Chief Shepherd should be the one adopted by the undershepherds. We can minister Christ only as we teach what he taught in the manner in which he taught it.

If the leaders have this spirit of Christ, the individuals of the fellowship will have a correct and formative model of how they should respond to and bear their communications with God. Of course there *is* a subordination within the fellowship of believers, but it is not one that comes from a clever or crude struggle for ascendancy. Rather it stems solely from authority given by experience in the Way and by the speaking of what is truly God's word. If we count on Christ (whose church it is) to bring about the *right* kind of subordination, we shall see the true unity and power of the glorious body of Christ, the living temple inhabited by God. Fully realized, this unity is the light of the world, the end and aim of all human history.

Keeping a balance. We must never forget, however, that the social and outward dimension of the church is not the whole—nor ultimately even the basic dimension—of redemption. The social dimension in all its glory is derived only from the *individual's communion* with God.

The advice of St. Francis de Sales to his student Philothea gives a proper practical balance between the individual and social dimensions of our life in Christ. Describing as "inspirations" all of "those interior attractions, motions, reproaches and remorses, lights and conceptions which God excites in us," he directs her as follows:

> Resolve, then, Philothea, to accept with a ready heart all the inspirations it shall please God to send to you. When they come, receive them as ambassadors sent by the King of Heaven, who desires to enter into a marriage contract with you. Attend calmly to His proposals, think of the love with which you are inspired, and cherish the holy inspiration. Consent to the holy inspiration with an entire, a loving and a permanent consent.[17]

Then St. Francis wisely directs his friend back into the fellowship of the church, saying, "but before you consent to inspiration in things which are of great importance, or that are out of the ordinary way, always consult your advisor."[18]

Joyce Huggett passes on similar advice, which she received from her friend Jean Darnall: "If you believe God has told you to do something, ask him to confirm it to you three times: through his word, through circumstances, and through other people who may know nothing of the situation."[19] This precept of three witnesses is not a law, but it is a good rule of thumb in an area where rules of thumb are badly needed.

No man or woman is an island, though we always remain much more than the sum of our relationships to others—even in the Christian community. Our relationships to others, essential and helpful as they may be, must rest finally on our personal relationship to God himself. When *both* relationships are right, we find perfect safety, and

> this full and perfect peace!
> Oh, this transport all divine!
> In a love that cannot cease,
> I am His and He is mine.[20]

Some Topics for Reflection

1. Do you agree with what has been said about the limited ability of stories and signs to increase our faith, whether in guidance or elsewhere?

2. "We *mistakenly* try to think of God's dignity in terms of what we see in the experience of the 'great ones' among human beings. But God's dignity and greatness are seen precisely in his lowliness and accessibility to all." Do you have any problems with this statement?

3. What do you understand by the term *naturalism,* and how does it affect the possibility of God's speaking to the individual?

4. Do you personally think that science makes the idea of hearing God questionable? Can you trace out your thinking on this matter in detail? Or can you articulate the thinking of someone you know well on this matter?

5. What are the main characteristics of a cultic style of leadership? Have you noticed any cultic behavior in the religious groups you are associated with or informed about? What would it cost organized religious groups to give up such behavior?

6. How do you think you should relate your private experiences of God's speaking to your own spiritual traditions (for example, denominational traditions) and to your present fellowship and its leaders?

Five

The Still Small Voice
& Its Rivals

Then Eli perceived that the LORD was calling the boy. Therefore Eli
said to Samuel, "Go, lie down; and if he calls you, you shall say,
'Speak, LORD, for your servant is listening.'"
1 SAMUEL 3:8-9

And, behold, the LORD passed by, and a great and strong wind rent
the mountains, and brake in pieces the rocks before the LORD; but the
LORD was not in the wind: and after the wind an earthquake; but the
LORD was not in the earthquake: and after the earthquake a fire; but
the LORD was not in the fire: and after the fire a still small voice.
1 KINGS 19:11-12 (KJV)

ONE ASPECT OF HEARING GOD IS RECEIVING HIS GUIDANCE. AS
previous chapters have established, guidance is a process where
some person, thing or sequence of events is brought to follow a
definite course.

In the most inclusive sense the train is guided by the rails upon which it runs,
the driver guides the car, the writer guides the pen or keyboard, the radar guides
the airplane pilot, the stars guide the ship's captain, the teacher guides the class,
and the parent guides the child. God could certainly *determine* the course of our
lives by manipulating our thoughts and feelings or by arranging external circumstances—what is often called the "closing" and "opening" of doors in the
"sovereign will" of God. But he can and does also guide us by *addressing* us.
Humanity's actual experience of God, profusely documented in history, shows this.

God addresses us in various ways: in dreams, visions and voices; through the Bible and extraordinary events; and so forth. Once again this is obvious in humanity's experience of God in general. It is also clearly marked out within the biblical accounts. But those who seek to live a life within God's will can be confused about the *significance* of the various ways God speaks with us.

Each way God communicates with us has its own special uses, but all the ways are not equally significant for our life with him. In terms of overall importance the written Word and Jesus, the living Word, are not even to be compared to a voice or vision used by God to speak to an individual. And from among the individual's experiences of hearing God, the "still small voice" has a vastly greater role than anything else.

What is this still small voice? The phrase is taken from the story of Elijah quoted at the beginning of this chapter. The translation might just as well read "a gentle whisper of a voice" or "a gentle whispering." Each expression places the emphasis on the *unobtrusiveness* of the medium through which the message came.

In the still small voice of God we are given a message that bears the stamp of his personality quite clearly and in a way we will learn to recognize. But in contrast with other cases, the *medium* through which the message comes is diminished almost to the vanishing point, taking the form of thoughts that are our thoughts, though these thoughts are not *from* us. In this way, as we shall see, the human spirit becomes the "candle of the LORD" (Prov 20:27 KJV).

Unfortunately this gentle word may easily be overlooked or disregarded, and it has even been discounted or despised by some who think that only the more explosive communications can be authentic. If their view is followed through, a *life* of hearing God must become a life filled with constant fireworks from heaven. But that does not square with the actual course of daily life. This has in turn led many to attack dramatic visions and the like as illusions or even as automatically satanic. A cloud of confusion and mistrust spreads over the whole issue of hearing God's voice. We can dispel that cloud if we examine and understand the many forms of God's speaking in relation to each other.

A Personal Appearance of Jesus?

A letter sent out by the staff of *Guideposts* magazine tells of an ordinary suburban housewife who one day, for reasons unknown to her, began to weep and continued weeping for four days.

> On the morning of the fourth day, alone in her living room, there was a sudden hum and crackle in the air. She saw a ball of white light through a window, spraying showers of multicolored light in its wake and approaching her with amazing speed. Then it was right there, beside her, and as she looked at it she saw a face.
>
> 'He is perfect,' was her first thought. His forehead was high. His eyes were large, but she could not fix their color any more than she could the color of the sea. His features were lost in the overwhelming impression of life brimming over with power and freedom.
>
> Instantly she knew this was Jesus. She saw his utter lack of condemnation, that nothing she had ever done or ever would do could alter the absolute caring or the unconditional love in his eyes.[1]

According to her account, Jesus was present with her in this way for three months, and then his presence began to fade. When this woman, Virginia Lively, last saw him, he said to her, "I will always be with you." She, like Thaddaeus (Jn 14:22), asked Jesus *how* she would know it if she could no longer see him. He replied, "You will see me," and then he was gone. Some years later while speaking to a church group, she found his eyes looking into hers again—but the eyes belonged to a woman in the second row. "And suddenly she saw his eyes looking at her from the eyes of every person in the room."[2]

It will be useful to acknowledge certain standard reactions to stories such as Ms. Lively's. Some people immediately conclude that the whole thing is of the devil because "even Satan disguises himself as an angel of light" (2 Cor 11:14), and we cannot simply dismiss their concern. In fact such experiences are always dangerous, for various reasons. But we must also not overlook the fact that light only serves as Satan's disguise because God really *is* light (1 Jn 1:5), because we are children of light (Eph 5:8) and saints in light (Col 1:12) and because God "maketh . . . his messengers a flaming fire" (Ps 104:4 KJV). It would be strange if we came to shun the genuine simply because it resembled the counterfeit.

Some will suppose that Ms. Lively hallucinated or perhaps suffered a nervous breakdown due to some stress she could not cope with or even face. Others may simply be at a loss to explain what happened, yet they remain unconvinced by her claim that Jesus Christ himself came to her.

At the other end of the spectrum are those who will consider her to be especially favored by God, placed above all those who have not had such an experience. They may go so far as to confuse the medium with the message and will worship the experience rather than the One who, supposedly, was present through it. These people often feel spiritually inferior until something similar happens to them.

This insecurity is one of the dangers of religious groups that insist their members must reproduce the experiences of their leaders. In this situation members will be tempted to try to *make* the great event happen, in whatever specific form it must take, and may even deceive themselves or pressure others into faking it. They may judge those without the required experience to be incapable of any significant spiritual ministry or service to God or even incapable of being received into heaven when they die.

Unusual experiences, like the one described by Ms. Lively, clearly pose problems for our understanding of guidance and for our understanding of the spiritual life in general.

The Primacy of the "Inner Voice"

Far be it from me to deny that such spectacular experiences occur or that they are, sometimes at least, given by God. But a major point of this book is that the still small voice—or the interior or inner voice, as it is also called—is the preferred and most valuable form of individualized communication for God's purposes. God usually addresses individually those who walk with him in a mature, personal relationship using this inner voice, proclaiming and showing forth the reality of the kingdom of God as they go. We must therefore compare and contrast it to the other, more dramatic ways in which God encounters human beings.

It is important to bear in mind that you may not be very self-conscious about hearing the voice; it need not force itself to the front of your thoughts. And one need have no theory or doctrine *about* this voice in order to hear it. When the voice came to little Samuel (1 Sam 3), Samuel did not know what it was or even that there was such a thing. Indeed I believe it is also possible for someone who regularly interacts with the voice of God not even to recognize it as something special. In contrast to those who have some of the more spectacular experiences, those most adept at the divine-human conversation are often reluctant to speak much about the inner voice. And that is completely as it should be. God's communication with the individual is not for show-and-tell any more than intimate interchanges between two people generally are.

If, however, we are seeking to understand how God's speaking works, a discussion of the voice is indispensable. We need to consider the various ways in which God addresses men and women. For only then can we hope to gain a better understanding of the nature and function of the way that is most common and most suited to communion between God and humankind: his still small voice. To begin with, I would like to take a look at a brief catalog of encounters with God, taken chiefly from the Bible. Most of these are like those reported in extrabiblical and even non-Christian sources, but the biblical accounts should be regarded as normative.

Reaffirming Our Participation in Biblical Experience

First, however, it is worth reminding ourselves to read the biblical accounts as if what is described is happening to *us*. We must make the conscious effort to think that such things *might* happen to us and to imagine what it would be like if they were to happen.

This will be difficult at first, for most people have become accustomed to thinking that God does such marvelous things only with *other* people. But remember what I wrote earlier (in chapter two) about how Elijah, Moses and Paul were people just like us, subject to like passions as we are. When misunderstood or mistreated they felt as we would in the same situation. They experienced hunger, weariness, nervousness, confusion and fear just as we do. They doubted their abilities and self-worth just as we do. Just like us—witness Moses and Gideon—they often said, "Oh, no! Not *me*. I can't do it."

Generally speaking, God will not compete for our attention. Occasionally a Saul gets knocked to the ground and so on, but we should expect that in most cases God will *not* run over us. We must be open to the possibility of God's addressing us in whatever way he chooses, or else we may walk right past a burning bush instead of saying, as Moses did, "I must turn aside and look at this great sight, and see why the bush is not burned up" (Ex 3:3). I say in all seriousness that we may mistake the voice of God for the sound of someone's radio turned up too loudly, for some accidental noise or—more likely still—for just another one of our own thoughts.

The reality of God's voice does not make seeking for it unnecessary. When I seek for something, I look for it everywhere. It is when we *seek* God earnestly, prepared to go out of our way to examine anything that might be his overture toward us—including the most obvious things like Bible verses or our own thoughts—that he promises to be found (Jer 29:13). But we will be able to seek him only if we honestly believe that he might explicitly address us in ways suitable to his purposes in our lives.

Biblical Stories of People Who Hear God

Bearing this in mind and remembering that we need to use our imagination to identify with the experiences we shall be considering, we turn now to six ways in which people are addressed by God within the biblical record:

☐ a phenomenon plus a voice

☐ a supernatural messenger or an angel

☐ dreams and visions

☐ an audible voice

☐ the human voice

☐ the human spirit or the "still small voice"

A phenomenon plus a voice. This first category of divine-human encounter is richly represented in the events of Scripture. God's covenant with Abraham, a major foundation of the Judeo-Christian tradition, was solemnized upon just such an occasion. Fire from God passing through the air consumed the sacrifice Abraham had prepared while God intoned the promise to Abraham and his seed (Gen 15:17-18).

Moses received his call to deliver Israel from Egypt by the hand of God while he stood before the bush that was burning yet unburned and from which God spoke (Ex 3:3-6). The nation of Israel as a whole was called to covenant by God's voice from within a mountain on fire, pulsating with the energy of his presence (Deut 5:23). Ezekiel was addressed in the context of a meteorological display that defies all but poetic description (Ezek 1—2).

At Jesus' baptism the heavens appeared to open up, and the Spirit visibly descended upon him in conjunction with a voice from heaven that said, "This is my Son, the Beloved, with whom I am well pleased" (Mt 3:17). Saul's encounter with Christ on the road to Damascus involved a blinding light from heaven and an audible voice heard not only by Saul but by those with him as well (Acts 9:3-8).

A supernatural messenger or an angel. In his book on angels Mortimer J. Adler, a distinguished philosopher and a historian of ideas, describes the opposition he received from his scholarly colleagues when he wished to include *angels* among the great ideas of Western humanity in a major publication.[3] There is no doubt whatsoever that—in terms of the amount of attention they have received not only in religion but also in art, literature and philosophy—angels deserve the place in Western civilization assigned to them by Adler. And it is certainly not going too far to describe the Bible itself as a book full of angels, from Genesis 16:7 onward.

Strictly speaking, the word *angel* means nothing more than "emissary" or "messenger," but it is normally understood that such messengers, while they are persons, are not mere human beings. They are supernatural beings on a divine mission. God addresses humans through them, though they do not always reveal their identity.

Sometimes in the biblical record it is difficult to determine whether an angel or the Lord himself is on the scene. In Genesis 18, for example, we have an account of three men appearing at the door of Abraham's tent. In the middle of this chapter the text casually shifts from "they" and "the men" to "the LORD." This is then followed by the well-known dialogue between Abraham and the Lord concerning the fate of Sodom.

Strangely at the opening of Genesis 19 only two angels appear to Lot in Sodom to finish off the episode. (The three men of Genesis 18 were apparently two angels accompanied by the Lord.) Hebrews 13:2 is taken by some as referring back to this story in Genesis when it exhorts, "Do not neglect to show hospitality to strangers, for by doing that some have entertained angels without knowing it."

In front of the city of Jericho (Josh 5:13-15) Joshua encounters "a man standing before him with a drawn sword in his hand," who has come to help as "commander of the army of the LORD." He directs Joshua to take off his shoes because the ground he stands on is holy. The "army of the LORD" here consists mainly of angels, no doubt the same as the legions that became visible in 2 Kings 6:17, as was discussed in chapter four, and that later stood at the beck and call of our incarnate Lord (Mt 26:53). ("LORD of hosts" becomes a primary name for God as redemptive history progresses through the Old Testament; see for example Ps 24:10; 46:7; 59:5.) A few verses later, at Joshua 6:2, the commander now seems to be the Lord himself, explaining that famous and unorthodox military strategy whereby the walls of Jericho were to be brought down.

Human beings are so commonly addressed by angels in Scripture that I shall list only a few more of the outstanding cases: Balaam (Num 22:22-35), Gideon (Judg 6:11-24), the parents of Samson (Judg 13), Isaiah (Is 6:6-13), Daniel (Dan 9:20-27), Joseph (Mt 1:20-25), Zacharias (Lk 1:11-20), Mary (Lk 1:26-38), the women at the empty tomb (Mt 28:2-7), Peter (Acts 5:19-20) and Paul (Acts 27:23-26).

We should take note that these people encounter angels in an otherwise normal state of mind, as distinct from encountering them in dreams and visions, although the content of the conversations recorded sometimes suggests (as with Gideon, Samson's parents and Zacharias, for example) that the people involved felt things were more than a little strange.

Dreams and visions. These two categories of divine communication—dreams and visions—can be treated together here, since our purposes do not require scholarly depth and precision. Sometimes they seem to coincide, perhaps because they often come at night and the recipients may have been unable to tell with certainty whether they were awake or asleep. So it was with Paul: "During the night Paul had a vision: there stood a man of Macedonia pleading with him and saying, 'Come over to Macedonia and help us' " (Acts 16:9; see also Acts 18:9; 2 Cor 12:1). Both visions and dreams involve some degree of a trancelike condition, a certain detachment from the person's actual surroundings, which marks them off from ordinary waking consciousness.

On the other hand some visions are clearly not dreams, as with Ananias, to whom the Lord spoke in a vision (Acts 9:10-13), and Peter in his rooftop trance, which is also specifically called a vision (Acts 10:9-19). Many dreams are not visions, as was the case with Jacob (Gen 28:11-17), Joseph (Gen 37:5-9), Joseph's jail mates (Gen 40:5-19), Pharaoh (Gen 41:1-7) and Nebuchadnezzar (Dan 4:4-18).

Gustave Oehler points out that the difference between a dream and a vision is not sharply marked out in the Bible.[4] But he does concede that the dream is regarded as a lower form of communication from God than a vision. Both are unusual states of consciousness, but the dream characteristically requires greater interpretation, often with considerable difficulty, in a manner that the vision does not.

By the time of Jeremiah the understanding of the ways in which God speaks had progressed to the point where the dreaming prophet was treated with some disdain. The dream is like straw or chaff when compared to the wheat of God's *word* (Jer 23:25-32). His word is like fire, like a hammer that crushes the rock. The dream has no comparable power.

Oehler sees emerging here "the principle that a clear consciousness when receiving revelation is placed higher than ecstasy or other abnormal states of mind."[5] This is a vital point to keep in mind as we attempt to understand our *own* experiences of God's communications and the significance of the different ways in which he meets us today.

An audible voice. However we are to understand the mechanisms involved, it is clear that on some occasions God has addressed human beings through what was experienced as an audible voice alone.[6] Something like this, though involving an angel from heaven, seems to have occurred with Abraham on Mount Moriah as he was about to sacrifice his son Isaac (Gen 22:11-12, 15-18).

A most touching, informative and profound story is that of the child

Samuel as he learns to recognize God's voice, which he clearly experienced as an audible voice (1 Sam 3). As this young boy lay on his pallet in the temple one night, he heard someone calling his name. He rose and ran to his old master, Eli, thinking that it was he who had called. This was during a period in Israel's history when God rarely spoke and gave no visions. Such things as voices and visions were not commonly discussed at that time. Hence, "Samuel did not yet know the LORD, and the word of the LORD had not yet been revealed to him" (3:7).

The third time Samuel came to Eli, saying, "Here I am, for you called me," Eli finally recognized what was happening. He told Samuel to go back and lie down, and he said, "If he calls you, you shall say, 'Speak, LORD, for your servant is listening'" (3:9-10). And so it happened. With this there began one of the most remarkable careers of any person who has ever lived before the Lord, fully justifying the use of the phrase "conversational relationship."

That brings us to the two most important ways in which God speaks to us: in conjunction with the language of human beings and through the inner voice of our own thoughts. These two ways are the most suited to God's presence in our lives as a close personal friend, a presence shared by the whole Christian community, and to the development of our individual personalities into his likeness.

The human voice. We have seen that an audible voice coming from no visible speaker was present with the boy Samuel, at the baptism of Jesus and on the road to Damascus. But no means of communication between God and us is more commonly used in the Bible or the history of the church than the voice of a definite, individual human being. In such cases God and the person he uses speak *conjointly.* It may be that the one spoken *to* is also the one spoken *through.* It is frequently so with me. In this case the word is at once the word of God, God's message, and the word of the human being who is also speaking.

The two do not exclude each other any more than humanity and divinity exclude each other in the person of Jesus Christ. We can say that God speaks through us as long as this is not understood as automatically ruling out *our* speaking *with* God and even, in an important sense, *through* God. The relationship must *not* be understood as an essentially mechanical one with God simply using us as we might use a telephone. No doubt that would be

God's option should he choose, but usually he does not.

Samuel Shoemaker has written this excellent description of our experience of God in this respect.

> Something comes into our own energies and capacities and expands them. We are laid hold of by Something greater than ourselves. We can face things, create things, accomplish things, that in our own strength would have been impossible. . . . The Holy Spirit seems to mix and mingle His power with our own, so that what happens is both a heightening of our own powers, and a gift to us from outside. This is as real and definite as attaching an appliance to an electrical outlet, though of course such a mechanical analogy is not altogether satisfactory.[7]

I believe I can say with assurance that God's speaking in union with the human voice and human language is the primary *objective* way in which God addresses us. That is, of all the ways in which a message comes from *outside* the mind or personality of the person addressed, it most commonly comes through a human being.

This is best suited to the purposes of God precisely because it *most fully engages the faculties of free, intelligent beings who are socially interacting with agape love in the work of God as his colaborers and friends.* This is obvious from the contents of the Bible. And of course the Bible is itself a case of God's speaking along with human beings—usually so in the process of its delivery to humankind and now always as it continues to speak to us today.

When God speaks conjointly with human beings, it often seems that weaker vessels are purposely chosen. In Moses' encounter with God through the burning bush, Moses' last line of protest against the assignment that God was giving him was that he did not speak well: "O my Lord, I have never been eloquent, neither in the past nor even now that you have spoken to your servant; but I am slow of speech and slow of tongue." (Ex 4:10). The Lord's reply was that he, after all, had made human mouths and presumably could assist them to accomplish his assignments: "Now go, and I will be with your mouth and teach you what you are to speak" (4:12).

When Moses still begged God to send someone else, God angrily gave him Aaron as *his* spokesman: "You shall speak to him and put the words in his mouth; and I will be with your mouth and with his mouth, and will teach you what you shall do. He indeed shall speak for you to the people; he shall serve as a mouth for you, and you shall serve as God for him. Take in your hand this staff, with which you shall perform the signs" (4:15-17).

Some New Testament passages suggest that the apostle Paul was not an eloquent man either. We know from his own statements that whether by choice or necessity, he did not come among the Corinthians "proclaiming . . . in lofty words or wisdom"; rather he came "in weakness and in fear and in much trembling. My speech and my proclamation were not with plausible words of wisdom, but with a demonstration of the Spirit and of power, so that your faith might rest not on human wisdom but on the power of God" (1 Cor 2:1-5). His only confidence was in God speaking *with* him, electrifying his words, as it were, when he spoke.

It is significant, I believe, that those chosen by our Lord to bear his message and carry on his work were for the most part "uneducated and ordinary" people (Acts 4:13). The pattern seems to prove amply that in God's selecting them there would be no mistake as to the source of their words and authority. God would use ordinary human beings and would dignify them by their association with him. But just as this is wholly suitable to his redemptive purposes, so it is wholly appropriate that everyone—and especially the individuals involved—should be clear about the source of the power manifested.

There must be no misallocation of glory not because God is a cosmic egotist, but because it would destroy the order that is in the blessedness of life in Christ. It would direct us away from God. Hence Paul writes, "Let the one who boasts, boast in the Lord" (1 Cor 1:31). The success of the redemptive plan therefore requires that "not many of you were wise by human standards, not many were powerful, not many of you were of noble birth" (1:26). Moses and Paul, two of the people most responsible for the human authorship of the Bible, were accordingly weak with words so that they might have the best chance of clinging constantly to their support in God who spoke in union with them and so that they might unerringly connect their hearers with God.

Does the word of God then literally overpower us? In some parts of the Bible record, those who speak with God seem compelled by force, as we see in the case of Balaam. Balak, king of Moab, offered Balaam great riches and honor if he would curse Israel. He knew that Balaam spoke in unison with God—"whomever you bless is blessed, and whomever you curse is cursed" (Num 22:6). Balaam was obviously greatly tempted by the offer. Even after God told him not to go to Balak and not to curse Israel because Israel was indeed blessed (22:12), Balaam kept toying with the idea. Eventually he thought that he had God's permission at least to go to Balak (22:20). But even while he was in Balak's camp he was simply *unable* to curse Israel. He explained to Balak that he did not have any power at all to say anything: "The word God puts into my mouth, that is what I must say" (22:38). When the moment came for him to curse Israel, after elaborate preparations, only a stream of blessings came forth (23:7-10), to the exasperation of Balak.

It would be a great mistake, however, to take these and similar cases to mean that the person who speaks with God, and thus speaks the word *of* God, literally cannot help speaking. Perhaps this is true in some cases. It is certainly true that people cannot force *God* to speak with *them*. But the compulsion upon the individual to speak, though often great, is normally still resistible. Human beings are not mere tools.

Jeremiah's experience in this respect has been replicated innumerable times in the experience of those who understand what it is to speak for and with God. Speaking God's word had made him a laughing stock among those who knew him, and he resolved to speak no more for the Lord:

> If I say, "I will not mention him,
>   or speak any more in his name,"
> then within me there is something like a burning fire
>   shut up in my bones;
> I am weary with holding it in,
>   and I cannot. (Jer 20:9)

The prophets often treat the word of the Lord as a *burden*. Later in his sermon against the false prophets, Jeremiah cries,

> My heart is crushed within me,
>   all my bones shake;

I have become like a drunkard,
    like one overcome by wine,
because of the LORD
    and because of his holy words. (23:9)

The prophet may also exult in the power he feels surging within him, as Micah did:

But as for me, I am filled with power,
    with the spirit of the LORD,
    and with justice and might,
to declare to Jacob his transgression
    and to Israel his sin. (Mic 3:8)

Jeremiah also experienced God's word to be of great power, like a fire that scorches and like a hammer that breaks rocks. J. B. Phillips said somewhere that while he was doing his well-known translation of the New Testament, he often felt like an electrician working on the wiring of a house with the power on.

Later in this book we will explore in detail the idea of the word of God as an agency, a substantial power in the cosmos and in human affairs: an agency that could come "to John . . . in the wilderness" (Lk 3:2), have dominion over unclean spirits (Lk 4:33-36), be like the finger of God (Lk 11:20), be spirit and life (Jn 6:63, 68), increase (Acts 6:7), grow and multiply (Acts 12:24), not be bound in prison (2 Tim 2:9), function as the sword of the Spirit (Eph 6:17)—being more dexterous and powerful than any mere two-edged, human sword. It has a life of its own and is so acute that it can dissect thoughts and intentions (Heb 4:12)—and simultaneously hold all of creation together (Col 1:17). This complex picture of the word of God must be examined closely before we conclude our study. For the time being, however, we rest with the fact that that word can and does come to us through the living personalities, minds and bodies of other human beings as they speak to us in unison with God.

The human spirit or the "still small voice." The final means through which God addresses us is our own spirits—our own thoughts and feelings toward ourselves as well as toward events and people around us. This, I believe, is the primary *subjective* way in which God addresses us. That is, of all the ways in which a message comes from *within* the experience of the person addressed (such as dreams and visions or other mental states), for those who are living in harmony with God it most commonly comes in the form of their own thoughts and attendant feelings. Of all the possible subjective routes this mode is best suited to the redemptive purposes of God because, once again, *it most engages the faculties of free, intelligent beings involved in the work of God as his colaborers and friends.*

Thus the familiar King James Version of Proverbs 20:27 says, "The spirit of man is the candle of the LORD, searching all the inward parts of the belly." This is possibly better put in the Jerusalem Bible: "Man's spirit is the lamp of Yahweh, searching his deepest self."

In a passage of great importance to our exploration here, the apostle Paul makes a comparison between humans and God with respect to self-knowledge: "For what human being knows what is truly human except the human spirit that is within? So also no one comprehends what is truly God's except the Spirit of God" (1 Cor 2:11). Paul then points out that we have received the Spirit of God and concludes that we can therefore search out and know the very mind of God by means of his Spirit—in contrast to the proverb quoted above, which emphasizes *the Lord's* use of *our* spirit. After quoting the question from Isaiah 40:13, "Who has directed the spirit of the LORD, or as his counselor has instructed him?" the apostle replies, "But we have the mind of Christ" (1 Cor 2:16).

So God uses our self-knowledge or self-awareness, heightened and given a special quality by his presence and direction, to search us out and reveal to us the truth about ourselves and our world. And we are able to use his knowledge of himself—made available to us in Christ and the Scriptures—to understand in some measure *his* thoughts and intentions toward us and to help us see his workings in our world.

In the union and communion of the believer with God, their two beings are unified and inhabit each other just as Jesus prayed: "I ask . . . that they may all be one. As you, Father, are in me and I am in you, may they also be in us, so that the world may believe that you sent me" (Jn 17:20-21). As we grow in grace, God's laws increasingly form the foundation of our hearts; his love is our love, his faith our faith. Our very awareness of our actions, intentions and surroundings then bears within it the view that God takes, bringing things into the clarity of *his* vision just as a candle might illuminate what is on our dinner table.

Therefore, the spirit of the individual truly is the "candle of the Lord," in the light of which we see ourselves and our world as God sees. In this way we are addressed by him, spoken to by him, through *our own thoughts.* This is something you can and should test by experiment. Those who begin to pray that God will enlighten them as to the nature and meaning of the processes that go on in their own soul will begin to understand. They will begin to see their spirit functioning as the candle of the Lord.

The soul's self-awareness applies to every part of the self: it touches upon one's family, possessions, profession and health; it reaches to one's fear of death, attitudes toward God, sexuality, preoccupation with reputation, concern with appearance and countless other areas of one's life. Our spirit, as a candle in the Lord's hands, may shed light on many other things apart from our own internal condition, although the primary point of the passage from Proverbs is the illumination of the inner life. Russ Johnston points out the importance of *recurrent thoughts* in God's communication with his children:

> We would see wonderful results if we would just deal with the thoughts that continue in our minds in a godly manner. But most people don't.... As thoughts come into your mind and continue, ask God, "Do you really want me (or us) to do this?" Most of us just let those thoughts collapse—and God looks for someone else to stand in the gap.[8]

But are not all our thoughts inherently bad? This well-intended but mistaken teaching about our thoughts has done much harm to the understanding of hearing God's voice.

The great Puritan minister Thomas Goodwin wrote a powerful discourse on *The Vanity of Thoughts,*[9] taking as his text Jeremiah 4:14 (KJV): "How long shall thy vain thoughts lodge within thee?" Goodwin is quite careful and helpful in the manner in which he describes these "vain" thoughts, but he leaves an impression, which is widely shared and emphasized, that if a thought is *our* thought, it could not possibly be trusted. Does God not say in Isaiah 55:8, "For my thoughts are not your thoughts"? And does Jeremiah not tell us that our hearts are desperately wicked, beyond our powers of comprehension (Jer 17:9)?

Of course there is an important point in all of this that stresses the difference between God's view of things and the view of the normal person apart from God. But this point must not obscure the simple fact that God comes to us precisely in and through our thoughts, perceptions and experiences and that he can approach our conscious life *only* through them, for they are the substance of our lives. Therefore, we are to be transformed by the *renewing of our minds* (Rom 12:2). God's gracious incursions into our souls can make our thoughts his thoughts. He will help us learn to distinguish when a thought is ours alone and when it is also his.

Chapter eight will deal at length with the question of how we can know which thoughts are from God. But for now just keep this practical advice in mind: when thoughts recur, always stop prayerfully to consider whether this may be an appearance of the Lord's "candle" or whether the thoughts may have some other significance. Although reoccurring thoughts are not *always* an indication that God is speaking, they are not to be lightly disregarded.

So the thoughts and feelings in the mind and spirit of one who is surrendered to God should be treated as if God were walking through one's personality with a candle, directing one's attention to things one after the other. As we become used to the idea that God is friendly and helpful, that he desires to straighten, inform and correct us for our good as well as to comfort and encourage, and that he really does love us, then we can begin to pray heartily with the psalmist, "Search me, O God, and know my heart; test me and know my thoughts" (Ps 139:23).

As we do this we are asking God, "Bring the light to bear upon my life, please," just as we might go to a dentist or doctor and say, "Examine me, please, and see if corrections to my physical condition are needed. Find out what is wrong and repair it." One's own spirit can then work together with the Almighty God, using one's thoughts and feelings to bring the truth of his word and his understanding to bear upon one's heart, life and world.

Having looked at the major ways in which, according to the biblical record, God addresses the conscious mind and will in order to inform and guide, let us now give some thought to their meaning for our own quest to hear his voice.

God Speaks Today

Perhaps the first thing to say is that there is no foundation in Scripture, in reason or in the very nature of things *why any or all of these types of experience might not be used by God today.* No one should be alarmed or automatically thrown into doubt by such experiences coming to them or by reports that other people have experienced them. As always we should simply follow Paul's admonition in 1 Thessalonians 5:19-22: "Do not quench the Spirit. Do not despise the words of prophets, but test everything; hold fast to what is good; abstain from every form of evil."

It is true that the existence and history of the church and the presence of the full written Scripture change the circumstances of and give new dimensions to the way in which God deals with human beings. But there is nothing *in* Scripture to indicate that the biblical modes of God's communication with humans have been superseded or abolished by either the presence of the church or the close of the scriptural canon.

This is simply a fact, just as it is simply a fact that God's children have continued up to the present age to find themselves addressed by God in most of the ways he commonly addressed biblical characters. The testimony of these individuals—where they are generally admitted to be honest, clear-minded and devout and including, as they do, many of the very greatest Christians throughout the ages—should not be discarded in favor of a blank, dogmatic denial. Of course at any time there may be some degree of fakery and confusion, well intended or not. But such a blank denial has no scriptural foundation. Moreover it is often no more than an attempt to substitute safety and deadness for living communications from God, to look to the ponderous scholars or letter-learned scribes for their interpretation of God's word rather than hearing for oneself the voice that is available to people even of the plainest sort or to resign oneself to hear only what God has said in Scripture rather than listen for the specific word he might have for one today.

The close of the scriptural canon marks the point in the (still ongoing) divine-human conversation where the principles and doctrines that form the substance of Christian faith and practice are so adequately stated in human language that nothing more need be said *in general.* Biblical Christians believe that nothing further will be said by God to extend or contradict those principles. But a biblical Christian is not just someone who holds certain beliefs *about* the Bible. He or she is also someone who *leads the kind of life demonstrated* in the Bible: a life of personal, intelligent interaction with God. Anything less than this makes a mockery of the priesthood of the believer.

Surely one of the most damaging things we can do to people's spiritual prospects is to suggest that God will *not* deal with them specifically, personally, intelligibly and consciously or that they cannot *count on* him to do so as he knows best. Once we have conveyed this idea to them, it makes no sense to attempt to lead them into a personal relationship with God.

Conversing with God

Rosalind Rinker relates how after years of service on the mission field and many fruitless efforts at a satisfactory prayer life, she found herself rebellious and spiritually empty. Then through a serious illness and other grave difficulties, "God began to take care of my rebellions through his great love. He began to teach me to listen to his voice."[10]

Almost by "chance," as she was praying with a friend for some of their students, she interrupted her friend's prayer with thanksgiving on a point that was being prayed for. After a moment of awkward silence and after they had sat back and laughed with great relief, they settled down again to prayer but now "with a sense of joy, of lightness, of the Lord's presence very near." They then asked if the Lord was trying to teach them something about prayer. "Should we give Thee more opportunity as we are praying to get Thy ideas through to us? Would that give the Holy Spirit more opportunity to guide us as we pray?" Then Rinker stopped praying and said to her friend, "Do you know what? I believe the Lord taught us something just now! Instead of each of us making a prayer-speech to Him, let's talk things over with Him, including Him in it, as we do when we have a conversation."[11]

I recall very clearly the effect of her book *Prayer: Conversing with God* when it arrived on the scene in the United States. Group after group was brought to life as they learned to listen to God as well as "make prayer-speeches" at him. Their talk of "a life with God" now had real, objectively shareable content.

Silence Is *Not* an "Answer"

Nowhere is it more important to be in a conversational relationship with God than in our prayer life. Often God does not give us what we ask for, but I believe that he will always answer, always *respond* to us in some way. It is interesting that we commonly speak of answered prayer only when we are *given* our requests. When a request is denied, does this then mean that there has been no response?

Some people say that God's silence is an answer in these cases. But I think that if we know how to listen, God will normally *tell* us something when he does not give us our requests. We will hear it and grow through it if we have learned to recognize and acknowledge his voice.

This was certainly true in the case of Paul's famous "thorn in the flesh," which he begged the Lord to remove from him three times (2 Cor 12:7-8). God was not silent, even though he turned down Paul's request: *"But his answer was:* 'My grace is all you need; power is most fully seen in weakness.' " (2 Cor 12:9 REB, italics added).

God is not impassive toward us like an unresponsive pagan idol; he calls us to grow into a life of personal interchange with him that does justice to the idea of our being his children.

Do We Need Anything More Than the Bible?

To many this is an inflammatory question, but it is one that must be posed. One of the arguments for disallowing any significant continuing use of voices, visions, dreams, prophetic people or individual thoughts as communications from God is that these allegedly are no longer needed. "We have the Bible, and we have the church. Let *them* speak for God," runs the argument. A number of things should be said in response to this.

First of all, if by what is "needed" we mean what is minimally required to enable human beings to know God, this, according to the Bible itself, is available independently of the Bible and the church. Hence they too would not be "needed"—yet here they are. For as Paul states in Romans 1:19-21,

> For what can be known about God is plain to them, because God has shown it to them. Ever since the creation of the world his eternal power and divine nature, invisible though they are, have been understood and seen through the things he has made. So they are without excuse; for though they knew God, they did not honor him as God or give thanks to him.

However, if by what is "needed" we mean what is required for a truly redemptive, personal *relationship* between God and the individual, then the existence of the Bible and the church is certainly not enough. These must at least, in addition to merely being there, have an individualized function in the life of each person. And in order for this to happen they—both the church and the Bible—must become the means through which God personally and uniquely addresses each individual.

Referring to the question "Were not the miracles and gifts of the Spirit only for the apostolic church?" Andrew Murray replied,

> Basing my views on scripture, I do not believe that miracles and the other gifts of the Spirit were limited to the time of the primitive Church, nor that their object was to establish the foundation of Christianity and then disappear by God's withdrawal of them. . . . The entire scriptures declare that these graces will be granted according to the measure of the Spirit and of faith.[12]

He further dismisses the idea that such a particularized presence of the hand of God was only necessary in the early days of Christianity: "Ah, no! What about the power of heathenism even today wherever the gospel seeks to combat it, even in our *modern society,* and in the midst of the ignorance and unbelief which reigns even in the Christian nations."[13]

One of the most amazing conceits that creeps from time to time into the Western branches of the church is the following attitude: "We are so much better now than in more primitive times that it is enough to have a written Word of God without the kind of divine presence and interaction with humanity described in that written Word." How obviously mistaken this is now at the turn of the millennium, as biblical truth and ideas serve less and less to guide the course of human events and as service to the old gods and goddesses of the pre-Christian world is explicitly reasserting itself in the highest levels of culture.

With such ideas of "progress" we shut ourselves off from God's resources for life and ministry in the present. C. H. Spurgeon is right on the mark with his comments on Psalm 103:2.

> Ought we not to look upon our own history as being at least as full of God, as full of His goodness and of His truth, as much a proof of His faithfulness and veracity, as the lives of any of the saints who have gone before? We do our Lord an injustice when we suppose that He wrought all His mighty acts, and showed Himself strong for those in the early time, but doth not perform wonders or lay bare His arm for the saints who are now upon the earth. Let us review our own lives. Surely in these we may discover some happy incidents, refreshing to ourselves and glorifying to our God. Have you had no deliverances? Have you passed through no rivers, supported by the divine presence? Have you walked through no fires unharmed? Have you had no manifestations? Have you had no choice favours? . . . Surely the goodness of God has been the same to us as to the saints of old.[14]

Bible Deism

Today something that could aptly be called "Bible deism" is prevalent, particularly in conservative religious circles. Classical deism, associated with the extreme rationalism of the sixteenth to eighteenth centuries, held that God created his world complete and perfect and then went away, leaving humanity to its own devices. There was no individualized intervention in the lives of human beings, no miracles. Bible deism similarly holds that God gave us the Bible and then went away, leaving us to make what we could of it, with no individualized communication either through the Bible or otherwise.

Bible deism is very like the Sadducean doctrine current in the time of Jesus and Paul which taught that God stopped speaking when he finished speaking with Moses and that no alleged communications via angels or spirits could possibly be valid. They did not accept individual communications with God, and they rejected angels and disembodied spirits as well as the idea of a resurrection and an afterlife. Paul, who was himself a

Pharisee and had actually dealt with angels and spirits, was able to divide his accusers on one occasion and defuse a dangerous situation by invoking the resurrection that the Pharisees, but not the Sadducees, accepted. The Pharisees sided with Paul to make a point that was important to them, saying, "We find nothing wrong with this man. What if a spirit or an angel has spoken to him?" (Acts 23:9).

Like the Sadducees, far too many believers, in their effort to honor the Bible, adopt an unbiblical teaching about God's relationship to his children.

Ministers: Turning People On, Not Off

Speaking pastorally, one of the greatest harms church leaders can do to those under their care is to convince them that God is not going to meet them personally or that he is really doing so only if *the leaders* approve of what is happening. If our gospel does not free the individual up for a unique life of spiritual adventure in living with God daily, we simply have not entered fully into the good news that Jesus brought.

God does take care of his church, and all our efforts as leaders must be directed toward fostering each person's individual adventure with him. We can trust him and nothing else, not even the sterling soundness and sobriety of our own "faith and practice." If we trust anything else, we as leaders will cause those in our charge to trust something else as well, and we may end up, at best, with very proper spiritual corpses filling our pews. We should shudder before these words of Jesus to the ministers of his day: "Woe to you, scribes and Pharisees, hypocrites! For you cross sea and land to make a single convert, and you make the new convert twice as much a child of hell as yourselves" (Mt 23:15).

There are dangers to encouraging people to hear from God. Of course there are. The adventure can get disastrously out of hand. We know that people do go off the deep end, and this problem must be addressed. Yet after gravely warning that death and disaster may also come from going off the *shallow* end, what must be done pastorally is to lead people into an understanding of the voice of God and how it works in their lives.

Most important and right at the outset, they must be helped to see that recognizing God's voice is something they *must learn to do through their own personal experience and experimentation.* They must especially be encouraged to do so if they do not already expect God to speak to them. And we may even have to help identify the voice of God for them and instruct them in how to respond. Those who are older in the Way should be prepared to do this from their own experience.

How wonderful that Eli recognized what was happening to young Samuel and could tell him what to do to begin his lifelong conversational walk with God! It might well have been years, in the prevailing circumstances, before Samuel would have found his way by himself. We must not mistakenly assume that if *God* speaks to someone, he or she automatically knows what is happening and who is talking. If Samuel did not know, surely many others also would not.

How wonderful that Abraham could assure his puzzled servant that God was guiding him back to the city of Nahor to find a wife for Isaac (Gen 24:1-7)! How wonderful that the servant could come to an utterly new understanding of God because he *did* experience guidance and was indeed guided into knowledge of guidance itself! If you turn to that great story now, you will enjoy reading and meditating on one person who certainly learned by experience to work with our God *who is available.*

The Priority of the Voice

Knowledge and experience of hearing God teaches us many things that can keep us from harm and keep us from harming others in our spiritual adventure of life in God's kingdom. One of the most important things we can learn is *the superiority of the voice*—however the "voice" may come, even as the still small voice within the silence of our own minds—over the other types of encounters. This superiority lies in two things: the clarity of its content and the advanced spiritual condition of those who can hear and receive it.

In Numbers 12 we find Aaron and Miriam, brother and sister of Moses, criticizing him because he had taken a woman from Ethiopia for a wife. In fact they were jealous of the way God spoke to Moses, saying, "Has the LORD spoken only through Moses? Has he not spoken through us also?" (12:2). The fact that God spoke through others certainly was no problem for Moses himself. He wanted everyone to prophesy (11:29), and he was a very unassuming man. But God did not disregard what Miriam and Aaron were saying. He called the three of them into the meeting tent. He then came down in a cloud and called Aaron and Miriam forward and said,

Hear my words:
> When there are prophets among you,
>> I the LORD make myself known to them in visions;
>> I speak to them in dreams.
> Not so with my servant Moses;
>> he is entrusted with all my house.
> With him I speak face to face—
>> clearly, not in riddles;
>> and he beholds the form of the LORD.

Why then were you not afraid to speak against my servant Moses? (Num 12:6-8)

"Not in riddles"—this phrase is important for our contemporary understanding of God's voice and guidance. Riddles are obscure, barely intelligible sayings. They lie on a par with the gibberish of "ghosts and the familiar spirits that chirp and mutter" from which people sought guidance in Isaiah's day as well as today (Is 8:19). We cannot know for sure what riddles mean, and they provide an all too fertile field for wild conjectures and manipulative interpretations.

Many who claim to speak for God refer to their visions, dreams and other unusual phenomena—or to their vague impressions or feelings—but they can articulate no clear, sane meaning. This does not mean that they have *not* truly been spoken to. But Moses was spoken to directly—"mouth to mouth" or *conversationally.* His meaning when he spoke for God was therefore always specific, precise and clear.

As Bible history proceeds, we notice that in the process of divine communication the greater the maturity of the listener, the greater the clarity of the message and the lesser the role played by dreams, visions and other strange phenomena and altered states.

Of course, it is impossible to argue conclusively from silence. But in the lives of New Testament personalities—especially Jesus himself—there is a great preponderance of strictly spiritual—nonphysical—communications between God and his people. Visions, dreams and angels continue to play some part—as I think they may do today. It would not be too much to say, however, that where these phenomena were the main, as opposed to occasional, means of interaction, *it indicates a less developed spiritual life both in the individual and in the church group.* I am not trying to be judgmental here; I am merely trying to be helpful in pointing out the kind of life with God into which we should expect to grow—a life in which one hears from God amid and within frequent times of conversational prayer.

I have found much help in the words of E. Stanley Jones, who so firmly believed in and practiced interaction with God's voice throughout his life:

> God cannot guide you in any way that is not Christ-like. Jesus was supreme sanity. There was nothing psychopathic about Him. He went off into no visions, no dreams. He got His guidance through prayer as you and I do. That is, He got His guidance when in control of His faculties, and not when out of control as in dreams. I do not say that God may not guide through a vision or dream; but if He does, it will be very seldom, and it will be because He cannot get hold of our normal processes to guide them. For God is found most clearly and beneficially in the normal rather than in the abnormal. And Jesus is the Normal, for He is the Norm.[15]

The More Spectacular Is the Less Mature

As I have said above, I believe that the predominance of the spectacular encounter generally goes along with the *less mature* levels of the spiritual life—though the mere absence of such spectacular events must not be taken as indicating great spiritual development. After all, such an absence is also consistent with utter deadness.

And it is well that this should be so. The spectacular encounters are obscure in their content and meaning, perhaps for our protection. In general, knowledge tends to be destructive when held by anything less than a mature personality thoroughly permeated by love and humility. That is true even in the secular areas of life. Few things are more terrifying in the spiritual arena than those who *absolutely know* but who are also unloving, hostile, proud, superstitious and fearful. That Aaron and Miriam *could* be jealous of Moses is a sure indication that God could not trust them with the kind of knowledge he shared freely with Moses. That Moses was untroubled by their attack and glad to share the prophetic ministry just as surely indicates that he could be trusted with such knowledge.

When the spectacular is *sought,* it is because of childishness in the personality. Children love the spectacular and show themselves as children by actively seeking it out, running heedlessly after it. It may sometimes be given by God—it may be necessary—because of our denseness or our hardheartedness. However, it is never to be taken as a mark of spiritual adulthood or superiority. If spectacular things do come to them, those who are more advanced in the Way of Christ never lightly discuss them or invoke them to prove that they are right or "with it" in some special way.

How Obscurity Can Serve Us

Having said that, it is important to understand that God in his mercy often speaks to us in obscure ways in order to allow us the room and time we need to respond. He lets us know that we are indeed being addressed but also that we need to stretch out in growth in order to receive the message. Perhaps we often think, *Well, God, why don't you just come out and say it? Tell me in detail how to live.* But we are usually full of mistaken ideas about what that would actually mean.

Our minds and values have to be restructured before God's glory, but at the same time our own interests are truly appreciated and understood. We may be tempted to cry out, like Isaiah, for God to rend the heavens, come out of hiding and stand before us telling us what to do (Is 64:1), but we do not really understand what it is we are asking for when we ask that. Probably it would literally kill us or at least unbalance us if it actually happened. So God in his mercy continues to approach us obliquely, in one way or another, but increasingly less so as we mature—even until that time when we can safely know him as he knows us (1 Cor 13:12).

It is therefore natural and right that God's word comes to us in forms that we must struggle to understand. This is even true of the Bible, which is very explicit in many respects but still requires persistent and energetic work to understand it. In the process of struggling we grow to the point where we can appropriate and assimilate the content of truth *as* it becomes clear. It is one of the oldest and most common stories of human life that in its most important moments we have little more than the foggiest idea of what it is we are doing and saying. And our ignorance is partly for our own good.

Did you *really* know what was happening when you entered the university or military training, got married or brought a child into the world? In some vague sense you did, perhaps, but you also had very little idea of what it meant in the long run. Had you appreciated all that it meant at the time, you probably would not have had the courage to proceed. Then you would have missed out on much good that has come to you through those events.

In faith also we come very slowly to appreciate what is happening to us. James and John came to Jesus and said, in effect, "Lord, when you become president we want to be your vice president and secretary of state." Jesus replied, "You do not know what you are asking. Can you drink the cup that I will drink of, be baptized with my baptism?" With great assurance they replied, "Oh yes, Lord, we are able to do that; bring it on" (Mk 10:37-39, paraphrase).

In fact they had no idea what they were asking. In the end it turned out that by the Lord's mercy they *were* able to drink his cup and take his baptism. They were prepared when the time came. James was the first one of the apostles to be martyred. According to tradition, John lived longer than any of the apostles. He was tortured with hot oil, and we know that he was exiled on the barren island of Patmos where he received a revelation of Jesus Christ in a form utterly new to all previous experience recorded in the book of Revelation.

These things were not what James and John had in mind by any means, but they did very well with them when the suffering came because God was with them. They grew to the vision and the task as they stepped forward in faith. They lived and finally died as the friends and colaborers of Jesus and of their heavenly Father.

The "Signs" Are Not the Reality

Bob Mumford, discussing the spectacular forms of communication from God, remarks that signs are given to us, because God meets us on the level where we operate. . . . In guidance, when God shows us a sign, it doesn't mean we've received the final answer. A sign means we're on the way. On the highway we may pass a sign saying, "New York: 100 miles." The sign doesn't mean we've reached New York, but it tells us we're on the right road.[16]

But on the other hand,

God wants to bring us beyond the point where we need signs to discern His guiding hand. Satan cannot counterfeit the peace of God or the love of God dwelling in us. When Christ's abiding presence becomes our guide, then guidance becomes an almost unconscious response to the gentle moving of His Holy Spirit within us.[17]

How glad I am that humankind was finally ready to be addressed by the still small voice of Jesus! How good it is that God left the spectacular forms that had been necessary—and perhaps still are necessary for some purposes—and came to deal with us by the very whispers of his Spirit. Who among us would really know what to do if the great God came down in splendor and somehow stood before us? As Job said, "These are indeed but the outskirts of his ways; and how small a whisper do we hear of him! But the thunder of his power who can understand?" (Job 26:14)

The incarnate Son comes without strife, so gentle that his voice is not to be heard above the chatter of the street (Mt 12:19). It is because of this approach that the Gentiles, or people generally, will finally come to have confidence in him.

I am so thankful for the quiet written Word, for the history and presence of the church of the Lamb, for the lives of the saints and for the tireless, still conquests of the Spirit of God. These approach me. These *I* can approach, and through them I can approach God while he safely draws ever closer to me.

The rivals of God's voice—still and small, still and within—continue to be necessary, then, and have their place. But once we are earnestly seeking God and get beyond the need to have big things happening to reassure us that somehow we are all right—and possibly that others are not—then we begin to understand and rejoice that, as Jesus so clearly lived and taught, the life of the kingdom is "righteousness, peace and joy in the Holy Spirit" (Rom 14:17).

Then we begin to understand that God's whole purpose is to bring us to the point where he can walk with us quietly, calmly and constantly, leaving us space to grow to be his (often fumbling) colaborers—to have some distance from him and yet be united with him because we are being conformed to the image of his Son, bearing the family resemblance.

Beyond Words

Even at the merely human level one of the highest forms of communication is that kind of communion in which no overt word is needed or wanted. What are we to make of a poet (Ben Jonson) who says, "Drink to me only with thine eyes / And I will pledge with mine"? He has touched upon an element of what God would finally bring us to in communion with him: a union sometimes beyond communication, a life constantly before him in this world and the next.

There is, finally, a *silence that speaks*—which, paradoxically, "says" all:

Love culminates in bliss when it doth reach
A white, unflickering, fear-consuming glow;
And, knowing it is known as it doth know,
Needs no assuring word or soothing speech.
It craves but silent nearness, so to rest,
No sound, no movement, love not heard but felt,
Longer and longer still, till time should melt,
A snow-flake on the eternal ocean's breast.
Have moments of this silence starred thy past,
Made memory a glory-haunted place,
Taught all the joy that mortal ken can trace?
By greater light 'tis but a shadow cast:
So shall the Lord thy God rejoice o'er thee,
And in His love will rest, and silent be.[18]

Some Topics for Reflection

1. Do you see any reasons to be concerned about Virginia Lively's story?

Should such testimonies be suppressed in a local congregation or encouraged?

2. What do you think of Gustave Oehler's "principle that a clear consciousness when receiving revelation is placed higher than ecstasy or other abnormal states of mind"? How would this relate to cases like Moses and the burning bush or Joshua and the "commander of the army of the LORD"?

3. The cases of an "audible voice alone" are today most likely to be associated with mental unbalance. Is this justified? Is there any well-based objection to God's simply producing the sound waves appropriate to audible language? Or does skepticism about such cases really rest on outright disbelief in God?

4. Have you experienced any cases that could be described as God's speaking to you *with the words of some other human being*? Biblical words? Those of a contemporary? What is it about those cases that leads you to describe them as such?

5. It is very common to hear church leaders speak of having a *personal relationship* with God through Jesus Christ. In your opinion, can such a personal relationship make sense *without* God's speaking directly to the individual?

6. Some reasons are given above for regarding the voice as the superior form of God's communication, given God's announced purposes in interacting with humanity. Do you find those reasons convincing?

7. What do you understand by "Bible deism"? Have you ever seen it in action? What makes it attractive?

Six

The Word of God
& the Rule of God

By the word of the LORD the heavens were made,
and all their host by the breath of his mouth.
PSALM 33:6

He sends out his command to the earth;
his word runs swiftly.
He gives snow like wool;
he scatters frost like ashes.
PSALM 147:15-16

Then they cried to the LORD in their trouble;
and he saved them from their distress;
he sent out his word and healed them,
and delivered them from destruction.
PSALM 107:19-20

Where the word of a king is, there is power.
ECCLESIASTES 8:4 (KJV)

THE VERY PHRASE "STILL SMALL VOICE" MIGHT SEEM TO SUGGEST that what lies at the heart of a relationship with God is something weak and marginal. But that is far from the truth. One who hears God's voice is operating from the very foundation and framework of all reality, not from the fringe. But what does this mean? What place do words and God's Word have in reality? This is a difficult question, but answering it will bring rich rewards. It is all about understanding the larger context in which we hear God. Let us explore further.

Astonishing Faith in the Power of Words

He is known to us only as "a certain centurion" (Lk 7:2 KJV). He was a Gentile, a Roman soldier of considerable rank: the top man, possibly, in the area of Capernaum. He was also a good governor who sacrificed his private wealth to help his subjects (Lk 7:5) and a good man who loved his servant, sick to the point of death. And he was humble. But all this was not what impressed Jesus when the man came to request healing for his servant. Jesus was particularly impressed by the quality and magnitude of the man's faith. The centurion seemed to understand, from his own experience of authority, how Jesus accomplished what he did. Therefore he had complete trust in Jesus' power. In an almost casual and offhand manner he said to Jesus,

> Don't trouble yourself, Sir! I'm not important enough for you to come into my house—I didn't think I was fit to come to you in person. Just give the order, please, and my servant will recover. I am used to working under orders, and I have soldiers under me. I can say to one, "Go," and he goes, or I can say to another, "Come here," and he comes; or I can say to my slave, "Do this job," and he does it. (Lk 7:6-8 Phillips)

Jesus looked at this man with astonishment. Then turning to the group following along after him, he said, "I have never found faith like this anywhere, even in Israel!" (Lk 7:9 Phillips). What? Did John the Baptist not have greater faith? What about those who heralded and welcomed the child Jesus as the Messiah? Did his own family and disciples not have greater faith than this Gentile soldier? Apparently not.

Great faith, like great strength in general, is revealed by the *ease* of its workings. As "the quality of mercy is not strained," so also with faith. Most of what we think we see as the struggle *of* faith is really the struggle to act *as if* we had faith when in fact we do not. We will look again at this centurion later. He has much to teach us about faith and about its dependence on a proper understanding of the word of God.

Words and *the* Word

God *created,* God *rules* and God *redeems* through his word. God's creating,

God's ruling and God's redeeming *is* his word. This is the single basic truth about the overall relationship that he has to his creatures. And in this truth we see the all-encompassing mediation of Jesus his Son. If we wish to understand God's personal relationship to us, including how he speaks to us individually today, we must understand what the word of God is in general and how both the Son of God and the Bible are the Word of God.

First, however, we must consider what words are. If you find a word written on a wall or simply overhear one spoken in a crowd, you cannot tell whose word it is. Its ownership does not reside within itself, considered merely as a mark or a sound. In contrast *my* word is not just *a* word. It is I who am speaking or writing. But even my name written ever so clearly on a check is not my word or my signature if *I* did not write it and thereby express my *self*—my thoughts and my intentions.

What is essential to a person's word is the meaning given to it by that person—the thought, feeling or action *that person* associates with it and hopes to convey to others. Through our words we literally give to others a piece of our mind. Through others' words we may know their thoughts and feelings and share in their lives.

Through words, soul impacts soul, sometimes with a great spiritual force. As marks or sounds alone, words are nothing. It is their mental side, their spiritual force, that hooks into the hidden levers of mind and reality and gives them their immense power. If we do not understand Spanish or Greek, we hear the sounds, but they have little or no effect because they are without meaning for us.

The power of the word lies finally in the personality that it conveys. Children learn to say, "Sticks and stones may break my bones, but words can never hurt me." Adults teach them to say this in order to ease the terrible pain that really is inflicted on them by the words of their playmates. How deeply children can be hurt by words! The school playground can become a chamber of horrors where young souls are left permanently crippled and scarred by malicious or mindless chatter.

Jesus saw this, no doubt, for *he* had eyes that saw. He also saw adults ravaging the lives of little children with their words. Surely it was largely his sense of the damage done in this way that made him say, "If any of you put a stumbling block before one of these little ones who believe in me, it would be better for you if a great millstone were fastened around your neck and you were drowned in the depth of the sea" (Mt 18:6).

The true view of the power of words is forcefully given in the book of Proverbs: "Death and life are in the power of the tongue" (18:21); "a soft tongue can break bones" (25:15); "a gentle tongue is a tree of life, but perverseness in it breaks the spirit" (15:4). This theme is carried into the New Testament. James remarks that the tongue is "a small member, yet it boasts of great exploits. How great a forest is set ablaze by a small fire!" (Jas 3:5). Jesus himself regarded words as a direct revelation of our inner being: "For by your words you will be justified, and by your words you will be condemned" (Mt 12:37).

Words as Spiritual Forces

In trying to understand the great power of words we cannot afford to overlook their *spiritual* nature. Spirit is unbodily, personal force. It is personal reality that can and often does work independently of physical or bodily forces. It can also work in conjunction with them. We can most clearly see spirit in our own selves as the force that belongs to thought, emotion and intention. In the biblical view spirit reaches far beyond these— and beyond our limited understanding—and ultimately serves as the foundation of all reality. "God is spirit" (Jn 4:24).

The view of words as spiritual forces is common to both Scripture and pagan philosophers. Once when his followers were struggling to understand him and were overemphasizing the material realm, Jesus said to them, "It is the spirit that gives life; the flesh is useless. The words that I have spoken to you are spirit and life" (Jn 6:63). This meant that through his words Jesus imparted *himself* and in some measure conferred on those who received his words the powers of God's sovereign rule. Through him they "have tasted the goodness of the word of God and the powers of the age to come" (Heb 6:5). This imparted power is referred to in Jesus' later explanation that "if you abide in me, and my words abide in you, ask for whatever you wish, and it will be done for you" (Jn 15:7).

Plato, the great philosopher of ancient Greece, also spiritualized words by treating our very thinking as an inner "conversation" that the soul holds with itself.[1] In treating thought as a kind of language—as words, but as words hidden away in the nonphysical real—he set a pattern that many thinkers have followed up to the present day.

St. Augustine carried that tradition on, joining it to Christian thought, in saying that "he who thinks speaks in his heart." He explicitly founded his view,[2] in part, on Gospel passages such as Matthew 9:2-4, where "some of the scribes *said to themselves,* 'This man is blaspheming' " (italics added; see also Lk 12:17).

The word as *a person's speaking* is therefore to be understood as a spiritual power—whether of ourselves, of God or of some other personal agency and whether for evil or for good. It is the power of the one who is speaking. It is precisely in this realm that God seeks for those who would worship him "in spirit and truth" (Jn 4:23). He desires truth in the "inward being" and "will teach me wisdom in my secret heart" (Ps 51:6).

William Penn says, with a characteristically Quaker emphasis,

> For the more mental our worship, the more adequate to the nature of God; the more silent, the more suitable to the language of the spirit.
>
> Words are for others, not for ourselves: nor for God who hears not as bodies do; but as spirits should. If we would know this dialect we must learn of the divine principle in us. As we hear the dictates of that, so does God hear us.[3]

The *word of God,* when no further qualification is added, is his speaking, his communicating. When God speaks, he expresses his mind, his character and his purposes. Thus he is always present with his word.

All expressions of his mind are "words" of God. This is true whether the specific means are *external* to the human mind—as in natural phenomena (Ps 19:1-4), other human beings, the incarnate Christ (the Logos) or the Bible—or *internal* to the human mind—in our own thoughts, intentions and feelings. God's rule over all things, including the affairs of humankind, is carried out through his word, understood in this way.

A Kingdom of Words

We are under constant temptation to think of the universe as a place in which there are only certain physical or mechanical relationships between things. Our dominant idea systems lead us to think of blind forces pushing and pulling among physical objects as the way in which all things relate to one another. This is the naturalistic outlook discussed in chapter four. Such a view, however, can never bring understanding of the common deeds and affairs of human beings, let alone of higher culture or the religious life. After centuries of attempts at such understanding, it still falls pathetically short of that goal as we enter the twenty-first century.

In contrast, the religious life and the religious outlook on the universe—especially the outlook identifiable with the mind of Christ and with life in his footsteps—is one that sees the universe as a *kingdom.* A kingdom does not work merely by pushes and pulls. Essentially it works by the *communication* of thoughts and intentions through words or other symbols, for a kingdom is a network of personal relationships.

This is a point about the nature of social reality that we cannot afford to miss. Some of our greatest problems in understanding and entering into life in the kingdom of God come from an inadequate appreciation of how that kingdom—like all kingdoms—works: that is, by communication, the speaking or use of words for the expression of minds and intentions. The Scriptures are the best place to look for illustrations of how the speaking of a word works in the kingdom of God.

Creation by Words: God's and Ours

We begin, naturally enough, with the first chapter of the first book of the Bible, at creation. We are told that in the beginning God created the heavens and the earth. How did he do it? By speaking, by a sequence of directly creative words.

It should come as no surprise, given what we know of the physical universe, that God's first creative act was to create light, a form of physical energy (Gen 1:3). How did he create light? According to the record he *said,* "Let there be light." God's speaking—the word of God—is simply the expression of his mind. By the expression of his mind, then, he created light.

The coming into being of light and the result (light itself) are both to be viewed as a word of God. The writer of Hebrews observes (Heb 1:1-3) that the things that are seen (light and so on) were not made of things that are visible. The word of God is *invisible;* it is the spiritual reality that produces all that *is* visible (cf. 2 Cor 4:18; 2 Pet 3:5-7).

Is it possible to clarify these passages from Genesis in some small measure by reflecting on how we ourselves create? I think so. You may express your own mind both through the creation of things and in what you create. But you will usually have to do more than just "speak" these into being. For example, if you are to create a bouquet of flowers or a cake, you cannot just think or say, "Let there be a bouquet!" or "Let there be a chocolate cake!"

In this way we can see the meaning of our finiteness. Finiteness means limitation or *restriction.* You and I are under some restrictions regarding how we can make a cake. We must work with and through the eggs, the flour, the sugar, the heat of the oven and the time. We must adapt ourselves and our actions to our ingredients. The structures already within the substances with which we must work dictate the order and limitations of our actions. God, by contrast, dictates the structure and order in all things.

Eventually, however, the cake is finished if we know what we are doing, and it is an expression of ourselves, our thoughts, feelings and intentions. Without them it would not exist. The husband or wife or child who just eats the cake without comment has not grasped that point. He or she must find it good and say so. Better yet, he or she must say, in so many words, "How good of you to make this cake for me!" For *you,* the cook, are invested in that cake.

At a still more creative level of human life we have inventions. Normally a cake will be thought of just as something nice that you produced by following a recipe or knowing how to make it. But if a person conceives of a new type of engine, clothing or communicative device, that is an invention. It too is an expression, at a deeper level of individuality, of the mind of its creator. Hence we glorify inventors and authors as special kinds of people. Here also, thought—the internal word—governs events in the material world;

yet here also, it works under restrictions. We cannot create a jet engine just by saying or thinking, "Let there be a jet engine!"

There is, however, one arena where the human mind simply "speaks" and what it wishes is done. This is in the voluntary motions of the body—such as the hands, the feet and the face—and the voluntary wide-ranging journeys of our inward thoughts.

God is *always* able to speak and to create without going through channels, without working under restrictions (though he does not always choose the direct route). This constitutes his infinity. Within a certain range—very narrow, in contrast to God's—we too have been given a similarly unrestricted ability in our own natural powers. In the realm of our finiteness we must *learn how* to do things. We learn how to break the eggs and how to stir the batter, how to steer the car and how to apply the brakes. But we do not *consciously learn how* to move our fingers, our tongues or our feet. Here there are no channels we must go through under normal circumstances. The action is immediate, and in our conscious processes there is no "how" about it. The thought, the intent, is there, and the body, with all the physical intricacies involved, just moves in obedience.

Similarly we know or can learn how to interpret a passage of Scripture, read music, solve a crossword puzzle or dissect an argument. There is therefore also a "how to" aspect across broad ranges of the mental life. But at a certain point you can only think *directly* of some things or decide on a course of action. If I ask you to think of a kitten, you do so immediately without first thinking, "*How* shall I think of a kitten?" for that makes no more sense than asking, "How shall I move my little finger?"

This all goes to make the following point. Here in this restricted range of direct action, God has given us a power that, so far as our conscious control is concerned, is as immediately creative as his own. A realization of how our own thoughts (inner words) translate themselves into an act of creation is absolutely vital if we are to gain any concrete sense of God's rule through his word. Only if we have some understanding of what it means for his word to *act* will we have any grounds for believing that God can have a personal, guiding relationship with us.

Returning to Genesis 1, we see God continuing to create by the direct action of his word on the results of his first creative word—the one that produced light and energy from itself alone, energy that we now know to be the substance of matter. Thus we read

> And God said, "Let there be a dome in the midst of the waters, and let it separate the waters from the waters. . . . Let the waters under the sky be gathered together into one place." (vv. 6, 9)

He spoke and thereby formed these specific things into existence.

> And God said, "Let there be lights in the dome of the sky. . . . Let the waters bring forth swarms of living creatures. . . . Let the earth bring forth living creatures of every kind. . . . Let us make humankind in our image, according to our likeness." (vv. 14, 20, 24, 26)

In all these cases, as God spoke the object concerned came into existence—whether in an instant or over a more or less extended period of time does not matter—in the same way that your hand moves in response to your thought and intention. *That* is the creative power of the word of God.

The word of God—the thought and mind of God—continues its presence in the created universe, *upholding* it. "Lasting to eternity, your word, Yahweh, unchanging in the heavens: your faithfulness lasts age after age; you founded the earth to endure. Creation is maintained by your rulings, since all things are your servants" (Ps 119.89-91 JB).

What we call natural laws, then, must be regarded as God's thoughts and intentions as to how the world should run. Because of this, as the Christian philosopher and Anglican bishop George Berkeley said long ago, echoing Psalm 19, "God himself speaks every day and in every place to the eyes of all men."[4] The events in the visible, material world—the unfolding of a rosebud, the germination of a seed, the conception and growth of a child, the evolution of galaxies—constitute a visible language manifesting not only a creative mind but, as Berkeley continues,

> a provident Governor, actually and intimately present, and attentive to all our interests and motions, who watches over our conduct and takes care of our

minutest actions and designs throughout the whole course of our lives, informing, admonishing, and directing incessantly, in a most evident and sensible
manner.[5]

With all this in mind you may wish to interrupt your reading here to
undertake a meditative and worshipful study of Psalm 104!

The Word of God as the Son of God

At a certain point in history this word—this visible language, the upholding
order of the universe—came to us through the womb of Mary: "He was in
the world, and the world came into being through him; yet the world did not
know him. He came to what was his own, and his people did not accept him"
(Jn 1:10-11).

The *redemptive* entry of God upon the human scene was no intrusion into
foreign territory; it was a move into "his own"—a focusing of that divine
thought which is the order of all creation into the finite form of one human
personality. He, as the ancient prayer says, "did not abhor the Virgin's womb."
Even there, as always, the "control panel" of the entire universe lay ready to
hand. By voluntarily emptying himself (Phil 2:7) during his incarnation, he
refrained from all but a very selective use of it.

The apparent paradox of the incarnation is that Christ's "in-fleshment"
was really not an imposed restriction but rather the supreme exercise of the
supreme power, as the end of human history will make abundantly clear:

> Here is my servant, whom I have chosen,
>> my beloved, with whom my soul is well pleased.
> I will put my Spirit upon him,
>> and he will proclaim justice to the Gentiles.
> He will not wrangle or cry aloud,
>> nor will anyone hear his voice in the streets.
> He will not break a bruised reed
>> or quench a smoldering wick
> until he brings justice to victory.
>> And in his name the Gentiles will hope. (Mt 12:18-21)

The story of the New Testament is the story of people's increasing understanding of who Jesus was. Those among whom he was reared said, "This is Mary and Joseph's boy. We know him." His own disciples thought he might be Elijah or one of the old prophets risen from the dead. In a flash of divine revelation Peter announced, as Jesus quizzed the disciples on his identity, "You are the Messiah, the Son of the living God" (Mt 16:16).

Only in the later parts of the New Testament does there emerge the concept of Jesus as a *cosmic* Messiah: a ruler spanning all geographical and ethnic differences, providing the glue of the universe (Col 1:17) and upholding all things by the word of his power (Heb 1:3) or as the Jerusalem Bible beautifully translates it, "sustaining the universe by his powerful command." Thus he is, as described in the book of Revelation, the Alpha and Omega, the Faithful and True, The Word of God who leads the armies of heaven, the King of kings and Lord of lords (Rev 1:8; 19:11, 13, 16).

In all its manifestations in nature and in the incarnate Christ, the word of God is characterized by overwhelming power. It is the awareness of this power that brings the prophet Isaiah to contrast the thoughts of humankind with the thoughts of God, which in their expression are the *words* of God. Mere human thoughts, though effective within their appointed range, are as far below the power of God's thoughts (and words) as the earth is below the heavens (Is 55:8-9). For God says that with a force comparable to the forces of nature—the rain and seed bringing forth plants, seed and bread to nourish the hungry (55:10)—"so shall my word be that goes out from my mouth; it shall not return to me empty, but it shall accomplish that which I purpose, and succeed in the thing for which I sent it" (55:11).

The *unity* of the natural order with God's redemptive community under the word of God is seen in Psalm 29. Here the behavior of the waters and the forests are attributed to the voice of the Lord: "The voice of the LORD causes the oaks to whirl, and strips the forest bare" (v. 9). But while "the LORD sits enthroned over the flood," he will also "give strength to his people! May the LORD bless his people with peace!" (vv. 10-11). This same unity is exhibited in the life of Jesus. He could turn water into wine, calm the billowing waves with his word and walk on them as on a pavement. But he could also place the word of God's kingdom rule into people's hearts, where it would bring forth fruit a hundredfold, or sixtyfold, or thirtyfold (Mt 13:23).

This then is the Word of God and the Son of God, united in the ordering of the cosmos. To understand how the Word of God is related to the *family* of God, however, we must consider more closely the *role of ordinary human words* in ordinary human life. This should then, later in the chapter, help us to see how the *power of the Word of God,* operating among human beings, differs from superstition, magic and voodoo. That is crucial if we are to make sense of hearing God and to keep Christian spirituality clearly distinct from other spiritualities.

The Power of a Word

In the book of Ecclesiastes a wise man reflects in depth on how human life and society work. Among other things he considers how kings or governments function. Psalm 29 told how the Lord sat as King at the flood, and we know that he is indeed King over all the earth and master of the most terrible of situations. But a king, contrary to what is often thought, does *not* rule simply by brute force.

The emperor Napoleon Bonaparte was about to use great force to subdue a certain population when a wise lieutenant, one of his aides, said to him, "Monsignor, one cannot *sit* upon bayonets." This man understood that the use of brute force could not lead to a *settled* political rule. All government exists to some degree by consent of the governed. No one can totally rule a people by force alone. Instead the ruler rules by words, understandings, allegiances and alliances.

The writer of Ecclesiastes, himself a king, was amazed at what the word of a king could do. He observes that a king's word "is powerful, and who can say to him, 'What are you doing?' " (Eccles 8:4). Take his authority, his role, away from him, and a king is like any other person. But when he is indeed kingly, his smallest word has awesome effects: heads roll, nations prosper, cities burn, armies march, enemies are crushed. Seeing clearly the power of words at the merely human level may help us to understand the power of the creative word of God in *his* kingdom.

Words in the Kingdom of God

If we turn to the kingdom of God with an understanding that it *is* a kingdom and that it too works in large measure by words, numerous events from the life of Jesus on earth are easier to appreciate and enter into sympathetically.

At the opening of this chapter we met "a certain centurion." He had implicit faith in Jesus—not, it seems, on a religious basis but from his secular knowledge of the power of authoritative words. So far as one can tell from the story, he did not have any special degree of faith in God, though he was a good man and respected the Jewish religion. He simply knew how authority worked, and he recognized that Jesus was working with authority to heal.

When, as recorded in Matthew 8, Jesus entered the city of Capernaum one day, this centurion came to ask for help, saying, "Lord, my servant is lying at home paralyzed, in terrible distress" (v. 6). Without being asked Jesus said, "I will come and cure him" (v. 7)—just like that! It seemed to be nothing extraordinary to him. For Jesus his healing this servant would be like our saying, "Now I'll raise my hand."

The centurion was in a position to understand Jesus' response. He replied, "Lord, I am not worthy to have you come under my roof" (v. 8). This was both an act of humility and a courtesy on the part of the centurion, for he knew that he was speaking to a Jew and that proper Jews thought that entering into the house of a Gentile would defile them. So he said humbly to Jesus, "But only speak the word, and my servant will be healed" (v. 8).

"Only speak the word"? Yes, for where the word of a *king* is, there is *power!* The word is enough. The centurion understood this because he was like a king within his own small arena, who was authorized to speak for a higher king, Caesar.

In both Gospel accounts of his meeting with Jesus, the centurion is allowed to explain fully how it is that he knows that Jesus need "only speak the word" to heal his servant: "For I also am a man under authority, with soldiers under me; and I say to one, 'Go,' and he goes, and to another, 'Come,' and he comes, and to my slave, 'Do this,' and the slave does it" (Mt 8:9; cf. Lk 7:8).

What we see here is *trust* based upon *experiential knowledge of the power in the words spoken by authorized individuals.* In a personal universe (whether our own small arena or God's cosmos) the word directs actions and events. The centurion understood this, and Jesus marveled at his understanding: "When Jesus heard him, he was amazed and said to those who followed him, 'Truly I tell you, in no one in Israel have I found such faith' " (Mt 8:10).

At this point our practical atheism or skepticism may abruptly emerge, and we may find ourselves saying (or silently thinking), "Things just aren't like that!" But what is it exactly that we find wrong here? What is amiss with a universe in which reality responds to a word? What is wrong with a universe in which reality responds to thoughts and intentions? Surely we live in precisely such a universe. But our faith does not normally rise to believing it—at least not to the extent to which it is true. In part, no doubt, our skepticism comes from the fact that we often speak words unaccompanied by faith and authority. Such words do not have the effect on reality that words laden with faith, spoken in the fulfillment of an authoritative role, do have. Thus *our* experience, unlike the centurion's, hinders rather than helps our faith.

For the centurion, by contrast, it was all perfectly easy because he recognized that he was dealing with someone in high authority. He knew what authority was. He knew what it was to command an event. He knew that Jesus was doing the same kind of thing, so it was a simple matter for him to step into the situation by faith. Where *he* had no authority—and thus could not himself say, "Be healed!"—he could recognize the one who did have such authority. In faith he could ask that one, Jesus, to use his authority to direct processes within the material universe, namely, the healing of his servant.

This Power Given to Human Beings

To some who doubted in his day, Jesus said, " 'But so that you may know that the Son of Man has authority on earth to forgive sins'—he then said to the paralytic—'Stand up, take your bed and go to your home.' And he stood up and went to his home. When the crowds saw it, they were filled with awe, and they glorified God, who had given such authority to human beings" (Mt 9:6-8). C. H. Spurgeon appropriately comments that "miracles of grace must be the seals of our ministry; who can bestow them but the Spirit of God?"[6]

According to the biblical record, powerful words such as Jesus spoke *have* been given to other human beings to speak also. In Numbers 20:8-12 we find a fascinating case study on this point. The Israelites, on their wilderness wanderings, were dying for lack of water. Moses' leadership was under violent criticism from his people. This drove Moses to prayer, as was right. Then God appeared to him, telling him to command a rock that was close by to give forth water: "Thus you shall bring water out of the rock for them" (v. 8).

Instead of doing this, however, Moses took the rod that God had given him earlier as a sign and with Aaron called the people together, saying, " 'Listen, you rebels, shall we bring water for you out of this rock?' Then Moses lifted up his hand and struck the rock twice with his staff; water came out abundantly, and the congregation and their livestock drank" (20:10-11). Pretty impressive. But because Moses had struck the rock instead of speaking to it, God dealt sternly with him for his disobedience: he did not allow him to cross into the land of promise "because ye believed me not" (20:12 KJV). Was Moses' truly such a serious offense? Did it deserve such a strong reaction from God? And if so, why? Without understanding the matters discussed above, one might see little wrong in what Moses did.

Possibly by striking the rock Moses was attempting to answer those who criticized *his* power. Or possibly he did not believe that his merely *speaking* to a rock could bring water out of it. Possibly he misunderstood and thought he had to bring forth the water by his own physical strength—"Shall *we* bring water for you out of this rock?" he asked. But the rock he struck, as we learn in 1 Corinthians 10:4, was Christ. Rocks—if what we have come to understand about the Logos, or Word, within creation and nature is true—are things that might well respond to words spoken with the appropriate kingdom authority and vision of faith.

The transfer of the power of God's word to the words of ordinary humans was something that Jesus, during his days in human form, approached experimentally. *He* could exercise this power of God's government, but could it be transferred to his followers? That was the question they faced together.

He commissioned his disciples to do what they had so often seen him do, and he sent them on their way: "As you go, proclaim the good news, 'The kingdom of heaven has come near.' Cure the sick, raise the dead, cleanse the lepers, cast out demons. You received without payment; give without payment" (Mt 10:7-8; cf. Lk 9:1-10).

This first trial run was conducted only with his twelve apostles. When they returned and reported good success in acting in the power of God's word, the question was then whether this transfer of God's power could be extended beyond the close followers and on to more ordinary believers. And so, according to Luke 10:1, Jesus sent out "seventy others." It seems to me to be a matter of great significance that these "seventy others" were not his closest associates; they were not, we might say, the best-trained troops in the army of the Lord. Yet they too returned rejoicing in the knowledge that even demons were subject to them through the name of their Master (Lk 10:17).

This seems to have had the effect of settling the Lord's mind on what we might call "the extended incarnational plan" for delivering humanity. It was apparently only at this point that Jesus saw Satan in defeat, through the transfer of the word of God and its power to ordinary people who could then speak *for* God under his government (Lk 10:18).

In this touching passage (Lk 10:21-24) Jesus seems positively gleeful, as in no other scriptural passage. Luke says Jesus "rejoiced in the Holy Spirit"; the Greek word used here (*agalliao,* v. 21) suggests the state of mind in which people may jump up and down with joy. Then Jesus turned aside, perhaps, for a moment of thanks to his Father: "I thank you, Father, Lord of heaven and earth, because you have hidden these things from the wise and the intelligent and have revealed them to infants; yes, Father, for such was your gracious will" (v. 21).

Under the vivid realization of the meaning of these events, he then informed his followers with assurance that his Father had turned everything over to him—"All things have been handed over to me by my Father"—and that he, Jesus Christ, was to be totally in charge of the revelation of the Father to humanity (v. 22). He congratulated those around him on their good fortune in being able to witness what had happened, in seeing just plain folks succeed in operating with the power of God's authoritative word. Prophets and kings had longed to see this but had not been able (vv. 23-24).

In this way the governmental rule of God reaffirmed itself *through* the actions and words of human beings within the people of Israel just before it was removed from their exclusive control. Because they failed to fulfill their divine appointment of being the light of the world, of showing the world how to live under God, Jesus finally said to the Israelites of his day, "Therefore, I tell you, the kingdom of God will be taken away from you and given to a people that produces the fruits of the kingdom" (Mt 21:43). It was not as if the Jews were to be excluded as individuals from the exercise of the word of power in God's kingdom. Far from it. But this was no longer to be *exclusively* their role *as Jews.* The Jewish people would no longer be the exclusive people of God, God's official address on earth. The story of the transfer of the kingdom from the Jews to the church, which was indicated by Jesus in Matthew 21:43, is the story of the New Testament book of Acts, which begins in Jerusalem and ends in Rome. Today participation in the kingdom rule of God through union with Jesus is open worldwide.

Prayers, Actions and Words

A proper understanding of the ways of the word of God among humanity, within the kingdom rule of God, illuminates something that has troubled many thoughtful students of the New Testament. Rarely does Jesus ever *pray* for a need brought before him. Rather he normally *addresses* it or performs some *action* in relation to it.

Such a case is described in Mark 9. While Jesus was on the Mount of Transfiguration a man brought his child to be healed. The child was possessed of a spirit that rendered him mute. The disciples tried to cast the spirit out, but they failed. When the Master arrived back on the scene he scolded his disciples for their inability (v. 19). After some conversation with the child's father about the child's condition and about the father's own faith, Jesus cast the demon out with a command. When the disciples asked why they had not been able to cast it out—apparently they had previously had some success in such matters—Jesus replied, "This kind can come out only through prayer"

(v. 29). Yet Jesus himself did not pray on this occasion. What is the explanation?

I believe this is an illustration of the principle that (as experience readily shows) there are *degrees of power* in speaking the word of God and that prayer is necessary to heighten that power. Prayer is more fundamental in the spiritual life than is speaking a word and indeed is the indispensable foundation for doing so. The role of speaking the word of God has become limited today because of a widespread lack of understanding of such "speaking," coupled with the generally low quality of the life of prayer.

Certainly in some situations we will encounter, and perhaps in most, a *direct* word or action from God himself rather than from ourselves is what is required. And for that we can only pray. Sometimes, on the other hand, *we* should be in a position to speak, to say on behalf of God and in the name of Christ how things are to be. To do this will be more or less difficult, as Jesus indicates in Mark 9, depending on the specifics of the case. This kind of situation will frequently differ from other kinds and will call for other abilities, which we may or may not have available at the time. But I believe we are called to *grow* into this capacity to speak with God, in the degree of power appointed by him for us individually.

In the works done by the apostles of Jesus, we see the apostles *speaking with* God—as in the book of Acts and less so in the Gospels. They did not *always* pray to God for help in the matter at hand, and they certainly dealt with different situations in different ways. When Peter and John were confronted with the lame beggar as they entered the temple in Acts 3, Peter commanded the man in the name of Jesus Christ—that is, he commanded him on Jesus' behalf—to rise up and walk (v. 6). Then Peter took the lame man by the hand and pulled him to his feet (v. 7). Peter did not kneel down and pray for him, nor did he pass by saying, "We'll be praying for you!" He put his whole bodily self on public display as an agent of Christ. Scary, isn't it?

When dealing with Dorcas, the deceased sister who "was devoted to good works and acts of charity" (Acts 9:36), Peter put everyone out of the room. Did he learn this from Jesus (compare Mt 9:25)? Kneeling down, he prayed.

Then he faced the body and commanded Dorcas to arise, and she returned to life (Acts 9:40). Perhaps Peter also learned from Elisha's practice in a similar situation (2 Kings 4:32-35). Elisha was one of the greatest practitioners of kingdom rule with his God.

At Lystra, Paul spoke the redemptive word of God to a lame man whose faith had been raised by hearing Paul preach. Paul loudly commanded the man, " 'Stand upright on your feet.' And the man sprang up and began to walk" (Acts 14:10).

Today with the return of the *charismata,* the gifts of the Spirit, to prominence across all denominational boundaries, multitudes of disciples once again dare to *speak* in the name of Jesus to the needs and dangers that confront them. And the practice of so-called spiritual warfare has prepared countless others to "speak to the mountain," as Jesus said (Mk 11:23). Testimonies of remarkable results find their way into many fellowships and into an abundance of Christian literature. This is to be expected as we grow in our confidence that reality—including the material world—is ultimately a *kingdom* in which authority, personal relationship and communication are basic to the way things run. We have, of course, much still to learn.

We Are Called into Question

There are, however, many ways in which these matters might be misunderstood. They will be especially unsettling if we are already used to living our lives untouched by them and are convinced that they should have nothing to do with our faith or our service to God. The suggestion that we *should* possibly be healing the sick, casting out demons or raising the dead by our participation in the word and power of God may leave us baffled, angry, rebellious and guilt-ridden.

At a meeting where I had been speaking on accomplishing things through prayer, a woman confronted me in great agony and tears and with not a little anger. She had earlier believed that prayer could actually make a difference to the course of events around us, and she had tried very hard to make this work in her life. But for whatever reason, she had failed in the attempt, and that failure had left her feeling guilty and deeply hurt. To protect herself she had readjusted her faith—at least on the surface—to consist of believing the creeds, helping out at church and being a good person generally, as that is commonly understood in our society. My words had reopened the old wounds and disturbed her hard-won peace. I have since come to understand that she was representative of many fine people who are convinced that the biblical mode of life in God's kingdom simply cannot be a reality for them.

On another occasion I met a very devout woman who had been raised in a fellowship where stress was laid on receiving a "second work of grace." She had been driven to distraction in her frantic efforts to obtain this "deeper life" and cease being a second-class citizen among her religious friends. She too had "failed." She had moved to a different denomination and had recoiled into a life of mere mental assent to the truth about Jesus and some degree of effort for her local church. That day I had only been teaching about the joyous possibilities of life opened up by Jesus' invitation to enter his kingdom and about how gladly that invitation was received by his hearers. But this woman was thrown into agony by the talk of a life of real interaction with God in the manner described in the Old and New Testaments.

I cannot deal effectively here with all the issues involved in such cases, but there is one thing I can and must make clear: When we consider a life of participation in God's kingdom rule, we are not looking at anything that *we* must make happen. The extent of our obligation is to be honestly willing and eager to be made able.

If we are to exercise the word and rule of God in ways regarded as spectacular by human beings, Jesus is our model, as always. And that means above all that there will be nothing forced or hysterical about it and that we can count on God himself to lead us into whatever we are to do. He will do this in a way that is suitable to our lives and his calling for us.

Beyond this we should always keep in mind the words of Jesus to his seventy friends on their return from their mission: "Nevertheless, do not rejoice at this, that the spirits submit to you, but rejoice that your names are written in heaven" (Lk 10:20).

Keeping all this firmly in mind, I want to turn now to two final questions for this chapter: "How does a life in which one speaks the creative word of

God differ from a life of voodoo, magic and superstition?" and "What does the Bible have to do with the word of God as discussed so far?"

Voodoo, Magic and Superstition

The word *magic* in this context refers not to sleight of hand or trickery but to the attempt to influence the *actual course* of events, as distinct from their *appearance,* by manipulation of symbolisms or special substances such as effigies and incantations. Voodoo and witchcraft—sometimes lumped together under the term "black magic"—are the forms of magical practice most familiar to the Western mind.

Satanism and demonism, though they sometimes merge with magic in practice, operate on a quite different principle—service to or from a power that is personal but evil. Magic and witchcraft, by contrast, are forms of superstition. They work from belief that some action, substance or circumstance not logically or naturally (or even supernaturally) related to a certain course of events does nonetheless influence the outcome of those events if "correctly" approached. Prayer and speaking with God must be carefully distinguished from superstition.

The word *superstition* is derived from words that mean "to stand over," as one might stand in wonder or amazement over something incomprehensible. The famous Connecticut Yankee in King Arthur's court in Mark Twain's fictional portrayal was able—as the story goes—to get the ignorant and generally superstitious people of ancient England to attribute unusual powers to his own actions, while he himself understood the natural causes of the events he manipulated. Martin Buber rightly says that "magic desires to obtain its effects without entering into relation, and practices its tricks in the void,"[7] the void of ignorance and selfish obsession.

Superstition, then, is belief in magic; and magic relies on *alleged* causal influences that are not actually mediated through the natures of the things involved. Suppose, for example, someone says they can throw you into great pain or even kill you by mutilating a doll-like effigy of you, a practice common in voodoo and other forms of witchcraft. It is superstition or magic, for there is no real connection between someone's sticking a pin in a doll and your feeling pain.

I am sure that in some cases there is much more reality to the *effects claimed* than we might wish to credit, from either a commonsense or a scientific point of view. For example, there seems to be good evidence that in some settings people do suffer or die when certain rituals are performed with reference to them. However, it is not the mutilation of the doll or the incantations over it that produce the effects. Rather the effects—where there are effects—are produced from the realm of the mind or spirit in a social context where a certain set of beliefs about voodoo or magical rituals is shared. Possibly in some cases spiritual beings are also involved.

This does not mean that the effects are illusory or unreal, but whatever actual causation is involved has nothing *magical* about it. No causation has. The voodoo process is, so far as any effects are concerned, an entirely natural process achieved through the prevailing psychosocial order.[8] The power involved is not the power of the ritual itself. It is the power of personal force, often involving something like hypnotism, along with the social context and perhaps the satanic dimension of the spiritual realm.

The Christian's faith is not superstition. If we look at the ways in which Moses, Jesus, Peter and Paul did the work of God—exercising his rule by speaking and acting with his word—there is neither magic nor superstition to be found. The same can be said for the astonishing results of believers speaking God's words, results that are once again becoming a part of ordinary Christian life today.

Many people have difficulty accepting the more spectacular episodes of God's word at work, such as we have seen from Scripture. The same people, however, still believe in the healing power of prayer and in the capacity of some individuals or some rituals practiced by the church to minister at the physical level in the healing of the body and so forth. Is *this* not just more superstition?

The answer is that in our faith *we do not believe that the power concerned resides in the words used or in the rituals taken by themselves.* If we did, we would indeed be engaged in superstitious practices. Instead we regard the words and actions simply as ways ordained in the nature of things as established by God for accomplishing the matter in question. They work as part of life in the kingdom of God. They enlist the personal agencies of that kingdom to achieve the ends at their disposal and are not mere tools by which we engineer our desired result. We are under authority, not in control.

The specific condition of understanding, faith, love and hope that is present in those who work with the word of God is *in its very nature* connected with the effect to be brought about—relating the nature of the human body or mind (in the case of healing) to the creative and redemptive Spirit who is God. As part of the kingdom this condition forms the appropriate channel from the supply to the need. It forms a natural (though really supernatural) order of influence and causation.

This might be made clearer if we return briefly to the matters discussed at the beginning of this chapter. We saw there that it is the very nature of the material universe to be subject generally to the word of an all-present, all-powerful, all-knowing divine mind. (Recall this discussion in chapter four.) This mind is what mediates between the word spoken by God's servant on his behalf and the physical structure of the waves or the rocks or of the body or mind to be healed. That is why Moses, Jesus, Peter and Paul were not magicians and did not practice anything like voodoo.

Sometimes, however, I fear that we Christians do engage in truly superstitious uses of words and rituals, especially when our activities are not an expression of any understanding of the connection between the desired consequence and our faith and union with God—that is, when we really do not understand how the kingdom of God functions among us.

A few years ago, for example, many Christians in the United States were caught up in a fad involving the phrase "what you say is what you get" (or "name it and claim it"). Some still are. It was suggested that if you just affirmed what you wanted, you would get it. Further, if you said what you *did not* want—for example, if you voiced something you were worried might happen—that also would happen to you. Now this *is* superstition, placing us in the category of those people described by Jesus who "heap up empty phrases as the Gentiles do" in prayer, thinking "that they will be heard because of their many words" (Mt 6:7). Possibly many professing Christians have little *except* superstition in their religious activities. They may have no understanding at all of the nature of God's kingdom and of how he rules in the affairs of humanity through his word, especially within the family of the faithful. We must each search our own heart on this matter. We do not have to be superstitious if we seek above all the kingdom of God.

Legalism is superstition. The legalistic tendencies found throughout our religious and cultural life also thrust us toward superstition. Legalism claims that overt *action* in conforming to rules for explicit behavior is what makes us right and pleasing to God and worthy of blessing. Jesus called legalism "the righteousness . . . of the scribes and Pharisees" (Mt 5:20).

Legalism, superstition and magic are closely joined by their emphasis on controlling people and events. Legalists are forced toward superstitious behavior because, in the interest of controlling life through their laws, they depart from the natural connections of life. They bypass the realities of the heart and soul from which life really flows. That is why Jesus tells us we must go *beyond* the righteousness of the scribes and Pharisees if we are truly to enter into life.

Life does not come by law (Gal 3:21), nor can law adequately depict or guide life. The law is the letter, and "the letter kills, but the Spirit gives life" (2 Cor 3:6). Legalists are evermore forced into merely symbolic behavior, which they superstitiously suppose to have the good effects they seek. Magic or superstition, as is well known, also place absolute emphasis on doing everything "just right," which is the essence of legalism.

"Speaking the word" confused with magic: Two biblical cases. Living and acting from the power of God through reliance on Christ has nothing to do with superstition, as it has nothing to do with legalism or salvation through the law. In two different cases in the book of Acts the word and work of God were *mistaken* for magic by those without understanding.

The first case is that of Simon the sorcerer in Acts 8. Seeing how Peter and John conferred the Holy Spirit on others, with the attendant manifestations, Simon offered money to them if they would give him power to do the same (vv. 18-19). Peter saw from this that Simon, though apparently a believer (v. 13), did not have his heart right with God. He rebuked him severely for thinking that he "could obtain God's gift with money" (v. 20).

In Acts 19 there is a rather more humorous story. A traveling troupe of Jewish exorcists, the seven sons of Sceva, saw the miracles worked by God with Paul and Paul with God. They listened to the *words* Paul used, mistaking them for incantations rather than intelligent, rational discourse within a society or kingdom.

They then tried exorcism by pronouncing the name of Jesus over a person possessed of demons, saying, "I adjure you by the Jesus whom Paul proclaims" (v. 13). The scriptural account of what happened then is so good that it must simply be quoted: "But the evil spirit said to them in reply, 'Jesus I know, and Paul I know; but who are you?' Then the man with the evil spirit leaped on them, mastered them all, and so overpowered them that they fled out of the house naked and wounded" (vv. 15-16).

This vastly impressed everyone in Ephesus, and the name "Lord Jesus" was held in great respect. Believers who had been using spells and practicing magic forsook such practices, realizing the great disparity between the realm of the magical and the kingdom of God. They burned magic books worth fifty thousand pieces of silver; while for its part "the word of the Lord grew mightily and prevailed" (v. 20).

As followers of Christ we are not to believe or act on things that make no sense and that we only hope to make work for our own ends, no matter how respected those things might be.

The Bible and the Word of God

Finally, how are we to understand the relationship of the Bible to this word of God that we have just seen growing mightily and prevailing around Ephesus and to the Word that is God and that upholds the world?

The Bible is *one* of the results of God's speaking. It is the *unique* written Word of God. It is inerrant in its original form and infallible in all of its forms for the purpose of guiding us into a life-saving relationship with God in his kingdom. It is infallible in this way precisely because God never leaves it alone.

The inerrancy of the original texts is rendered effective for the purposes of redemption only as that text, through its present-day derivatives, is constantly held within the eternal living Word. Inerrancy by itself is not a sufficient theory of biblical inspiration because as everyone knows, the Bible in our hand is not the original text. Inerrancy of the originals also does not guarantee sane and sound, much less error-free, interpretations. Our dependence as we read the Bible today must be on God, who now speaks to us in conjunction with it and with our best efforts to understand it.

In light of our discussions so far it is clear that *while the Bible is the written Word of God, the word of God is not simply the Bible.* The way we know that this is so is, above all, by *paying attention to what the Bible says.*

If you take just the passages studied so far and carefully examine what they say about the word of God, you will see that that word is much greater than the Bible, though inclusive of it. The Bible is the Word of God in its unique *written* form. But the Bible is not Jesus Christ, who is the *living* Word. The Bible was not born of a virgin, crucified, resurrected and elevated to the right hand of the Father.

Neither is the Bible the word of God that is settled eternally in the heavens as the psalmist says (Ps 119:89), expressing itself in the order of nature (Ps 19:1-4). The Bible is not the word of God that, in the book of Acts, expanded and grew and multiplied (Acts 12:24). It is not the word that Jesus spoke of as being sown by the active speaking of the ministry (Mt 13). But *all* of these are God's *words,* as is also his speaking that we hear when we *individually hear God.*

So the Bible is the unique, infallible, written Word of God, but the word of God is not just the Bible. If we try to dignify the Bible by saying false things about it—by simply *equating* the word of God with it—we do not dignify it. Instead we betray its content by denying what it says itself about the nature of the word of God.

God reigns in his kingdom through his speaking. That speaking is reserved to himself, but it may in some small measure be communicated through those who work in union with him. The Bible is a finite, written record of the saving truth spoken by the infinite, living God, and it reliably fixes the boundaries of everything he will ever say to humankind. It fixes those boundaries *in principle,* though it does not provide the detailed communications that God may have with individual believers today.

The Bible has its own special and irreplaceable role in the history of redemption. We can refer any person to it with the assurance that if they will approach it openly, honestly, intelligently and persistently, God will meet them through its pages and speak peace to their souls. This is assured to any person whose deepest self cries out,

> Beyond the sacred page I seek Thee, Lord;
> My spirit pants for Thee, O Living Word.[9]

Paul therefore instructed his protégé Timothy that "the sacred writings . . . are able to instruct you for salvation through faith in Christ Jesus. All scripture is inspired by God and is useful for teaching, for reproof, for correction, and for training in righteousness, so that everyone who belongs to God may be proficient, equipped for every good work" (2 Tim 3:15-17).

The word of God in the larger sense portrayed *in* the Bible is therefore available to every person *through* the Bible, the written Word of God. All may hear the living Word by coming to the Bible humbly and persistently, with burning desire to find God and live in peace with him.

As for others the Bible may prove a deadly snare, as it did for those in Christ's earthly days who actually used Scripture to dismiss him and his claims on them (Jn 5:36-47). Because of this we are warned in the Bible that we can even destroy ourselves by Bible study: specifically by the study of Paul's epistles, for "some things in them [are] hard to understand, which the ignorant and unstable twist to their own destruction, as they do the other scriptures" (2 Pet 3:16).

Our only protection from our own pride, fear, ignorance and impatience as we study the Bible is fellowship with the living Word, the Lord himself, invoked in constant supplication from the midst of his people, as we see here—

> O send Thy Spirit, Lord, now unto me,
> That He may touch my eyes, and make me see;
> Show me the truth concealed within Thy word,
> And in Thy book revealed, I see thee Lord.[10]

and here—

> Light up Thy word; the fettered page
> From killing bondage free:
> Light up our way; lead forth this age
> In Love's large liberty.

> O Light of light! Within us dwell,
> Through us Thy radiance pour,
> That word and life Thy truths may tell,
> And praise Thee evermore.[11]

Some Topics for Reflection

1. How is it that words can have such power? Is it through their relationship to personality? What is that relationship? In what way are words spiritual?

2. Relate words, in the full sense explained above, to creation: creation by God and creation by us.

3. How is a kingdom a verbal, not a merely physical, reality?

4. How are natural laws related to God's word?

5. Compare the Word as the Son and the Word as the Bible.

6. What exactly was it that the Roman centurion knew, and how did it relate to his faith in Jesus?

7. Explain the relationship between prayer and speaking *with* God.

8. "The 'rock' that Moses struck was Christ." What do you make of this statement (see 1 Cor 10:4)?

9. Do you feel threatened in any way by the contents of this chapter? Did anything in this chapter encourage you?

10. How can you distinguish Christian faith in the power of God's word from voodoo?

Seven

Redemption Through the Word of God

He says, "It is too small a thing that You should be My Servant
To raise up the tribes of Jacob, and to restore the preserved ones of Israel;
I will also make You a light of the nations
So that My salvation may reach to the end of the earth."
ISAIAH 49:6 (NASB)

You are the light of the world.
MATTHEW 5:14 (NASB)

TO UNDERSTAND HOW GOD SPEAKS WE MUST TO SOME EXTENT understand what the word of God is. In the Way of Christ, as I have said, discerning God's voice is essentially *just one dimension* of a certain kind of life, the *eternal* kind of life, a life lived in conversational relationship with God (Jn 17:3).

We must study of the word of God so that we might better understand what the eternal life is, how we by the graciousness of God are to take part in it and especially how hearing God is part of it. We will truly be at ease hearing God only if we are at home with the word of God, with his speaking throughout creation and redemption. Hearing God is not a freakish event.

God does not speak only for us and our purposes, nor does he speak primarily for our own prosperity, safety or gratification. Those who receive the grace of God's saving companionship in his word are by that very fact also fitted to show humankind how to live. They, and they alone, are at home in the universe as it actually is. In that sense they are the light of the world. Their transformed nature automatically suits them to this task, which, therefore, is not optional or an afterthought. The light that they radiate is not what they do but who they *are*.

Individuals close at hand, along with world events at large, demonstrate what great need there is for light on how to live. The popular media of newspaper, radio and television, as well as scholarly research and publications, constantly update us on our burgeoning social and personal problems. These problems remain unsolved because of the confusion, ignorance or perversity both among our leaders and among most of the world's population with regard to the fundamental causes of human happiness and misery.

Solutions to the problems of humanity—problems that range from incest to atomic warfare, from mental illness to poverty and pollution—are by no means easy or simple. But what we know of human nature seems clearly to indicate that insight on how to live can be provided effectively only by those who are prepared to lead the way by example. Only by *showing* how to live can we teach how to live. It is by our example—more precisely, by the kind of life that is in us and makes us examples of God's indwelling—that we reveal the basis for the communication of God's redeeming word and Spirit to an ever larger circle of human beings. This is the pattern set forth in the New Testament book of Acts and at subsequent points of Christian history. In us as in Jesus Christ himself, *the life* is to be "*the light* of all people" (Jn 1:4).

Collectively the "called-out" people of God, the church, is empowered to stand up for wandering humanity to see, like the cloudy pillar by day and the pillar of fire by night that guided the Israelites through the desert (Ex 13:21-22). When faced with starvation, crime, economic disasters and difficulties, disease, loneliness, alienation and war, the church should be, because it alone *could* be, the certified authority on how to live to which the world looks for answers. The resources of God's government are at the church's disposal. However dimly, we sense this and announce it when we say, "Christ is the answer!" Although you might not actually have thought of these problems as "questions," they do present the precise difficulties of life that Jesus alone can resolve.

Individually the disciple and friend of Jesus who has learned to work shoulder to shoulder with his or her Lord stands in this world as a point of contact between heaven and earth, a kind of Jacob's ladder by which the angels of God may ascend from and descend into human life (Jn 1:51; Gen 28:12). Thus the disciple stands as an envoy or a receiver by which the kingdom of God is conveyed into every quarter of human affairs (Lk 10:1-11). This, as Hannah Hurnard has so beautifully described it, is the role of the intercessor:

> An intercessor means one who is in such vital contact with God and with his fellow men that he is like a live wire closing the gap between the saving power of God and the sinful men who have been cut off from that power. An intercessor is the contacting link between the source of power (the life of the Lord Jesus Christ) and the objects needing that power and life.[1]

But what is the *process* by which we can be fully transformed into children of light—"blameless and innocent, children of God without blemish in the midst of a crooked and perverse generation, in which you shine like stars in the world . . . holding fast to the word of life" (Phil 2:15-16)? How are we to understand the ongoing process—which involves hearing God's voice—by which our present life is to be redeemed, shaped and conformed to the likeness of the Son (Rom 8:29)? And what is the role of the word of God in this process? When these questions are answered, we shall be in a position to deal in a practical manner—in chapters eight and nine—with hearing God's voice.

An Additional Birth by the Word of God

How are we to fulfill the following words of Scripture?

> Let the same mind be in you that was in Christ Jesus.
> (Phil 2:5)

> For to this you have been called, because Christ also suffered for you, leaving you an example, so that you should follow in his steps. "He committed no sin, and no deceit was found in his mouth." When he was abused, he did not return abuse; when he suffered, he did not threaten; but he entrusted himself to the one who judges justly. (1 Pet 2:21-23)

In the light of the previous chapter on the word of God, we can now give a clear and thorough answer to the question about the process of redemption—one that goes beyond mere figures of speech and poetic language. *It is through the action of the word of God upon us, throughout us and with us that we come to have the mind of Christ and thus to live fully in the kingdom of God.*

As we have seen, the word of God is a creative and sustaining substance, an active power, not limited by space and time or physical constraints. It organizes and guides that which it is directed to by God and by people in union with God. It is what lies at the foundation of all the kinds of life and being there are.

What is life? In all its various levels and types, life is *power to act and respond in specific kinds of relations.* For example, a cabbage has certain powers of action and response and a corresponding level of life. There is a big difference between a cabbage that is alive and one that is dead, though the dead one still exists. This can also be said of a snail or a kitten.

But a live cabbage can make no response to, say, a ball of string. That is precisely because of the *kind* of life that is in it. Though alive as a cabbage, it is *dead* to the realm of play. Similarly a kitten playing with the string can make no response to numbers or poetry, and in that sense the kitten is dead to the realms of arithmetic and literature. A live cabbage, though dead to one realm (that of play) is yet alive in another—that of the soil, the sun and the rain. The situation is similar with the kitten.

Human beings were once alive to God. They were created to be responsive to and interactive with him. Adam and Eve lived in a conversational relationship with their Creator, daily renewed. When they mistrusted God and disobeyed him, that cut them off from the realm of the Spirit. Thus they became dead in relation to it—much as a kitten is dead to arithmetic. God had said of the forbidden tree, "in the day you eat of it you shall die" (Gen 2:17). And they did.

Biologically they continued to live, of course. But they ceased to be responsive and interactive in relation to God's cosmic rule in his kingdom. It would be necessary for God to confer an additional level of life on them and their children, through "being born from above," (Jn 3:3) in order for them once again to be alive to God, to be able to respond toward him and to act within the realm of the Spirit.

Human beings "born of water" (Jn 3:5)—that is, through natural birth—are alive in the flesh, in the biological and psychological realm of nature. But in relation to God they remain "dead through the trespasses and sins" (Eph 2:1). Therefore they inhabit a world "without hope and without God" (Eph 2:12 NIV). They can, however, be born a second time, "born from above" (Jn 3:3). This is not merely to be born again in the sense of *repeating* something or to make a new start from the same place. Instead it is a matter of an *additional* kind of birth whereby we become aware of and enter into the spiritual kingdom of God. Imagine an otherwise normal kitten that suddenly begins to appreciate and compose poetry, and that image will give you an impression of the huge transition involved in this additional birth.

This additional birth is brought about by God's word and Spirit, and it is spiritual in its effects. "What is born of the flesh is flesh, and what is born of the Spirit is spirit" (Jn 3:6).

The Teacher Who Did Not Know

A respected spiritual leader of the Jews was very impressed with what he had seen of Jesus and approached him with the words, "Rabbi, we know that you are a teacher who has come from God; for no one can do these signs that you do apart from the presence of God" (Jn 3:2). Thus Nicodemus, this leader, complimented Jesus, yet at the same time he complimented himself on being an insider who had the good sense to recognize God at work.

Jesus' reply to him was a stinging rebuke, though it was delivered in such a gentle way as to be digestible and helpful. In effect Jesus said that Nicodemus had not the slightest idea what he was talking about. Nicodemus came claiming to be able to recognize, to see God at work. Jesus said, "No one can see the kingdom of God without being born from above" (Jn 3:3). Without this birth we cannot recognize God's workings: we do not possess the appropriate faculties and equipment. We are like kittens trying to contemplate a sonnet.

Nicodemus was immediately tripped up by this simple observation, revealing the true limits of his understanding. He could only think of the usual sort of birth. So he gropingly inquired, "How can a grown man have *that* again?" Then Jesus explained that unless someone has had the usual birth ("of water") and an additional birth (of Spirit) she or he cannot participate in God's governance, his kingdom.

Those born of the Spirit manifest a different kind of life. Remember that a life is *a definite range of activities and responses.* The spiritually born exhibit a life deriving from an invisible spiritual realm and its powers. In natural terms one cannot explain what is happening with them, where they come from or where they go (Jn 3:8). But just as with the invisible wind and its effects, we recognize the presence of God's kingdom in a person by its effects in and around them.

Birth Through the Spirit and the Word of God

We have already seen how the words of Jesus are Spirit and in what sense the Spirit is also Word. The additional birth that brings a person to life in the realm of God is attributed both to the Spirit (Jn 3:5-8) and to the Word. In 1 Peter 1:23 those who are alive to God are described as being "born anew, not of perishable but of imperishable seed, through the living and enduring word of God." And James 1:18 tells us that "in fulfillment of his own purpose he gave us birth by the word of truth."

This testimony of James and Peter was based on their observations of the effects that the word of God through Christ had on them and of the effects that God's word through them and the early church had on others. Paul expressed this as a sober matter of fact: "So faith comes from what is heard, and what is heard comes through the word of Christ" (Rom 10:17).

As the word of God in creation brought forth light and matter and life, so the gospel of Christ comes to us while we are biologically alive but dead to God. The gospel both empowers and calls forth a response by its own power, enabling us to see and enter the kingdom of God as participants. It opens the door of the mind and enters the heart. From there it is able to progressively transform the whole personality. Thus "the sower sows the word" of the kingdom (Mk 4:14). When this takes root in the heart and mind, a new life enters our personality and increasingly becomes *our* life as we learn to "be guided by the Spirit" (Gal 5:25) and "sow to the Spirit" (Gal 6:8).

Redemption in this respect is simply a further aspect of creation—a new creation. This new creation is the only thing that matters in our relation to God, as Paul says (Gal 6:15). Without it we have no relation to God, in the sense of something in which we *live,* and from it arise all further developments of God's rule in our individual souls.

This is what C. H. Spurgeon had to say on the matter:

> Even so we have felt the Spirit of God operating upon our hearts, we have known and perceived the power which he wields over human spirits, and we know him by frequent, conscious, personal contact. By the sensitiveness of our spirit we are as much made conscious of the presence of the Spirit of God as we are made cognizant of the existence of souls, or as we are certified of the existence of matter by its action upon our senses. We have been raised from the dull sphere of mere mind and matter into the heavenly radiance of the spirit-world; and now, as spiritual men, we discern spiritual things, we feel the forces which are paramount in the spirit-realm, and we know that there is a Holy Ghost, for we feel him operating upon our spirits.[2]

The Word of God Planted in Our Hearts

James, the brother of Jesus, uses the image of planting to portray the relationship of the additional life in the Spirit to our natural, fleshly life. He encourages us to "welcome with meekness the implanted word that has the power to save your souls" (Jas 1:21).

After the "additional" life has been planted in us, our natural powers are not left to run their own way under or alongside the new life; they are to be channeled through and subordinated to that life from above. All are redirected to spiritual ends, appointed to higher purposes, though they remain in themselves normal human powers.

The uniqueness of each individual personality remains in the beauty and goodness of its natural life. But a holy radiance rests upon it and shines through it because it is now the temple of God, the area over which the larger and higher power of God plays. An additional, spiritual life comes through the word of God as that word possesses and redirects the energies of the natural life to promote the ends of God's kingdom.

Washed in the Word of God

A different description of the function of the word of God in our redemption is seen in Ephesians 5:25-27. Here, speaking of the church, the apostle says that Christ "gave himself up for her, in order to make her holy by cleansing her with the washing of water by the word, so as to present the church to himself in splendor, without a spot or wrinkle or anything of the kind—yes, so that she may be holy and without blemish."

Here Christ, the Word of God, is pictured as *washing away* the impurities and clutter that have permeated our human personalities during our life away from God. These impurities and distractions, which in fact do not automatically disappear at the additional birth, limit and attack both individual spiritual growth and the role intended for Christ's followers as the light of the world.

By his sacrificial death and triumphant resurrection Jesus Christ finished welding his immediate followers into a totally new kind of social unit—the redemptive community, the living temple of the living God (Eph 2:21-22). This community in turn provided an environment within which God's word would be present with such richness and power that the church *could* stand forth on the world scene as beyond all reasonable reproach. This is how it is to fulfill its calling to be the light of the world—the haven and guide of all humanity on the earth.

Just think for a moment about what happens when you wash a dirty shirt: the water and laundry soap move through the fibers of the shirt material and carry out the dirt lodged within those fibers. When we come to God our minds and hearts are like that dirty shirt, cluttered with false beliefs and attitudes, deadly feelings, past deeds and misguided plans, hopes and fears.

The word of God—primarily the gospel of his kingdom and of the life and death of Jesus on our behalf—enters our mind and brings new life through faith. As we open our entire life to this new power and as those sent by God minister the word to us, the word moves into every part of our personality, just like the water and soap move through the shirt's fibers. God's word pushes out and replaces all that is false and opposed to God's purposes in creating us and putting us in our unique place on earth.

We are transformed by the renewing of our minds and thus are able to "discern what is the will of God—what is good and acceptable and perfect"

(Rom 12:2). *Hearing God becomes a reliably clear and practical matter for the mind that is transformed by this washing of the word.*

The Amazing Extent of the Dirt

What a multitude of things must first be washed from the mind, and what an obstacle they pose to our hearing God! Only the powerful and living word of God is capable of removing them. For example, we usually think that if we are mean enough to people they will be good. We hope to control people by threatening them and punishing them. Yet this was not the way of Jesus. He let others punish him and said, "And I, when I am lifted up from the earth [on the cross], will draw all people to myself" (Jn 12:32).

We are also apt to believe that we must serve ourselves or no one else will. But Jesus knew that those who would save their life must lose it (Lk 9:24-25). We are pretty well convinced that we gain by grabbing and holding. But Jesus taught us, "Give, and it will be given to you" (Lk 6:38). An untold number of other false ideas and attitudes corrupt our minds and lives and must be washed out by the entry of God's word. "The unfolding of your words gives light" (Ps 119:130).

Even for many of us who already profess to follow Christ, much inward change will still be needed before we will be able to hear God correctly. When trouble comes—for example, when we have car problems or get into a dispute with someone in our family or at work—how long does it take us to get around to bringing it to God in prayer? When we see an accident or some violent behavior or we hear an ambulance down the street, do we even think to hold those concerned up to God in prayer? When we go to meet with a person for any reason, do we go in a spirit of prayer so that we would be prepared to minister to them, or they to us, in all ways possible and necessary? When we are alone, do we constantly recognize that God is present with us? Does our mind spontaneously return to God when not intensely occupied, as the needle of the compass turns to the North Pole when removed from nearer magnetic sources? Our answers to these questions make us sadly aware of how our mind is solidly trained in false ways.

Today with all our knowledge, all our technology and all our sophisticated research, we find our world in the same basic situation as that described by Isaiah many centuries before Christ:

> We wait for light, and lo! there is darkness;
>   and for brightness, but we walk in gloom.
> We grope like the blind along a wall,
>   groping like those who have no eyes;
> we stumble at noon as in the twilight,
>   among the vigorous as though we were dead. (Is 59:9-10)

This is all because our minds—perhaps our very brains—need to have the false thoughts and habits washed out of them. They so badly need to be washed that we rarely understand what life would be like if they *were* cleaned, and many of us do not even sense the need for cleaning.

A recent report from a mental health clinic told how the removal of coffee from the waiting rooms transformed the patients' behavior. Before, while the coffee was available, there was constant bickering and even violence between patients as well as between the patients and the staff. After the coffee was removed and the stimulation of caffeine was withdrawn, there were only two or three unpleasant scenes per week. Like the caffeine, the poisonous thoughts, beliefs, fears, lusts and attitudes inhabiting our minds compel us to destructive behavior that we ourselves do not understand and whose source we do not recognize.

Earlier I explained that a word is fundamentally an expressed thought or feeling. The *literal* truth is that Christ through his word removes the old routines in the heart and mind—the old routines of thought, feeling, action, imagination, conceptualization, belief, inference—and in their place he puts something else: *his* thoughts, *his* attitudes, *his* beliefs, *his* ways of seeing and interpreting things, *his words*. He washes out our minds, and in the place of confusion and falsehood—or hatred, suspicion and fear, to speak of emotions—he brings clarity, truth, love, confidence and hopefulness.

So where there was fear, there is now hope; where there was suspicion, there is now confidence; where there was hate, there is now love; and all are based on a new understanding of God conveyed into us by his word. Vessels of wrath become vessels of patience and kindness. Where there was covetousness and lust, there is now generosity and courteous consideration. Where there was manipulation and possessiveness, there is now trust toward God and encouragement of others toward liberty and individuality. We now have the *character* to which listening for God's voice is natural.

Union with Christ

Until now we have been dealing with the word of God as it comes to, upon and through us. But in the progress of God's redemptive work *communication* advances into *communion* and communion into *union*. When the progression is complete we can truly say, "It is no longer I who live, but it is Christ who lives in me" (Gal 2:20) and "For me, living is Christ" (Phil 1:21).

Communication often occurs over a certain distance, even amidst possible opposition. We can still communicate with those with whom we are at war. God communicates with us even while we are his enemies, dead in our sins. When communication between two people rises to the level of communion, there is a distinctness but also a profound sharing of the thoughts, feelings and objectives that make up our lives. Each recognizes the thought or feeling as his or hers, while knowing with joy that the other is feeling or thinking in the same way.

When communion advances into union, however, the sense of "mine" and "thine" may often be absent. There is only "ours," and while "mine" does mean mine, it no longer thereby also means "not thine." This condition of union is realized in a marriage where the two partners have indeed become one. For this reason marriage can serve as a picture of the relation between Christ and his church, and between the soul and God.

It is this union beyond communion that Paul speaks of when he says the redeemed have the mind of Christ (1 Cor 2:16) as well as when he exhorts us to have the mind of Christ (Phil 2:5). Jesus prays the faithful might have this same union: "that they may be one, as we are one, I in them and you in me, that they may become completely one, so that the world may know that you have sent me and have loved them even as you have loved me" (Jn 17:22-23).

For the good that Christ offers us in the redeemed life to become real in ourselves, we must at some point begin to appreciate the *literal* character of the Scriptures that speak of Christ's being *in* us. Jesus Christ imparts himself to his church. In what may have been his first attempt to make this plain, he told his followers, "Very truly, I tell you, unless you eat the flesh of the Son of Man and drink his blood, you have no life in you. Those who eat my flesh and drink my blood have eternal life, and I will raise them up on the last day; for my flesh is true food and my blood is true drink" (Jn 6:53-55).

Those who heard these words were deeply offended, for they did not understand that when he spoke of his flesh and blood he was speaking in the most concrete terms of himself. As he immediately explained, his actual flesh, when taken apart from his *spiritual, personal reality,* would do them absolutely no good at all (Jn 6:63). In this same verse he goes on to describe his *words* as "spirit and life."

It was through his words that he literally, not figuratively, imparted himself while he lived and taught among the people of his day. On the foundation of his words to his followers, the powerful events of Calvary, the resurrection and Pentecost brought forth a communion and then a union later described by the apostle Paul as the great mystery of the ages, "Christ in you, the hope of glory" (Col 1:27).

Christ's Faith as My Faith

The faith by which Jesus Christ lived, his faith in God and his kingdom, is expressed in the gospel that he preached. That gospel is the good news that the kingdom rule of God is available to humankind here and now. His followers did not have this faith within themselves, and they long regarded it only as *his* faith, not theirs. Even after they came to have faith *in him,* they did not share his faith.

Once, in the middle of the Sea of Galilee, the disciples' boat was almost beaten under by the waves while Jesus slept calmly. His disciples woke him crying, "Lord, save us! We are perishing!" (Mt 8:25). Jesus reproachfully replied, "Why are you afraid, you of little faith?" (8:26). Now the disciples obviously had great faith in Jesus. They called upon him, counting on him to save them. They had great faith in him, but *they did not have his great faith in God.* It was because they did not have *his* faith that he spoke of how little faith they had.

Some Christians too commonly demonstrate that the notions of "faith *in* Christ" and "love *for* Christ" leave Christ *outside* the personality of the believer. One wonders whether the modern translations of the Bible are not being governed by the need to turn our weakened practice into the norm of faith. These exterior notions of Christ's faith and love will never be strong enough to yield the confident statement, "It is no longer I who live, but it is Christ who lives in me" (Gal 2:20). They can never provide the unity of the branches with the vine, where the life that is in the branch is literally that which flows to it through the vine and is the very life of the vine to which it is attached (Jn 15:1-4).

Such exterior notions cannot provide the mutual abiding (Jn 15:5) that causes us branches to bring forth much fruit and without which we can do nothing. It is as such abiding branches that we "were reconciled to God through the death of his Son, [so] much more surely, having been reconciled, will we be saved by his life" (Rom 5:10).

Our additional life, though it is still our life, is also God's life in us: his thoughts, his faith, his love, all *literally* imparted to us, shared with us, by his word and Spirit.

Paul on Salvation

The substance of Paul's teachings about salvation is drained off when we fail to take literally his words about our union and identification with Christ. Without this his writings can be handily subjected to elaborate plans of salvation or made into a "Roman road" of doctrinal assents, by which we supposedly gain God's approval *merely* for believing what every demon believes to be true about Jesus and his work. James S. Stewart's profound book *A Man in Christ* deals with this tendency in interpreting Paul and forcefully corrects it:

> Beyond the reproduction in the believer's spiritual life of his Lord's death and burial lies the glorious fact of union with Christ in His resurrection. "Like as Christ was raised up from the dead by the glory of the Father, even so we also should walk in newness of life" (Romans 6:4). Everything that Paul associates with salvation—joy, and peace, and power, and progress, and moral victory—is gathered up in the one word he uses so constantly, "life." Only those who

through Christ have entered into a vital relationship to God are really "alive."
. . . But what Paul now saw with piercing clearness was that this life into
possession of which souls entered by conversion was nothing else than the life
of Christ Himself. He shared His very being with them.[3]

Stewart points out how Paul speaks of "Christ who is your life" (Col 3:4)
and of "the life of Jesus" being "made visible in our bodies" (2 Cor 4:10).
He points to Paul's contrast of the law of sin and death with "the law of the
Spirit of life in Christ Jesus" (Rom 8:2). And he emphasizes that "this life
which flows from Christ into man is something totally different from anything experienced on the merely natural plane. It is different, not only in
degree, but also in kind. It is *kainotēs zōēs* (Rom 6:4), a new quality of life,
a supernatural quality."[4] This is what Paul means when he says that if one is
in Christ, one is a new creation (2 Cor 5:17).

It is this identity between the additional life of the regenerate, or restarted,
individual and the person and life of Christ himself that turns believers into
"a colony of heaven" (as Moffatt translates Phil 3:20) and enables them to
fulfill their call to be the light of the world, showing the world what it is really
like to be alive.

Focusing on Our Aliveness to God

The person who has been brought into the additional life by the creative action
of the word of God now lives between two distinct realms of life and power: that
of the natural or fleshly and that of the supernatural or spiritual. Even while dead
in our sins and unable to interact constructively with God, we are still capable of
sensing the vacuum in the natural life apart from God and of following up on the
many earthly rumors about God and where he is to be found. Once the new life
begins to enter our soul, however, we have the responsibility and opportunity of
ever more fully focusing our whole being on it and wholly orienting ourselves
toward it. This is *our* part, and God will not do it for us.

We can see how this happens by looking in Romans 7. Here Paul speaks
of a time when he found that the impulses of his personality, solidified
through lifelong training in the ways of sin, continued to move in their old
patterns and not in conformity with the new life that had entered his soul

when he encountered Christ. In this condition, he said, "I fail to carry out the things I want to do, and I find myself doing the very things I hate" (7:15 JB).

This condition is rather like that of a boat traveling through the water. The boat does not immediately shift to the direction the pilot wants at the very moment he moves the rudder. And it may even continue moving forward for some time while the engine is in full reverse. The pilot must learn how to direct the boat partly in terms of powers that move independently of his will and do not as such represent *his* intentions.

Paul chooses to identify with his new life. He *acknowledges, reckons and affirms* his union with what in himself cleaves to the good:

> When I act against my own will, that means I have a self that acknowledges that the Law is good, and so the thing behaving in that way is not my self but sin living in me. The fact is, I know of nothing good living in me—living, that is, in my unspiritual self—for though the will to do what is good is in me, the performance is not, with the result that instead of doing the good things I want to do, I carry out the sinful things I do not want. When I act against my will, then, it is not my true self doing it, but sin which lives in me. (Rom 7:16-20 JB)

Or, as the King James Version simply says, "It is no more I that do it, but sin that dwelleth in me" (Rom 7:20).

The "not I, but sin" of Romans 7 must be taken in conjunction with the "not I, but Christ" of Galatians 2:20. Of course some people might say such things and only be seeking to excuse themselves from responsibility for their inner sinfulness, as referred to in Romans 7, or from responsibility for their sinful actions, as referred to in Galatians 2. But not Paul. Paul—and he speaks for hosts of men and women who have come to life in Christ throughout the ages—is beyond the point of excusing or accusing. He has accepted the full measure of his guilt. He is now concerned with how to enter into the new life to its fullest.

This requires that *we* take a stand as to *who we are* in this new life, that we identify *with* the Christ-life in us and *against* the sin still present in our selves and that we settle in our will the question of who we intend to be. This is what it means to "consider" ourselves "dead to sin and alive to God in Christ Jesus" (Rom 6:11).

As men and women of the additional birth, we stand at the intersection of the merely natural (fleshly) and the spiritual. St. Thomas Aquinas coined a word to express just this state: *aevum,* as distinct from *tempus* and *aeternitas. Aevum* is the mean between eternity and time, sharing in them both. It is two lives, two streams of awareness and power, mingling together in the individual who must choose which one he or she will truly be.

Our identification with the one life or the other is not a fact to be discovered by subtle examinations of theological treatises or of our soul-life and state of mind. It is a *set of the will.* Is it my will to be in the old, dead life of sin? Or is it my will to be in the resurrection life of Christ, which has entered into me through the impact of God's word?

If you choose the latter, you still "work out your own salvation with fear and trembling; for it is God who is at work in you, enabling you both to will and to work for his good pleasure" (Phil 2:12-13). It *is* I. Yet it is *not I,* but Christ. We move beyond mere communication and communion toward union with him, and we have the opportunity of progressively unifying all aspects of our personalities with him so that, literally, "to me, living is Christ and dying is gain" (Phil 1:21).

The Written Word in the Progress of Redemption

Once the life of Christ has entered into us there are many things that we may do to increase the extent and depth of our identification and union with him. But the proper use of the *written* Word is most central to our cooperative efforts with God toward full conformity with Christ.

The written Word may come to us in many ways. It may come through sermons, through art, through casual conversation, through dramatic performances, literature or song. All of these are important. For many centuries the contents of the Bible were present to the people of Europe through the architecture and artistry of their great cathedrals and churches. Indeed even today Christians who have read the Bible and know its contents well are often powerfully impacted on first seeing the content of the Bible communicated in magnificent stone and rich, sweeping stained-glass windows, such as are found in the cathedral at Chartres, France.

Although all these means are good and helpful, however, the person who wishes to grow in grace is by far best advised to make a close and constant companion of *the book*—the Bible. I do not mean that it should be worshiped. Its uniquely sacred character is something that does not need to be exaggerated or even insisted on, because it is self-authenticating to any earnest and open-minded user. For just as openness to and hunger for God leads naturally to the Bible, if it is available, so the eager use of the Bible leads naturally and tangibly to the mind of God and the person of Christ.

The written Word of God is an expression of God's mind just as surely, though in a different manner, as are creation and Jesus, the living Word. As we read and study it intelligently, humbly and openly, we come increasingly to share God's mind.

This use of the Bible is not superstitious or magical, because a *natural connection* exists between a proper use of the Bible and its ideal result—union with Christ. The Bible expresses the mind of God since God himself speaks to us through its pages. Thus we, in understanding the Bible, come to share his thoughts and attitudes and even come to share his life through his Word. Scripture is a *communication* that establishes *communion* and opens the way to *union,* all in a way that is perfectly understandable once we begin to have experience of it.

We will be spiritually safe in our use of the Bible if we follow a simple rule: *Read with a submissive attitude.* Read with a readiness to surrender all you are—all your plans, opinions, possessions, positions. Study as intelligently as possible, with all available means, but never study merely to find the truth and especially not just to prove something. Subordinate your desire to *find* the truth to your desire to *do* it, to act it out!

Those who wish to hear the word and know the truth are often not prompted by their desire to *do* it. The light that such people find frequently proves to be their own snare and condemnation.

"Praying" the Scriptures

William Law comments, "Therefore the Scriptures should only be read in an attitude of prayer, trusting to the inward working of the Holy Spirit to make their truths a living reality within us."[5]

There is a simple technique that every believer, no matter how trained or untrained, can follow with assurance that the very bread of life will be spread out for them on the pages of the Scriptures. It is a practice very similar to one encouraged by Madame Guyon in her little book *Short and Very Easy Way of Prayer,* first published in 1688 in Lyons, France. This book is still available today, republished with some modifications under the title *Experiencing the Depths of Jesus Christ.* The first four chapters of it could usefully be read as a supplement to what I am about to say here.

When we come to the Scriptures as a part of our conscious strategy to cooperate with God for the full redemption of our life, *we must desire that his revealed will should be true for us.* Next, we should *begin with those parts of Scripture with which we have some familiarity,* such as Psalm 23, the Lord's Prayer, the Sermon on the Mount, 1 Corinthians 13 or Romans 8.

You may think that this is not a big beginning. But keep in mind that your aim is not to become a scholar or to impress others with your knowledge of the Bible—a dreadful trap for so many fellowships aiming to be biblical. That aim will only cultivate pride and lay a foundation for the petty, quarrelsome spirit so regrettably, yet so commonly, observed in those outwardly identified as the most serious students of the Scriptures.

It may help to remember these words of Thomas à Kempis:

Of what use is it to discourse learnedly on the Trinity, if you lack humility and therefore displease the Trinity? Lofty words do not make a man just or holy; but a good life makes him dear to God. I would far rather feel contrition than be able to define it. If you knew the whole Bible by heart, and all the teachings of the philosophers, how would this help you without the grace and love of God?[6]

Your aim must be only to nourish your soul on God's word to you. Go first to those parts of the Bible you already know, therefore, and count on your later growth and study to lead you to other parts that will be useful.

Do not try to read a great deal at once. As Madame Guyon wisely counsels, "If you read quickly, it will benefit you little. You will be like a bee that merely skims the surface of a flower. Instead, in this new way of reading with prayer, you must become as the bee who penetrates into the depths of the flower. You plunge deeply within to remove its deepest nectar."[7]

You may have been told that it is good to read the Bible through every year and that you can ensure this will happen by reading so many verses per day from the Old and New Testaments. If you do this you may enjoy the reputation of one who reads the Bible through each year, and you may congratulate yourself on it. But will you become more like Christ and more filled with the life of God? It is a proven fact that many who read the Bible in this way, as if they were taking medicine or exercising on a schedule, do not advance spiritually. It is better in one year to have ten good verses transferred *into the substance of our lives* than to have every word of the Bible flash before our eyes. Remember that "the letter kills, but the Spirit gives life" (2 Cor 3:6). We read to open ourselves to the Spirit.

Come to your chosen passage as to a place where you will have a holy meeting with God. Read a small part of the passage and dwell on it, praying for the assistance of God's Spirit in bringing *fully* before your mind and into your life the realities expressed. Always ask, "What is my life like since this is true, and how shall I speak and act because of this?" You may wish to turn the passage into a prayer of praise or request.

Perhaps you are reading the great "God is love" passage from 1 John 4. You find written here, "There is no fear in love, but perfect love casts out fear; for fear has to do with punishment, and whoever fears has not reached perfection in love" (v. 18). You may prayerfully dwell on the ways in which love—God's love for us, our love for him, and love among people on earth—pushes fear out of all relationships. You may think of the fearless child surrounded by loving parents, of how loving neighbors give us confidence and relieve our anxieties. You may dwell on how the assurance of God's love given to us in the death of his Son suggests that we will never be beyond his care. You may seek God's help in comprehending this and in seeing what your fear-free life might be like. Then you may lift your heart in joyful praise as you realize how things are for you, living in God's kingdom. God's word now speaking in you, not just *at* you, creates the faith that appropriates the fact *for you.*

Or you may read, "The LORD is my shepherd, I shall not want" (Ps 23:1). First, you will find *information,* which you may not automatically transfer to yourself. You may say, "This was true just for David, the psalmist." But as you dwell prayerfully on the plain information, a *yearning* that it might be so for *you* may arise. You may express this, saying, "I wish the Lord were my shepherd; that the great God would have for me the care and attention that the shepherd has for his sheep!" And as you meditate on the psalm, *affirmation* may arise, as it has for so many people ("It must be so! I will have it be so!") followed then perhaps by *invocation* ("Lord, make it so for me") and *appropriation* (the settled conviction that it *is* so, that it is a statement of fact about you.)

Do not hurry. Do not *dabble* in spiritual things. Give time for each stage to play itself out fully in your heart. Remember, this is not something you are doing by yourself. *Watch* and pray.

Now practice again with those great passages from Romans 8, beginning with verse 28, "We know that all things work together for good for those who love God, who are called according to his purpose," and ending with the declaration of triumph that no matter what befalls us "we are more than conquerors through him who loved us" (v. 37). Again, the general train of development is as follows:

1. *information*
2. *longing* for it to be so
3. *affirmation* that it *must* be so
4. *invocation* to God to make it so
5. *appropriation* by God's grace that it *is* so

This last stage must not be forced or, especially, faked. The ability for it will be given as you watch for God to move in your life.

When there is an inner agreement between our minds and the truth expressed in the passages we read, we know that we have part of the mind of Christ *in us as our own.* For these great truths conveyed by Scripture were the very things that Jesus believed. They constituted the faith, hope and love in which he lived. As they become our beliefs, his mind becomes our mind. We are fitted out then to function as true colaborers with God as brothers, sisters and friends of Jesus in the present and coming kingdom of God. And we are in a position to know and understand fully how God speaks now to his children.

For a deeper treatment of this kind of devotional use of the written Word, so very important for our participation in the process of redemption, you will need to study the practice of *lectio divina* followed by many Christians.[8] In order for the written Word of God to have its best effect, it should be made part of an overall plan of disciplines for the spiritual life.[9]

Some Topics for Reflection

1. Redemption is understood in this chapter to cover whole persons and their lives. It is not merely a matter of the forgiveness of sins, to guarantee our entrance into heaven when we die. Do you regard this view of redemption as biblical? Does it make sense in your theological background? In what way is a *redeemed life* automatically the light of the world?

2. What is life, say, in a cabbage or in a kitten? Can you characterize the "life from above" in terms of its presence in day-to-day human existence?

3. Planting and washing are two metaphors relating to the additional life of the Christian. Can you explain the meaning of each metaphor and illustrate each in a practical context?

4. Did the discussion of communication, communion and union make sense to you in terms of experiences you have had or know about on a purely human level? What about in terms of your experience of Jesus?

5. What is the distinction between the faith *of* Christ and faith *in* Christ? What difference does the distinction make? Which is saving faith? What does such faith save, in fact?

6. What does it mean to "*consider* ourselves dead to sin" (Rom 6:11)? What will be the results of not doing this?

7. Our identification with the sin-life or with the Christ-life in us "is not a fact to be discovered by subtle examinations of theological treatises or of our soul-life and state of mind. It is a set of the will." What is this about? Do you agree?

8. Experiment several times with praying the Scriptures, and summarize the results of the exercise. Share them with a friend.

Eight

Recognizing the Voice of God

The shepherd of the sheep . . . calls his own sheep by name
and leads them out. . . . He goes ahead of them,
and the sheep follow him because they know his voice. . . .
I am the good shepherd. I know my own and my own know me. . . .
My sheep hear my voice. I know them, and they follow me.
JOHN 10:2-4, 14, 27

The doctrine of the inner light is not sufficiently taught.
To the individual believer, who is, by the very fact
of relationship to Christ, indwelt by the Holy Spirit of God,
there is granted the direct impression of the Spirit of God
on the Spirit of man, imparting the knowledge
of his will in matters of the smallest and greatest importance.
This has to be sought and waited for.
G. CAMPBELL MORGAN, *GOD'S PERFECT WILL*

WHEN A WORD OR THOUGHT COMES TO US—THROUGH OTHERS, the inner voice, some special experience, the Bible or circumstances—*how* do we know whether or not it is a word from God to us? What is it about it that indicates it has a divine source?

We can, of course, know that the word is from God if it corresponds with the plain statement or meaning of the Bible, construed in such a way that it is consistent with soundly interpreted biblical teaching. We can all know at all times, for example, that God directs us not to worship an idol or be covetous.

Beyond this, however, the only answer to the question "How do we know whether this is from God?" is *"By experience."* Even a word-for-word quotation from the Bible can be put to a use that makes it only a message from the dear self or from Satan. The dangers of so-called proof texting—of taking biblical passages out of context to serve some preconceived purpose—are well-known. A single statement taken directly from the Bible, statements that are often invoked for personal application, may be used in ways *contrary* to the purposes of God, contrary to any meaning that he may have in mind for us. That is why *only the Bible as a whole* can be treated as the written Word of God.

In any case we must certainly go beyond, though never *around,* the words of the Bible to find out what God is speaking to us. As we have already seen, the teachings of the Bible, no matter how thoroughly studied and firmly believed, can never by themselves constitute our personal walk with God. They have to be *applied* to us as individuals and to our individualized circumstances, or they remain no part of our lives.

Voice Recognition in Nature

It is a remarkable fact that sheep and other domesticated animals and pets unerringly recognize the voice of their master or mistress. When they first hear that voice, they do not recognize who is speaking, but they learn to do so very quickly. They do not need a voice meter or other device to analyze it scientifically; they simply recognize it immediately.

I once saw on television a story about a man named Charlie Frank and his elephant Neeta. Frank raised Neeta from birth and trained her as a circus performer. On retirement he gave her to the San Diego Zoo. They had not seen each other for fifteen years at the point when the program filmed their reunion. Frank called to Neeta across a distance of about a hundred yards. She came to him immediately and performed her old routines on command. Her past experience gave her the power to recognize his voice. In a similar way we human beings learn from experience alone how to recognize the color red, with its various shades and characteristics, and to distinguish it from blue or yellow. A musician learns by experience to distinguish a minor key from a major one simply by hearing a melody.

Comparing humans with animals on this point echoes a prophetic theme. Isaiah marvels that "the ox knows its owner, and the donkey its master's crib; but Israel does not know, my people do not understand" (Is 1:3). Jeremiah makes a similar complaint with reference to nondomesticated creatures:

> Even the stork in the heavens
> knows its times;
> and the turtledove, swallow, and crane
> observe the time of their coming;
> but my people do not know
> the ordinance of the LORD. (Jer 8:7)

By contrast, the light that shines on every human being who comes into the world, according to John 1:9, vainly strikes the blinded eyes of fallen humanity. The word that has gone out to the very ends of the earth, according to Psalm 19:4, falls on deaf ears. But those who have been given the additional birth—the new birth through the redemptive message of Christ that has entered their lives—can learn by experience to hear God as he speaks, to recognize his word and confidently interact with it.

The simple statements from the Gospel of John, chapter ten, quoted at the beginning of this chapter are not merely a record of words that Jesus spoke. They are also an expression of John's own experience with Christ, his Lord and friend. The emphasis given in the opening of John's first epistle to seeing, hearing and touching the Word of Life (1 Jn 1:1, 3) is quite startling. But it was in the presence of the visible, touchable Jesus that John learned to recognize when God was speaking.

In the course of later experience John became so confident of the inner teacher that he could tell his children in the faith—even as he was warning them about those trying to deceive them—that they had no need of anyone other than the inner teacher, the Holy Spirit: "The anointing that you received from him abides in you, and so you do not need anyone to teach you. But as his anointing teaches you about all things, and is true and is not a lie, and just as it has taught you, abide in him" (1 Jn 2:27).[1]

John therefore speaks to us from the authority of his experience, just as Abraham spoke to his eldest servant when sending him into an unknown land to find a wife for Isaac (Gen 24) and just as Eli did to little Samuel (1 Sam 3). We may mistakenly think that if *God* spoke to us we would automatically know who is speaking without having to learn, but that is simply a mistake—and one of the most harmful mistakes for those trying to hear God's voice. It leaves us totally at the mercy of any stray ideas we have picked up about what God's speaking is like.

Perhaps our inability to recognize his voice right off is a result of our fallen and distorted condition. Or perhaps it lies in the very nature of all personal relations—certainly you and I did not recognize the voice of whoever is now most dear and intimate to us the first time we heard it. Or perhaps it is because of the very gentleness with which our heavenly Father speaks to us. Whatever the reason, it seems that at first we must be *told* that God is speaking to us and possibly even be helped to detect his voice. Only later do we come, without assistance, confidently to distinguish and recognize his voice as *his* voice. That ability comes only with experience.

With assistance from those who understand the divine voice from their own experience and with an openness and will to learn on our part, we can come to recognize the voice of God without great difficulty. On the other hand we should understand that it is in Satan's best interest to make an inherent mystery of God's word coming directly to the individual. In this way the power of God's specific word for our lives can be hindered or even totally lost. Without qualified help which works alongside our own desire to learn and readiness to cooperate, God's direct word will most likely remain a riddle or at best a game of theological charades. This is generally the condition of the church today, I suspect. This would explain why there is such great confusion and difficulty about what it means really to walk with God (Mic 6:8). Such confusion allows evil impulses to move into the vacuum and sweep us away.

The Three Lights
God's impressions within and his word without are always corroborated by his providence around, and we should quietly wait until those three focus into one

point. . . . If you do not know what you ought to do, stand still until you do. And when the time comes for action, circumstances, like glowworms, will sparkle along your path; and you will become so sure that you are right, when God's three witnesses concur, that you could not be surer though an angel beckoned you on.[2]

Many discussions about hearing God's voice speak of three points of reference, also called "three lights," that we can consult in determining what God wants us to do.[3] These are *circumstances, impressions of the Spirit* and *passages from the Bible*. When these three things point in the same direction, it is suggested that we be sure the direction they point is the one God intends for us.

If I could keep only one bit of writing on hearing God outside the Bible itself, it would be hard to pass over a few pages from Frederick B. Meyer's book *The Secret of Guidance*. Many other authors have very fine and helpful things to say on the subject, but Meyer draws the issues together in a complete and yet simple fashion; and the spirit of his remarks—as is usual with him—is so sane and so spiritual that I would choose him over most others who have written on this subject. According to Meyer,

> The circumstances of our daily life are to us an infallible indication of God's will, when they concur with the inward promptings of the spirit and with the Word of God. So long as they are stationary, wait. When you must act, they will open, and a way will be made through oceans and rivers, wastes and rocks.[4]

It is possible to understand this precious advice in such a way that it completely resolves any problem about hearing God's voice. I believe that this will normally be the case for those who have *already* learned to recognize the inner voice of God. Probably none knew it more clearly than Meyer himself.

For those who do not yet have a confident, working familiarity with this voice, however, trying do discern the three lights may speedily result in a swirl of confusion, leaving them hopelessly adrift or wrecked on the shoals of spiritual misadventures. These lights can be especially dangerous and disappointing for those without a deep experience and commitment in the

Way of Christ. Such people will almost certainly try to use them as a spiritual gimmick or quick fix. They will then fall prey to the desire to get their own way and to secure their own prosperity and security. Let us look more closely at the problem with using the three lights.

The Problem of Their Interdependence

A large part of the *practical* problem in working with the three lights comes from the simple fact that they are *interdependent.* It is difficult or impossible to tell what the one is saying without already knowing what the others are saying.

First of all, it is commonly understood that it is the Holy Spirit working through the Scriptures that makes them effective for guidance as well as redemption. A conference of biblical scholars has affirmed "that the Holy Spirit who inspired Scripture acts through it today to work faith in its message" and also that "the Holy Spirit enables believers to appropriate and apply scripture to their lives." Furthermore, the members of this conference denied "that the natural man is able to discern spiritually the biblical message apart from the Holy Spirit."[5]

Many people commonly regarded as evangelicals seem prepared to make even stronger statements on the role of the Holy Spirit in Bible study. Consider these comments made by William Law:

> Without the present illumination of the Holy Spirit, the Word of God must remain a dead letter to every man, no matter how intelligent or well-educated he may be. . . . It is just as essential for the Holy Spirit to reveal the truth of Scripture to the reader today as it was necessary for Him to inspire the writers thereof in their day. . . . Therefore to say that, because we now have all the writings of Scripture complete, we no longer need the miraculous inspiration of the Spirit among men as in former days, is a degree of blindness as great as any that can be charged upon the scribes and Pharisees. Nor can we possibly escape their same errors; for in denying the present inspiration of the Holy Spirit, we have made Scripture the province of the letter-learned scribe.[6]

But how are we to recognize or authenticate a thought or message as an intervention of the Holy Spirit—even in our studies of the Bible—*except* from the teachings of the Scriptures?

The biblical test of a spiritual impulse weighs the impulse by whether or not it confesses Jesus as Lord (1 Cor 12:3) or as Son of God (1 Jn 4:2-3); yet this test is not very helpful in practice when we are, for example, trying to decide whom to marry or which job to take. And testing of spiritual or mental impulses or messages cannot in general be done by invoking the teachings of Scripture if Scripture itself cannot be understood without spiritual assistance from those very impulses and messages.

Finally, the mere open or closed doors of circumstances cannot function independently of the other two lights or of some additional factor; for one does not know merely by looking at these doors who is opening or closing them—God, Satan or another human being. Indeed one often cannot tell whether they are open or closed until after one has acted. Therefore, it is not practically possible to use the criteria of openness or closedness by themselves to determine what to do. Scripture and inner promptings must be brought into consideration to determine whether doors are open or closed.

No doubt those who think they can make the three lights formula work will be very impatient with me for raising these difficulties. My experience suggests that people who for whatever reason do not really need help in the practical context of hearing God may think that this formula can be made to work *as* a formula—which is how it is normally presented. Those who do need help, on the other hand, frequently drive themselves to distraction trying to use it. Also, the formula is often thought to have worked *in retrospect*—after one has taken a certain alternative at the suggestion of the lights and all has turned out well. But by that stage such confidence is no longer needed.

It is, therefore, simply not true that we can get a reading of what circumstances say, a separate reading of what the Bible says and yet another separate reading of what the Spirit says. Consequently we cannot strengthen our reading of God's will from one of these sources just by mechanically checking it against the other sources, as we might get a safer reading of the time of day by consulting three clocks running independently of each other.

The Conditions of Responsible Judgment

All who have much experience in the Way of Christ, however, will know that it *is* somehow right, when trying to hear what God is saying to an individual, to look to circumstances, the Bible and inner impulses of the Spirit. And all will know that these three do *somehow* serve to correct each other. That is why Frederick B. Meyer's words are so valuable. While they provide no formula, no mechanism, for making decisions, they must not simply be abandoned. How are we to understand the role they play in hearing God's voice? The answer to this question comes in two parts.

First, a life lived by listening to God speaking is not one that excludes our own judgment. Listening to God does not make our own decision-making process unnecessary. We ourselves, as well as others who come under the influence of God's voice, are still the ones who make the decisions. This is something we have already discussed, and we shall consider a new and very important aspect of it in the next chapter. *The three lights are* simply *the factors that we must consider in the process of making a responsible judgment and decision about what we are to do.* To be responsible in judgment and action is to humbly and fully consider these factors.

Second, while neither one light taken individually nor all of them taken together simply *give* us God's word, each or all together may be and usually are the *occasion* of God's directive word coming to us. This is the way it usually works in practice.

The voice of God is not itself any one of the three lights nor is it all of them together. But the inner teaching of which John speaks in his first epistle—the voice or word of God coming to individuals, as repeatedly displayed in biblical events—*usually* comes to us in conjunction with responsible study and meditation on the Bible, with experience of the various kinds of movements of the Spirit in our heart and with intelligent alertness to the circumstances that befall us.

Although there are exceptions to the rule, God's directive voice does not usually come to us out of the blue. This point is important to us practically. *It enables us to do specific, concrete things that will help us as we seek to know the will of God.* These things we do—reflecting on the three lights— turn out to be the very things that go into exercising responsible judgment.

As we reflect on our circumstances, our impressions of the Spirit and passages we read in the Bible, we also listen for the divine voice. But when God speaks and we recognize the voice as *his* voice, we do so because our *familiarity* with that voice enables us to recognize it. We do *not* recognize it because we are good at playing a guessing game about how the occasions through which his direction comes do or do not match up with each other.

Three Factors in the Voice

> The voice of my beloved!
>> Look, he comes
> leaping upon the mountains,
>> bounding over the hills. . . .
>
> I slept, but my heart was awake.
> Listen! my beloved is knocking. (Song 2:8; 5:2)

To say that we learn to recognize the voice of God by experience is not, however, all that we can say or must say. Certain factors distinguish the voice of God, just as any human voice can be distinguished from another.

The most immediate factor in the human voice, which by itself is usually enough to tell those familiar with it whose voice it is, is a certain *quality* of sound. This is mainly a matter of which *tones* are produced and the manner in which they are modulated. Quality at the human level also includes the *style* of speech. For example, is it slow or fast, smooth or halting in its flow, indirect or to the point?

Besides quality a certain *spirit* attaches to the human voice. A voice may be passionate or cold, whining or demanding, timid or confident, coaxing or commanding. This is, of course, not merely a matter of sounds but also a matter of attitudes or personal characteristics that become tangibly present in the voice.

Finally, there is the matter of *content* or of information conveyed. Although this is rarely the most immediate sign of who is speaking, it is in the end the most conclusive mark, for it reveals the history and conscious experience of the speaker. No matter if quality and spirit were totally different, a specific bit of information could conclusively identify a speaker in certain cases. For example, we might identify someone's words even when those words are spoken by another (as we do when one person reads another's writings aloud) or when we read those words in written form without the author there to read them to us.

The three factors of *quality, spirit* and *content* by no means exhaust the complexity of the voice. Modern-day science and linguistics find in the voice vast fields for theoretical and practical study. From the philosophical point of view much more could be said.[7] But enough has been said here to allow us to turn next to an examination of the voice of God in our hearts.

The Weight of Authority

The question then is, "What are the factors of God's voice that enable us to recognize it as his?" Also in this case there is a distinctive quality with which we can become familiar—but it is not strictly the quality of sound as it would be with a human voice. In chapter five I explained how the voice of God will usually (though not always) take the form of certain *thoughts* or *perceptions* that enter our minds. These obviously are not sounds.

The quality of God's voice is more a matter of the *weight* or impact an impression makes on our consciousness. A certain steady and calm force with which communications from God impact our soul, our innermost being, incline us toward assent and even toward active compliance. The assent or compliance is frequently given before the content of the communication is fully grasped. At least I find it so and others do as well.

We sense inwardly the immediate power of God's voice. And once we have experienced it, we no longer wonder at the biblical phenomena of nature and spirits responding to this divine word. The unquestionable authority with which Jesus spoke to nature, humans and demons was but a very clear manifestation of this quality of the word of God.

Addressing the question of how we can distinguish the voice of God from the voice of our own subconscious, E. Stanley Jones says,

> Perhaps the rough distinction is this: The voice of the subconscious argues with you, tries to convince you; but the inner voice of God does not argue, does not

try to convince you. It just speaks, and it is self-authenticating. It has the feel of the voice of God within it.[8]

When Jesus spoke, his words had a weight of authority that opened up the understanding of his hearers and created faith in them: "for he taught them as one having authority, and not as their scribes" (Mt 7:29).

The authority of the scribe or the scholar comes only from his footnotes or his references to and associations with someone other than himself, someone who is really supposed to know. The word of God, on the other hand, comes with a serene weight of authority in the word itself. People left the presence of Jesus with heads and hearts full of thoughts and convictions that he had authored in them through the power of God's voice and word with which he spoke.

The immediate *qualitative* distinction of the voice of God is emphasized in John Wesley's first sermon, "The Witness of the Spirit." Here he poses the question, "But how may one who has the real witness in himself distinguish it from presumption?" He answers:

> How, I pray, do you distinguish day from night? How do you distinguish light from darkness; or the light of a star, or a glimmering taper, from the light of the noonday sun? Is there not an inherent, obvious, essential difference between the one and the other? And do you not immediately and directly perceive that difference, provided your senses are rightly disposed? In like manner, there is an inherent, essential difference between spiritual light and spiritual darkness; and between the light wherewith the Sun of righteousness shines upon our heart, and that glimmering light which arises only from "sparks of our own kindling": and this difference also is immediately and directly perceived, if our spiritual senses are rightly disposed.
>
> To require a more minute and philosophical account of the manner whereby we distinguish these, and of the criteria, or intrinsic marks, whereby we know the voice of God, is to make a demand which can never be answered: no, not by one who has the deepest knowledge of God.[9]

In my own experience I first became aware that it was God's word that was coming to me by the effects it had on myself and others around me. My main work for God is that of a teacher. I have occasionally received insights that, while perhaps of little significance in themselves, were experienced by me as literally staggering. Then as I became aware and began to trust that these insights were *God's* word, I immediately began to observe the qualitative difference that Wesley emphasizes. And I began to find that certain others also understood from their experience exactly what this difference was.

Adele Rogers St. John remarks (perhaps somewhat overconfidently but yet to the point), "The first time you receive guidance you will know the difference. You can mistake rhinestones for diamonds, but you can never mistake a diamond for a rhinestone."[10]

The Spirit of God's Voice

The voice of God speaking in our souls also bears within itself a characteristic *spirit*. It is a spirit of exalted peacefulness and confidence, of joy, of sweet reasonableness and of goodwill. It is, in short, the spirit of Jesus, and by that phrase I refer to the overall tone and internal dynamics of his personal life as a whole.

Those who had seen Jesus had truly seen the Father, who shared the same Spirit. It is this Spirit that marks the voice of God in our hearts. Any word that bears an opposite spirit most surely is not the voice of God. And because his voice bears authority within itself, it does not need to be loud or hysterical.

Bob Mumford has a vivid illustration of this point. One day the voice of God spoke to him when he was in Colombia, South America, and very distinctly said, "I want you to go back to school." His description of this experience brings out the quality and spirit of the voice:

It couldn't have been any clearer if my wife had spoken the words right next to me. It was spoken straight and strong and right into my spirit. It wasn't a demanding, urgent voice. If it had been, I would immediately have suspected the source to be someone or something other than the Lord. The vocal impression was warm, but firm. I knew it was the Lord.[11]

The sweet, calm spirit of God's voice carries over to the lives of those who speak with his voice: "But the wisdom from above is first pure, then peaceable, gentle, willing to yield, full of mercy and good fruits, without a trace of partiality or hypocrisy" (Jas 3:17). If we would only heed this statement, we would never lack for sure knowledge of who speaks for God and who does not.

Content

Finally, there is a *content* that marks the voice of God. This is a matter of what information the voice conveys to us. Perhaps we had better speak of a *dimension* of the content, since the specific content of an individualized word from God may not of itself be easily identifiable as having come from God. But this much we can say: The content of a word that is truly from God will always conform to and be consistent with the truths about God's nature and kingdom that are made clear in the Bible. Any content or claim that does *not* conform to biblical content is not a word from God. Period! As Charles Stanley comments, "God's Voice will never tell us to engage in any activity or relationship that is inconsistent with the Holy Scriptures."[12]

Evan Roberts, when he was in college studying for the ministry, was deeply moved by the sermons of Seth Joshua, who visited his school.

> Roberts could not concentrate on his studies after that and went to the principal of his college, and said, "I hear a voice that tells me I must go home and speak to the young people in my home church. Mr. Phillips, is that the voice of the devil or the voice of the Spirit?" Phillips answered, very wisely, "The devil never gives orders like that. You can have a week off."[13]

While this response may seem a little glib, it was basically right. Subsequent events in which he was involved strongly confirmed that Roberts was indeed directed by the Lord on this occasion.

The Principles Are What Count

In order to qualify as the voice of God, a thought, perception or other experience must conform to the principles—the fundamental truths—of Scripture. It is the *principles,* not the incidentals, of Scripture that count here. Study of the Scriptures makes clear that certain things are fundamental, absolute, without exception. They show up with stunning clarity as we become familiar with the overall content of Scripture.

In 1 Corinthians 11, for example, we find women being advised not to have short hair and men being informed that on them long hair is shameful. Such things are clearly *incidental*. On more serious matters, in Mark 10, Jesus tells the truly fine young man who had come to him that he must sell all he has and give the proceeds to the poor. This too, contrary to what many have thought, is *incidental to people generally* (for Jesus did not ask this of everyone he met). In the particular case of this young man, of course, Jesus' directive went right to the heart of his special problem with wealth. But it is not a principle to which all must conform. Why? Because it is not a teaching emerging from the whole of Scripture; and it should not, without further consideration and guidance, be taken as God's word to you or anyone else.

When you read the writings of John the apostle, however, and learn from him "that God is light and in him there is no darkness at all" (1 Jn 1:5), you are on to a *principle*—something that wells up from the whole Bible and the totality of the experience of God's people through history.

We are also discovering principles when we hear Jesus saying that the most basic of all the commandments is "you shall love the Lord your God with all your heart, and with all your soul, and with all your mind, and with all your strength" and that the second is "you shall love your neighbor as yourself" (Mk 12:30-31). And his declaration that "those who want to save their life will lose it, and those who lose their life for my sake, and for the sake of the gospel, will save it" (Mk 8:35) is also conveying a principle, as is his statement that we are to "strive for his kingdom, and these things will be given to you as well" (Lk 12:31). *No specific word that is from God will ever contradict such principles.* Such principles place an iron-clad restriction on what content can come with *God's* voice.

Principles of Scripture are to be identified most of all from the actions, spirit and explicit statements of Jesus himself. When we take him in his wholeness as the model to follow—and what else could it mean to *trust* him?—we will safely identify the content of the inner voice of God, for "whoever follows me will never walk in darkness but will have the light of life" (Jn 8:12). In the awareness of this we are set free to be open to the new and special things that God wants to do in us and through us. We will be free to develop the power and authority that come from the experience of dealing directly with God—free *and* safe within the pattern of Christ's life and teachings.

Beware the Spiritual Panacea

Something should also be said on the negative side about the content of voices. Any voice that promises total exemption from suffering and failure is most certainly not God's voice. In recent years innumerable spokespeople for God have offered ways we can use God and his Bible as guarantees of health, success and wealth. The Bible is treated as a how-to book, a manual for the successful life in the way of the Western world, which if followed will ensure that you will prosper financially, that you will not get cancer or even a cold and that your church will never split or lack a successful minister and program. To the question from the old hymn

> Shall I be carried to the skies
> On flowery beds of ease,
> While others fought to win the prize
> And sailed through bloody seas?[14]

these people shout, "Yes, most certainly!"

But if we consider those who stand throughout history as the best practitioners of the Way, we will find that they went through great difficulties, often living their entire lives and dying amidst these trials. The word of God does not come just to lead us out of trouble—though it sometimes does this—or to make sure that we have it easy and that everything goes our way. When we hear a suggestion that his word does in fact come to free us from all difficulties, we will need to recall this interchange between Jesus and Peter: "I'm going to go up to Jerusalem, and they are going to kill me," said Jesus. Peter—because he just *knew* it—replied, "Far be it from you, Lord. Such a thing shall not happen to you." Peter did not have such events in mind for himself, and hence they were not for his Messiah, the star to which he had hitched his wagon. But Jesus said to him, "Out of my sight, Satan; you are a stumbling block to me. You think as men think, not as God thinks" (Mt 16:23, paraphrase).

We must not be misled by wishful thinking. We are going to go through the mill of life like everyone else. We who are disciples are different because we *also* have a higher or additional life—a different quality of life, a spiritual life, an eternal life—*not* because we are spared the ordinary troubles that befall ordinary human beings. "Many are the afflictions of the righteous, but the LORD rescues them from them all" (Ps 34:19).

In summary, then, what we discern when we learn to recognize God's voice in our heart is a certain *weight or force,* a certain *spirit* and a certain *content* in the thoughts that come in God's communications to us. These three things in combination mark the voice of God. To those well experienced in the Way of Christ, these give great confidence and great accuracy in living day to day as the friends of Christ and as colaborers with God in his kingdom.

The Voice of Satan

There are other "spiritual voices," too. It is in *contrast* with the kind of voice I have just described that the voice of our adversary, Satan, is made known to us, for he too will speak in our heart once he sees he no longer holds us in his hand. Only if we learn to recognize this voice as well can we avoid many silly attributions of events to Satan ("The devil made me do it!"). And only so can we correctly identify and firmly resist him and make him flee from us (1 Pet 5:9; Eph 6:11).

Satan will not come to us in the form of an oversized bat with bony wings, hissing like a snake. Very seldom will he assume any external manifestation at all. Instead he will usually, like God, come to us through our thoughts and our perceptions. We must be alert to any voice that is in contrast with the weight, spirit and content of God's voice, for that may signify that we are under subtle attack.

The temptations of Jesus in Matthew 4 illustrate this well. It does not take much imagination to realize that if some bat-like creature suggested to Jesus that he turn the stones into bread, this would certainly have tended to curb his appetite. How then did the tempter come to him (v. 3)? Actually the Gospel passages give no indication as to how he came.

Perhaps—and this is just a suggestion—as Jesus suffered extreme hunger, the stones about him reminded him of—perhaps began to *look* like—the loaves from his mother's oven. Perhaps he began to *smell* them and then to think how easily he could turn those stones into such loaves—with butter. But then he also realized the *conflict* between this vision and the great truth that the word of God is a substance, a meat (Jn 4:32). He refused to allow himself to be turned away from learning that God's word is sufficient for his every need. Human beings live by every word that issues from God's mouth (Deut 8:3). The voice of temptation was clearly opposed in spirit and content to God's word, and Jesus recognized Satan and successfully resisted him in this and in the other temptations which followed.

Likewise, followers of Christ must be encouraged to believe that they can come to understand and distinguish the voice of God. They need only to look within their thoughts and perceptions for the same kinds of distinctions as they would find in spoken or written communications received from other human beings: a distinctive quality, spirit and content.

All of the words that we are going to receive from God, no matter what may accompany them externally or internally, will *ultimately pass through the form of our own thoughts and perceptions.* We must learn to find in them the voice of the God in whom we live and move and have our being.

Infallibility

But, someone may ask, when I am sure that God is speaking to me and sure about what he says, *could I not still be mistaken,* even though I have much apparently successful experience of hearing and understanding his voice? Yes, of course you *could* still be wrong. God does not intend to make us infallible by his conversational walk with us. You could also be wrong about most of the beliefs on which you very successfully base your life. But you are usually correct. You could also be wrong in believing that your gas gauge is working, that your bank is reliable, that your food is not poisoned. Such is human life. Our walk with the Lord does not exempt us from the possibility of error, even in our experienced discernment of what his voice is saying.

Infallibility, and especially infallibility in discerning the mind of God, simply does not fit the human condition. It should not be desired, much less expected, from our relationship with God.

The Centrality of the Bible (Once Again)

Personally I find great comfort and encouragement in the face of my fallibility by maintaining a close relationship with the Bible. In this book I have repeatedly emphasized the centrality of the written Word in hearing God's voice. It cannot be stressed too much that the permanent address at which the word of God may be found is the Bible. More of God's speaking to me has come in conjunction with study and teaching of the Bible than with anything else. As Frederick B. Meyer says, "The [written] Word is the wire along which the voice of God will certainly come to you if the heart is hushed and the attention fixed."[15]

Reading in the lives of the saints seems to confirm this. From the many available illustrations, I have selected a few words from John Bunyan:

> One day, as I was traveling into the country and musing on the wickedness and blasphemy of my heart, and considering the enmity that was in me to God, that scripture came into my mind: "Having made peace through the blood of His cross" (Colossians 1:20). By which I was made to see, both again and again, that God and my soul were friends by his blood; yea, I saw that the justice of God and my sinful soul could embrace and kiss each other, through his blood. This was a good day to me; I hope I shall never forget it.
>
> At another time, as I sat by the fire in my house and was musing on my wretchedness, the Lord made that also a precious word unto me: "Forasmuch then as the children are partakers of flesh and blood, he also himself likewise took part of the same; that through death he might destroy him that had the power of death, that is, the devil; and deliver them who through fear of death were all their lifetime subject to bondage" (Hebrews 2:14-15). I thought that the glory of these words was then so weighty on me, that I was both once and twice ready to swoon as I sat, yet not with grief and trouble, but with solid joy and peace.[16]

It is, once again, *by experience* that many have come to know that there is all the difference in the world between an experience of the Scriptures in which a word of God seizes me and an experience in which I am simply seizing the words on the page, however interesting this may be in the process of biblical scholarship.

In the former case I find myself addressed, caught up in all the individuality of my concrete existence by something beyond me. God acts toward me in a distinctively personal manner. This is the common testimony across wide ranges of Christian fellowship and history. I think it is this sense of being seized in the presence of the Scripture, in a manner so widely shared, that gives the Bible its power to assure us in the face of our continuing fallibility. We stand within a community of the spoken to.

Both in the experience of Scripture and of other things—circumstances, our own inner thoughts and impulses, the reading of history or biography— God's word frequently comes in a way that at least approximates the experience of an *audible* voice. When examined closely the data of Christian experience reveals that this is much more common than is generally thought. But the audibility of the voice is not anything essential to it, nor does it have any effect on the reliability of our experience of the voice. The essentials remain, once again, the distinctive quality, spirit and content that we have learned through experience to associate with the personal presence of God.

Scholarship too, both biblical and otherwise, is certainly important to the individual and to the church as a whole. It is a part of *our* part in responsible living before God. But it can never stand in the place of experience of the living voice of God; and it cannot remedy or remove our fallibility.

In general no person is totally dependent on the expertise of biblical or other scholars for a saving and living knowledge of God. Humble openness before the recorded Word of God is sufficient for receiving his saving and guiding word to us. Those who *know all about* the word of God may yet never have *heard* it and recognized it. And those who have heard it and who recognize it readily may have little to say *about* it. But we need many who both know it and know about it in order that it might come to have freer course and more competent reception in the community of believers and in the world. Only in this way will his people learn how to follow God's voice more successfully.

Practical Consequences

Knowing the voice of God, having a *practical understanding* of that voice in our minds and hearts, is not a luxury for the people of God, not something to be allocated to those who enjoy special spiritual high points. Let us consider four aspects of the importance of this understanding to a vibrant life in God's kingdom.[17]

1. Direct, daily kingdom access for all believers. First of all, without this direct communication with Christ, who is the head of the church, the rule of God will not be promoted through our lives as it should and could be. The understanding of the voice of God gives substance to the relationship between Christ and his church. *He talks to it.* That is a major part of what it means for his word to live in the church.

When we align ourselves with the kingdom of Christ, when we come into the family of God, we become an outpost of that kingdom. You might say, though these are crude metaphors, that we have the telephone installed so we can take the heavenly orders and participate in decisions as we do kingdom business; we have the computer terminal put in place, from which we can communicate, act and interact with God in his work. It is important that we have God's instructions and directions for what we do. And to repeat a crucial point, it is just not true that the Bible *alone,* or our subjective experiences *alone* or the interpretation of circumstances *alone* is going to give us the kind of direction we need. It was never so intended. We must be spoken to by God, specifically and concretely guided in thought and action to the extent and through the channels he chooses. In this book I have tried to make sense of what that might amount to.

2. Provision of confidence, comfort and peace. We as individuals, however, must also have the confidence and peace that comes from knowing we are indeed in communication with God himself.

Think of the benediction that contains the blessing of Moses upon God's people in Numbers 6:24-25: "The LORD bless you and keep you." What does this mean? "The LORD make his face to shine upon you." What does that mean? Have you ever watched a little child who loves her father when the father's face is *not* directed toward that child and shining upon her? Have you perhaps been in that place yourself? Do you remember what it was like to experience your father's or mother's turning away from you in anger and *withdrawal*—when their faces did not shine but instead scowled at you or ignored you? Communication was cut off. You were agonized by it until you learned to harden your heart against it. In a similar way a certain communication is absolutely necessary to our having the kind of confidence and peace appropriate to a child of God.

A little child's mother died. He could not be adequately consoled and continued to be troubled, especially at night. He would come into the room where his father was and ask to sleep with him. He would never rest until he knew not only that he was with his father but that his father's face was turned toward him. He would ask in the dark, "Dad, is your face turned toward me now?" And when he was at last assured of this, he was at peace and was able to go to sleep.

How lonely life is! Oh, we can get by in life with a God who does not speak. Many at least think they do. But it is not much of a life, and it is certainly not the life God intends for us or the *abundance* of life that Jesus Christ came to make available. Without real communication from God our view of the world is very impersonal, however glorious we may find God's creation. But there is all the difference in the world between having a fine general view that this is our Father's world—or even that an arrangement has been made for our eternal redemption—and having confidence, based in experience, that the Father's face, whether in the dark of the night or the brightness of the day, is turned toward us, shining upon us, and that the Father is speaking to us individually.

3. Protection from mad religionists and legalism. It is also important for us to know on a practiced, experiential basis how God speaks so that we might protect ourselves and others about whom we are concerned.

We all know what foolishness sometimes follows on the heels of the words "God told me." Indeed we all know not only what foolishness but even what tragedies can come when people say these words. We need to know what the voice of God is like, how it comes and what kinds of things it might say if we are to protect ourselves and those around us in the fellowship of the faithful from people who are malicious or who are being carried away with voices contrary to God, which they themselves may not understand.

It is of vital importance that we are able to recognize when people in positions of power and authority do not, even with all their authority, know what they are talking about or when they are being guided by evil. We need to understand how God's voice works for our own protection as well as for the protection of those we love and for the prosperity of the church as a whole. Hearing God's voice must therefore be taken out of the realm of superstition or mere guesswork and put in terms that everyone who wants to understand can understand.

We can clearly identify cultic leaders without exception if we understand what has been said above about the spirit and content of God's voice and if we understand the proper character of God's leaders. The tragedy of Jim Jones and Jonestown, for example—which we now know began long before Jonestown among the decent citizens of various cities across the United States—could have been stopped if even a few of the people he gathered around him had been in a position to see through his claims to speak for God. But they themselves had no competence in dealing with the voice of God as a practical, experiential matter, and through mystification of that voice and by "spiritual" bullying they were literally led to the slaughter.

Every few years a new version of this same tragedy is played out. Right this minute some less overtly destructive version of the Jonestown deception is being played out in hundreds or thousands of Christian settings throughout the earth. If those who try to bring others under their "guidance" knew that they would be examined by compassionate but strong individuals who have an understanding of such matters, things would go much better for our churches generally and for the individuals in them, not to mention our communities at large.

Danger comes not only from the wild side of religion, however; it can also come from the respectable side. In John 9 Jesus healed a blind man on the sabbath. The leaders of the people, proud of being Moses' disciples (v. 28), "knew" that Jesus could not possibly be of God because he did not observe their restrictions on working during the sabbath (v. 16). They just "knew" that this man Jesus was a sinner because they "knew" the Bible. And they "knew" that the Bible said you were not supposed to do the kinds of things Jesus was doing on the sabbath. Therefore, since this man Jesus did these kinds of things on the sabbath, he was a sinner.

They had good, reliable general knowledge of how things were supposed to be. For his part the man healed could only report, "I do not know whether he [Jesus] is a sinner. One thing I do know, that though I was blind, now I see" (v. 25). But *that* was not in the Bible, in the law. The leaders had their own guidance, and they thought it was sufficient. But it was not sufficient, though it was very *respectable.* For it allowed them to condemn the power and works of love in Jesus himself: "We know that God has spoken to Moses, but as for this man, we do not know where he comes from" (v. 29).

"We don't know!" That is perhaps the most self-damning statement they could possibly have made. They looked at what Jesus did and said, "We don't know what this person is doing. We don't know where he is coming from. We don't know that he is of God." Why didn't they know?

What they were really confessing was that they did not know who God is or what his works are. In their own way they shared Nicodemus's problem of not being able to see the kingdom of God—though they were sure that in fact they did. Many stand in that same place today. They could look at the greatest works of love and righteousness, and if those works did not conform either to their legalistic ideas of what the Bible or their church teaches or to what their own subjective experiences confirm, they could condemn those works without batting an eyelid, saying, "We *know* that this is wrong!" We all need to be delivered from such knowledge!

In the face of the mad religionist or the blind legalist, we really have no recourse, no place to stand, if we do not have *firsthand* experience of hearing God's voice, held safely within a community of brothers and sisters in Christ who also have such knowledge of God's personal dealings with their own souls.[18]

4. Realization of a biblical quality of life. Finally, experience and understanding of God's voice can alone make the events of the Bible real to us and allow our faith in its truth to rise beyond mere abstract conviction that it *must* be true. This is a theme that we have already touched on a number of times, but it is so important that it is worth returning to once again.

Consider, for example, the events recorded in 1 Samuel 16:1-13. This is the story of the selection of David as king over Israel. As with so much of the Bible, the passage is filled with "the LORD said to . . ." In this case, the Lord is speaking to Samuel.

> The LORD said to Samuel, "How long will you grieve over Saul? I have rejected him from being king over Israel. Fill your horn with oil and set out; I will send you to Jesse the Bethlehemite, for I have provided for myself a king among his sons." Samuel said, "How can I go? If Saul hears of it, he will kill me." "Take a heifer with you, and say, 'I have come to sacrifice to the LORD.' Invite Jesse to the sacrifice, and I will show you what you shall do; and you shall anoint for me the one whom I name to you." (16:1-3)

The sons of Jesse came before Samuel; the first was Eliab. Apparently Eliab was a fine-looking person, for Samuel said, "Surely the LORD's anointed is now before the LORD" (v. 6). But the Lord said to Samuel in words we should never forget, "Do not look on his appearance or on the height of his stature, because I have rejected him; for the LORD does not see as mortals see; they look on the outward appearance, but the LORD looks on the heart" (v. 7).

Abinadab, Shammah and all of Jesse's other sons (besides David, who was not present) then passed before Samuel with the same result. Finally, David was called out of the fields, where he was keeping the sheep. When he came before Samuel, "The LORD said, 'Rise and anoint him; for this is the one.' Then Samuel took the horn of oil, and anointed him in the presence of his brothers; and the spirit of the LORD came mightily upon David from that day forward" (vv. 12-13).

It is essential to the strength of our faith that we are in some measure capable of inwardly identifying with Samuel's experience as he *conversed with the Lord* in the midst of Jesse's family. Hopefully the earlier discussion of the nature of the inner voice will help in this.

King David's own conversational interactions with God are documented at many points in the Bible, nowhere more graphically than in 1 Chronicles 14. After he had taken the throne of Israel, the Philistines came to war against him. David "inquired of God" (v. 10) what he should do. This was probably done by standing before the ark of God. The ark had been used earlier in the history of Israel for such inquiry, and it had been recently relocated by David in an effort to place it in Jerusalem, which he had chosen as his capital city (see 1 Chron 13). "David inquired of God, 'Shall I go up against the Philistines? Will you deliver them into my hand?' The LORD said to him, 'Go up, and I will give them into your hand' " (v. 10).

And so it happened. The Philistines then regrouped and later set themselves in array once more in the same valley. "When David again inquired of God, God said to him, 'You shall not go up after them; go around and come on them opposite the balsam trees. When you hear the sound of marching in the tops of the balsam trees, then go out to battle; for God has gone out before you to strike down the army of the Philistines' " (vv. 14-15). It occurred just as God said.

One of the most interesting things about these cases and many other similar biblical passages is the *specific* information, the *clear and detailed cognitive content,* given in the movement of God on the minds of Samuel and David. What we have here are not mere impressions, impulses or feelings which are so commonly thought to be what God uses to communicate with us. Rather we have a specific and full cognitive or propositional content concerning what is the case, what is to be done and what will happen.

David and Samuel were not left to wonder about the meaning of their impulses to do this or that or their feelings about this or that. Nor did they have to test them against the Scriptures or circumstances. They were simply told. David did not have to speculate about the meaning of "the sound of marching in the tops of the balsam trees" (v. 14); he was *told* its meaning.

Plain Communication

It is possible to talk about hearing God in terms of mysterious feelings, curious circumstances and special scriptural nuances of meaning to the point where God's very character is called into question. We must reply to this tendency by stating emphatically that *God is not a mumbling trickster.*

On the contrary it is to be expected, given the revelation of God in Christ, that if he wants us to know something, he will be both able and willing to communicate it to us *plainly,* just as long as we are open and prepared by our experience to hear and obey. This is exactly what takes place in the lives of such biblical characters as those we have just seen.

We may be sure that "no prophecy ever came by human will, but men and women moved by the Holy Spirit spoke from God" (2 Pet 1:21). With very little exception the form such inspiration took was nothing more than thoughts and perceptions of the distinctive character that these people had come through experience to recognize as the voice of God in their own souls. The thoughts and perceptions were still *their* thoughts and perceptions. It could not be otherwise. But the thoughts and perceptions bore within themselves the *unmistakable stamp* of divine quality, spirit, intent and origination.

Thus we find that Paul distinguishes clearly between what the Lord said through him and what he was saying on his own (for example, 1 Cor 7:12). Yet when he composed his letters under divine inspiration, he did not stop thinking or set aside his own perceptions and feelings to become an unconscious writer or mindless voice box. His thoughts and perceptions were his, *but they were God's also.* Paul recognized them as such by virtue of the distinctive character that he knew so well and worked with in utter confidence.

When we have learned through experience to recognize the voice of God as it enters into the texture of our souls, the lives of biblical characters become real to us, and the life of God in them becomes something with which we can identify. Our faith is strengthened by this, and we are able to claim our part in the unified reign of God in his people throughout history on earth and in heaven.

Some Topics for Reflection

1. It is a fact of nature that sheep recognize and respond to the voice of the one who takes care of them (Jn 10:3-4). What do you make of how Jesus uses this metaphor to explain the interaction between his voice and his people (Jn 10:14-27)?

2. What are the "three lights" referred to in this chapter, and what problems arise because of their interdependence?

3. What are the "three factors in the voice" treated in this chapter? Do you regard any of them as more important than the others? If so, why?

4. God's voice or word does not usually come to us via sound waves unless he is speaking to us through and *with* a human being, as explained earlier. Does the lack of an audible quality diminish the reliability of our experience of his voice?

5. "Any voice that promises total exemption from suffering and failure is most certainly *not* God's voice." What do you think of this claim? Are there any spiritual panaceas for life's problems?

6. What would be some indications that a communication that comes to you is from Satan? From yourself?

7. Do you agree with what this chapter says about infallibility and hearing from God? What are some practical implications of the position I have taken? Or of *your* view on this matter?

8. Our ability to recognize the voice of God serves as protection against leaders on both the wild side and the respectable side of religion. Discuss or reflect on any examples of this you have experienced or know about.

Nine

A Life More
Than Guidance

To deliver the soul from the sin which is its ruin
and bestow on it the holiness which is its health and peace,
is the end of all God's dealings with His children;
and precisely because He cannot merely impose,
but must enable us to attain it ourselves, if we are really to have
the liberty of His children, the way He must take is long and arduous.
JOHN WOOD OMAN, *GRACE AND PERSONALITY*

If you indeed cry out for insight,
and raise your voice for understanding,
if you seek it like silver,
and search for it as for hidden treasures—
then you will understand the fear of the Lord
and find the knowledge of God.
PROVERBS 2:3-5

IN THE PREVIOUS CHAPTERS WE HAVE DEALT WITH MANY ASPECTS OF how God speaks individually to his children. This discussion may sometimes have seemed remote, scholarly or merely philosophical. It is an unavoidable fact, however, that *what we do or do not understand, in any area of our lives, determines what we can or cannot believe and therefore governs our practice and action with an iron hand.* You cannot believe a blur or a blank, and the blanks in our understanding can only be filled in by careful instruction and hard thinking. It will not be done on our behalf.

Contrary to what many in our culture will tell you, this does *not* cease to be true when we enter the realm of the religious life. I have seen a book for sale in the United States called *The Lazy Man's Guide to Riches*. Misunderstandings about faith and grace lead people to think that the Christian gospel is *The Lazy Person's Guide to Getting into Heaven When You Die* or perhaps *The Passive Person's Path to Paradise*. But it is not.

Faith is not opposed to knowledge; it is opposed to sight. And grace is not opposed to effort; it is opposed to earning. Commitment is not sustained by confusion but by insight. The person who is uninformed or confused will inevitably be unstable and vulnerable in action, thought and feeling.

Misunderstandings, mental confusions and mistaken beliefs about God's guidance—or more generally about God and communications between him and his creatures—make a strong walk with him impossible, even if we've chosen, in effect, not to think about it. I have seen repeatedly confirmed in often tragic cases the dire consequences of refusing to give deep, thoughtful consideration to the ways in which God chooses to deal with us and of relying on whatever whimsical ideas and preconceptions about his ways happen to be flying around us. That is very dangerous to our health and well-being.

Indeed when we refuse to make the effort to understand God's dealings with humanity or to study the Bible and whatever else may help us to understand it, we are in rebellion against the express will of God. For he commands us to love him with *all our mind* as well as with all our heart, soul and strength (Mk 12:30; cf. Prov 1—8). We can therefore say on scriptural grounds that it is the direct and inclusive will of God that we *study* his ways of communicating with us. The conscious rejection of thoughtful and careful study is not faith, and it does not spring from faith. It is the rejection of the God-appointed means to God-appointed ends.

But now you have made that study. You have endured the hardship of thinking carefully and in depth about hearing God's voice in general and about the presentation of it given within the Scriptures. It is time to bring our results to bear on the life that any serious disciple of Christ consciously undertakes from day to day. If the previous chapters have communicated successfully and if you are concerned about hearing God and knowing his will for you, you should be able to come to a place of rest and assurance where you can be confident that the Lord's face does indeed shine upon you.

The question that we will deal with in this final chapter is, therefore, essentially a how-to question:

☐ How may we come to live confidently and sensibly with God as a conversational presence in our lives?

This leads on to subordinate questions such as

☐ How much can we count on hearing God?

☐ What does it mean when we don't hear his voice?

☐ What are we to do then?

The Framework for Our Answers

Let us set out toward the answers to such questions from a brief summary of the fundamental points presented in the course of this book. Repetition counteracts our powerful habits and misconceptions about hearing God that are buried deeply in customary religious behavior and thought patterns.

While God's communications, including those intended to guide our specific choices, come through experiences of many kinds, the content or meaning of his detailed and individualized communications to us always finally takes the form of the inner voice, a characteristic type of thought or perception. Without this the accompanying events, appearances or biblical passages remain puzzling, mystifying and open to conjecture.

God may of course direct us mechanically *without* speaking to us and guiding us through our own understandings and choices. He *can* guide us just as we guide our car, without speaking. But whenever he guides us in our conscious cooperation with him as friends and collaborators, he does so by speaking to us, by giving to us thoughts and perceptions that bear within themselves the marks of their divine origination.

His speaking most commonly occurs in conjunction with study of and reflection on the Bible, the written Word of God, wherever the Bible is available. Less commonly, though still often, it comes in conjunction with a human being who is speaking to us. But it may come in any of the other ways God chooses.

Our ability to recognize God's voice in our souls and to distinguish it with practical certainty from other competing voices is acquired by effort and experimentation—both on God's part and ours. It does not come automatically by divine imposition and command.

Those who really want to live under God's guidance and who by proper teaching or other special provision made by God become convinced that he will speak and perhaps *is* speaking to them can proceed to learn through experience the particular quality, spirit and content of God's voice. They will then distinguish and understand the voice of God; their discernment will not be infallible, but they will discern his voice as clearly and with as much accuracy as they discern the voice of any other person with whom they are on intimate terms.

I emphasize once again that this does not mean that they will always correctly understand what God says to them or even that it will be easy for them to get his message straight. One great cause of confusion is that people make infallibility a condition of hearing God. It helps, I believe and hope, to understand that God's word is *communication* and that communication occurs constantly in contexts where infallibility is completely out of the question.

The infallibility of the *speaker*—as is the case when God is the speaker—does not and need not guarantee infallibility of the *hearer.* But fortunately, as we all know, speakers who are not even close to being perfect still communicate reliably and regularly. I know my children's voices well and would recognize them under a very wide range of circumstances. Generally I understand what they say. But I would know it was one of them speaking even if I could not understand what was said. (This has actually happened on numerous occasions!)

Indeed careful study of personal relationships shows that recognition of a certain voice is often the cue for someone to *stop* listening or even to distort the message in particular ways that are relevant to the specific nature of the relationship between the people involved. I am convinced that this often happens in the divine-human conversation, and it almost always happens when God speaks to those who are in covert rebellion against him.

One of Jesus' deepest teachings concerned the *manner* in which we hear.

This is so important that it cannot be emphasized enough. Specifically, Jesus alerted his hearers to the fact that they might not be using their ears simply for hearing but for other purposes as well—such as to filter and manage the message so it fits better their own lives and purposes: " 'Let anyone with ears to hear listen!' And he said to them, 'Pay attention to what you hear; the measure you give will be the measure you get, and still more will be given you. For to those who have, more will be given; and from those who have nothing, even what they have will be taken away' " (Mk 4:23-25). Listening is an *active* process that may select or omit from, as well as reshape, the message intended by the speaker. Both listening and our other ways of perceiving turn out to be fundamental displays of our character, our freedom and our bondages.

Those who really do *not* want to hear what God has to say—no matter what they may say to the contrary—will position themselves before God in such a way "that they may indeed look, but not perceive, and may indeed listen, but not understand; so that they may not turn again and be forgiven" (Mk 4:12). If we do not want to be converted from our chosen and habitual ways, if we really want to run our own lives without any interference from God, our very perceptual mechanisms will filter out his voice or twist it to our own purposes.

The doleful reality is that very few human beings really *do* concretely desire to hear what God has to say to them. This is shown by how rarely we listen for his voice when we are not in trouble or when we are not being faced with a decision that we do not know how to handle. People who understand and warmly desire to hear God's voice will, by contrast, want to hear it when life is uneventful just as much as they want to hear it when they are facing trouble or big decisions. This is a test that we should all apply to ourselves as we go in search of God's word: do we seek it only under uncomfortable circumstances? Our answer may reveal that our failure to hear his voice when we want to is due to the fact that we do not *in general* want to hear it, that we want it only when we think we need it.

Usually those who want a word from God when they are in trouble cannot find it. Or at least they have no assurance that they have found it. This is, I think, because they do not first and foremost simply want to hear God speaking in their lives in general. At heart they only want to get out of trouble or to make the decisions that will be best for them. I have spoken with many who think of divine communication only as something to help them avoid trouble.

That we lack the desire to receive God's word merely for what it is, just because we believe it is the best way to live, is also shown by a disregard of the plain directives in the Scriptures. Sanctification from sexual uncleanness (1 Thess 4:3) and a continuously thankful heart (1 Thess 5:18) are among the many specific things clearly set forth in God's general instructions to all people. It is not wise to disregard these plain directives and *then* expect to be hear a special message from God when we want it.

I do not mean to say that God absolutely will not, in his mercy, communicate and instruct those who have departed from the general guidance, the Word, he has given. Contrary to the well-meaning words of the blind man whom Jesus healed (Jn 9:31), God does on occasion "listen to sinners," and he speaks to them as well. But this cannot be counted on as part of a *regular and intelligible plan for living in a conversational relationship with God.* Anyone who rejects the general counsels of Scripture is in fact planning not to be guided by God and cannot then rely on being able to be delivered from their difficulties by obtaining God's input on particular occasions.

Many people, however, honestly desire God's word both in its own right and because God knows it is best for us. As a part of their total plan for living in harmony with God, these believers adopt the general counsels of Scripture as the framework within which they are to know his daily graces. These people will most assuredly receive God's specific, conscious words through the inner voice to the extent that it truly is appropriate in helping them become more like Christ. There *is* a limit to which such guidance is appropriate, and we will return to this point later. But it is true in general, as G. Campbell Morgan has written, that "wherever there are hearts waiting for the Voice of God, that Voice is to be heard."[1]

With this summary of what we have learned so far before us, we turn now to deal with some final practical questions.

Listening for God

James Dobson has given some of the best practical advice I have ever heard on how someone who really wants the will of God and who has a basically correct understanding of it should proceed. Describing how he does it himself, he says, "I get down on my knees and say, 'Lord, I need to know what you want me to do, and I am listening. Please speak to me through my friends, books, magazines I pick up and read, and through circumstances.' "[2]

The simplicity of this should not mislead us. When we are in a proper, well-functioning relationship with God, this is exactly what we are to do. And then we are, as Dobson says, to *listen.* This means that we should pay a special kind of attention both to what is going on within us and to our surrounding circumstances.

We are talking about practicalities now, so it might be a good thing, until it becomes a habit, to write down Dobson's simple prayer for guidance and put it somewhere—on the bathroom mirror, for example—where you can see and use it often. In conjunction with doing that it is important to observe *regular times for listening* with respect to the matters that especially concern you.

Frederick B. Meyer is once again helpful at this practical level:

> Be still each day for a short time, sitting before God in meditation, and ask the Holy Spirit to reveal to you the truth of Christ's indwelling. Ask God to be pleased to make known to you what is the riches of the glory of this mystery (Colossians 1:27).[3]

If we maintain this general habit, then when we are aware of a need for a particular word from God, we will be able to listen for it with greater patience, confidence and acuteness.

Personally I find it works best if after I ask for God to speak to me in this way, I devote the next hour or so to some kind of activity that neither engrosses my attention with other things nor allows me to be intensely focused on the matter in question. Housework, gardening, driving about on errands or paying bills will generally do. I have learned not to worry about whether or not this is going to work. I know that it does not *have* to work, but I am sure that it *will* work if God has something he really wants me to know or do. This is ultimately because *I am sure of how great and good he is.*

Often by the end of an hour or so there has stood forth within my consciousness an idea or thought with that peculiar quality, spirit and content that I have come to associate with God's voice. If so, I may write it down for further study. I may also decide to discuss the matter with others, usually without informing them that "God has told me. . . ." Or I may decide to reconsider the matter by repeating the same process after a short period of time. Remember Gideon (Judg 6:11-40). Remember too that scientists check their results by rerunning experiments. We should be so humble.

If, on the other hand, nothing emerges by the end of an hour or so, I am not alarmed. I set myself to hold the matter before God as I go about my business and confidently get on with my life. Of course I make it a point to *keep* listening. Very often, within a day something happens through which God's voice, recognizably distinct, is heard.

If this does not happen, I generally cease specifically to seek God's word on the matter in question. I do not cease my *general* attitude of listening. But I am neither disappointed nor alarmed, nor even concerned, as a rule, and I shall explain why as we proceed further. (I am not speaking here of prayer generally, where a different approach of greater persistence and tenacity is often called for.)

I have followed this simple method of listening for God's voice in many situations—in university teaching, research and administration; in family and business affairs; in writing and conducting sessions in conferences and seminars. It is the furthest thing from a legalism or formality for me, and God also takes ample occasion to slip up on me by speaking to me words that I am not seeking in this way. Generally it is much more important to cultivate the *quiet, inward space of a constant listening* than to always be approaching God for specific direction.

From my own experience, then, and from what I have been able to learn from the Scriptures and from others who live in a working relationship with God's voice, I am led to the following conclusion: Direction will always be made available to the mature disciple if without it serious harm would befall people concerned in the matter or the cause of Christ.

If I am right, the obedient, listening heart, mature in the things of God, will in such a case find the voice plain and the message clear, as with the experiences of the friends of God recorded in the Bible. This is a claim that must be tested by experience, and anyone willing to meet the conditions and learn from failures as well as successes can put it to the test. In every congregation we need a group of people who in front of everyone are explicitly learning and teaching about life in dialogue with God.

This Is Not a Gimmick

God often speaks *without* our initiating any such procedure of seeking his individualized word as I have just described. We must also not be misled into thinking that there is some sure-fire *technique* for squeezing what we want to know out of God. A life surrendered to God, a humble openness to his direction even when it is contrary to our wants and assumptions, experience with the way his word comes to us and fervent but patient requests for guidance—these do not constitute a *method* for getting an answer from him.

Hearing from God is not a gimmick. Talk of method is, strictly speaking, out of place here, although it is possible and helpful to lay down general, practical guidelines. After all God is not someone we "work up" for a result, even though certain behaviors before him are more or less appropriate. Above all we must beware of trying to *force* God to speak. This is especially true just when we are most likely to attempt it—that is, when we are not in peaceful union with him.

King Saul Forcing a Word

A scene from the life of Saul, the first king of Israel, poignantly illustrates the folly of such attempts. Saul certainly did not have waiting upon God to see his will done as his highest priority. To keep control over his armies in the face of the Philistines, he sacrificed without waiting as he should have for Samuel, the priest, to arrive. He blundered ahead on his own, even though it was not his place, and made peace offerings and burnt offerings (1 Sam 13:5-10).

When Samuel arrived at last, he asked Saul why he had sacrificed without him. Saul's reply goes to the very heart of his character: "When I saw that the people were slipping away from me, and that you did not come within the days appointed, and that the Philistines were mustering at Michmash, I said, 'Now the Philistines will come down upon me at Gilgal, and I have not entreated the favor of the LORD'; so I forced myself, and offered the burnt offering" (1 Sam 13:11-12).

Samuel immediately announced that Saul would lose his kingdom (1 Sam 13:13-14), for he clearly saw that Saul was a man who would take things into his own hands to get his way and that he would also find a "good reason" for doing so. Samuel knew that God would not stand by such a man.

A little later Saul disobeyed again—when he did not utterly destroy Amalek (1 Sam 15)—and once more he found a "good reason." He even pretended to Samuel that he had obeyed (v. 13), and when his deceit was uncovered he again blamed his disobedience on the people (v. 24). And again Samuel announced that the kingdom would be taken from him (v. 26).

Finally Saul came to his extremity, facing death (1 Sam 28). Samuel himself was dead by that time, and when Saul inquired of the Lord, "the LORD did not answer him, not by dreams, or by Urim, or by prophets" (v. 6). Now, as was his way, Saul tried to *force* the knowledge he sought. Even though he himself had banned witches from Israel, he sought out a witch and compelled her to call up the spirit of Samuel (vv. 7-11) to tell him what to do. Samuel arose "up out of the ground" (v. 13) and said to Saul, "Why have you disturbed me by bringing me up?" (v. 15).

Saul poured out his tale of woe: "I am in great distress, for the Philistines are warring against me, and God has turned away from me and answers me no more, either by prophets or by dreams; so I have summoned you *to tell me what I should do*" (v. 15, italics added). How sadly typical this is of the human view of God and his guidance! We treat him like a celestial aspirin that will cure headaches brought on by the steady, willful tendency of our lives away from and even against him. We treat him as a cosmic butler who is to clean up our messes. To compel him to serve us we seek gimmicks and tricks suited only to idols.

Samuel then read Saul's sentence to him: "Why then do you ask me, since the LORD has turned from you and become your enemy? . . . Tomorrow you and your sons shall be with me; the LORD will also give the army of Israel into the hands of the Philistines" (vv. 16, 19). At these words Saul fell flat on the ground, weakened by hunger and terror—a tragic picture. God refused to be used by him any longer.

Deciding "On Your Own"

With all of this clear in our minds, we turn to what surely is one of the greatest problems in the devout person's attempt to receive God's word. Even if we are not in disobedience to God, even if our hearts are attuned to his will, there will be many times in which God does not send a particularized word. What then *are* we to do?

We must not automatically assume that if God does not communicate with us on a particular matter we are displeasing to him. *If* that is the cause—which of course remains possible and should always be considered—there are ways of finding this out. It will be something that can be discovered and clearly known if we seek it out through honest examination of our lives, through counsel with Christian friends and ministers and through asking the Lord to reveal it to us.

It is crucial to remember that God will not play little games of hide-and-seek with us. As I emphasized earlier, it is very important that we believe God is the kind of person Jesus revealed him to be. Such a person will show us what the problem is and if there is a problem, provided that we sincerely and with an open mind pray and seek to be shown. He is not frivolous or coy; he will not tease or torture us. In our relationship with him there is no mysterious catch to receiving his word for us, no riddle to solve, no incantation to get just right—not with the God and Father of our Lord Jesus Christ! We must make a point of not thinking of him in terms of human beings (relatives, supervisors, authorities and others) who may have enjoyed tricking us by not explaining what we were supposed to do.

There are reasons other than his displeasure why a specific word may not be forthcoming to us in a particular case. One of the major other reasons is that in general, *it is God's will that we ourselves should have a great part in determining our path through life.* This does not mean that he is not with us. Far from it. God both *develops* and, for our good, *tests* our character by leaving us to decide. He calls us to responsible citizenship in his kingdom by saying—in effect or in reality—as often as possible, *"My will for you in this case is that you decide on your own."*

In his profound chapter titled "The Will of God," John Wood Oman gives us an excellent statement on this point:

> We can only be absolutely dependent upon God as we are absolutely independent in our own souls, and only absolutely independent in our own souls as we are absolutely dependent on God. A saved soul, in other words, is a soul true to itself because, with its mind on God's will of love and not on itself, it stands in God's world unbribable and undismayed, having freedom as it has piety and piety as it is free.[4]

From the apostle Paul and the saints through the ages rings out the full meaning of that robust and powerful saying, "I live! Yet not I, but Christ lives in me!" (see Gal 2:20). In this way individual human personality is not obliterated, but rather it is given its fullest expression.

We are dealing here with the essence of human personality as God has ordained it. A child cannot develop into a responsible, competent human being if he or she is always told what to do. Personality and character are in their very essence inner directedness. This inner directedness is perfected in redemption. That is Oman's point. Moreover a child's character cannot be known—even to himself—until he is turned loose to do what he wants. It is precisely what he wants and how he handles those wants that both reveal and make him the person he is.

What we want, what we think, what we decide to do when the word of God does not come or when we have so immersed ourselves in him that his voice within us is not held in distinction from our own thoughts and perceptions—these show *who we are:* either we are God's mature children, friends and coworkers, or we are something less.

There is also, after all, a neurotic, faithless and irresponsible seeking of

God's will: a kind of spiritual hypochondria, which is always taking its own spiritual temperature, which is far more concerned with being righteous than with loving God and others and doing and enjoying what is good. One can be over-righteous (Eccles 7:16). We may insist on having God tell us what to do because we live in fear or are obsessed with *being right* as a strategy for *being safe*. But we may also do it because we do not really have a hearty faith in his gracious goodwill toward us. If so, we need to grow up to Christlikeness, and nothing short of that will solve our problem. Certainly more words from God will not!

We may in our heart of hearts suspect that God is mean and tyrannical, and therefore we may be afraid to make a move without dictation from him. We may even have the idea that if we can get God to tell us what to do, we will no longer be responsible for our decisions. Far from honoring God, such an attitude is blasphemous, idolatrous and certain to prevent us from ever entering into that conversational relationship with God in which sensible words, clearly revealed and reliably understood, are given as appropriate. How much would you have to do with a person who harbored such low opinions about you?

Often we just do not think through the things we say about God. A well-known American minister of some decades ago, Bud Robinson, was called by a parishioner whose husband had recently died. The lady informed the minister that God had told her to give the husband's suits to him. Would he please come over, she asked, to see if the suits would fit? Pastor Robinson very sensibly replied, "If God told you to give them to me, they'll fit." How refreshing it is to hear from someone who actually believes in a competent God!

The Perfect Will of God

We cannot be groveling robots or obsequious, cringing sycophants and *also* be the *children of God!* Such creatures could never bear the family resemblance. A son or daughter is not their father's toady, and toadying does not come from either humility or worship before the God and Father of Jesus Christ. To suppose so is to live within a morbid and anti-Christian view of who God is. "The humility that cringes in order that reproof may be escaped or favor obtained is as unchristian as it is profoundly immoral."[5]

In this context I must say something about being in the *perfect* will of God. If our lives conform to the general counsels of God for his people as given to us in the written Word as a whole, then we are perfectly within God's general as well as moral will. If, in addition, we have received and obeyed a specific word of God to us concerning a particular matter, then we are *perfectly* in God's *specific* will for us, relevant to that matter.

But suppose that no such specific word has come to us on some matter of great importance to our lives. (For example, Should we enter this school or that? Should we live here or there? Should we change employment?) Does this mean that in the matter at hand we *cannot* be in God's perfect will or that we can be so only by chance, following some anxiety-ridden guessing game about what God wants us to do?

Most assuredly it does not! We must resolutely resist the tendency to blame the absence of a word from God automatically on our own wrongness. And we must equally resist the idea that it means we must be somewhat off the track and living in something less than God's perfect will. If we are living in sincere devotion to the fulfillment of God's purposes in us, we can be sure that the God who came to us in Jesus Christ will not mumble and tease and trick us regarding any specific matter he wants done. I cannot emphasize this point too much since the tendency to think otherwise is obviously so strong and ever present.

Think of it this way: no decent parents would obscure their intentions for their children. A general principle for interpreting God's behavior toward us is provided in Jesus' words, "If you then, who are evil, know how to give good gifts to your children, how much more will the heavenly Father give the Holy Spirit to those who ask him!" (Lk 11:13). How much more will our heavenly Father give clear instructions to those who sincerely ask him—in those cases where he has any to give? Where he has none to give, we may be sure that is because it is best that he does not. Then whatever lies within his moral will and whatever is undertaken in faith *is his perfect will.* It is no less perfect because it was not specifically dictated by him. Indeed it is perhaps more perfect precisely because he saw no need for precise dictation. He expects and trusts us to choose, and he goes with us in our choice.

Several different courses of action may, then, each be God's perfect will in a given circumstance. We should *assume* that this is so in all cases where we are walking in his general will, are experienced in hearing his voice and, on seeking, find no specific direction given. In these cases there are usually various things that would equally please God, though he directs none of them in particular to be done. All are perfectly in his will because none is better than the others so far as he is concerned, and all are good. He would not have you do other than you are doing. (Of course, being in his perfect will does not mean you are quite flawless yet! You can be in his perfect will without being a perfect human being.)

In his book *Decision Making and the Will of God,* Garry Friesen has done a masterful job of critiquing the view that God always has one particular thing for you to do in a given case, that correct decision-making depends on your finding out what that thing is and that if you miss it, you will only be in God's permissive will at best—and a second-class citizen in the kingdom of God. Arguing against this extremely harmful view, Friesen remarks,

> The *major point* is this: God does not have an ideal, detailed life-plan uniquely designed for each believer that must be discovered in order to make correct decisions. The concept of an "individual will of God" [in *that* sense] cannot be established by reason, experience, biblical example or biblical teaching.[6]

So the *perfect* will of God may allow, for a particular person, a number of different alternatives. For most people, for example, a number of different choices in selecting a partner (or none at all), various vocations, educational institutions or places of residence may all equally be God's perfect will—none being in themselves better or preferred by God in relation to the ultimate outcome desired by him.

The sincere seeker should assume that this is so and should move forward with faith in God if no specific word comes on the matter concerned after a reasonable period of time. All of this is consistent with there *sometimes* being only one choice that would perfectly fit God's will for us. Our choices must be approached on a case-by-case basis, just as life is lived one day at a time, trusting God.

Just as character is revealed only when we are permitted or required to do as we want, so also the degree and maturity of our faith are manifested only in cases where no specific command is given. It is not a great and mature faith that merely does what it is told. Rather—in the words of William Carey as he went out to India as a pioneer missionary—such a faith is one that "attempts great things for God and expects great things from God." It actively gets on with the work to be done, the life to be lived, confident in the good-hearted companionship of the Father, Son and Holy Spirit. Human initiative is not canceled by redemption; it is heightened by immersion in the flow of God's life. People with a mature vision of God and extensive experience in his ways have no need to be obsessively anxious about doing the right thing. For the most part they will simply *know* what is right. But their confidence is finally not in a word from the Lord but in the Lord who is with us.

Caught in Cosmic Conflict

Sometimes it is not because our Father wishes us to decide that we find ourselves without his specific communication. There are also times when we are face to face with the powers of darkness that inhabit our universe along with us. Many people have fallen under some affliction and have cast about desperately to find out what *they* did wrong; but often it was nothing, or whatever wrong they may have done was not what was responsible for their problem.

A battle is going on in the universe in which we live. As we live in this universe and share in God's activity both of creation and redemption, there are moments when we stand alone. Jesus knew what that was like. You will remember how he speaks in Luke 22:53 of the time when *his* hour would come—the hour of darkness, the hour of the powers of evil. In that hour he cried out, "My God, my God, why have you forsaken me?" (Mt 27:46).

You and I are going to face these hours too; though, I believe, we will never be *actually* forsaken and alone. As that magnificent little giant John

Wesley said at his death, "Best of all, God is with us!" But words from God, no matter how well we know his voice, will not spare us the times of grief and pain, as Jesus was not spared. Our confidence remains that these times also "work together for good" for those who love God and are called according to his purposes (Rom 8:28). In that we can rest and refuse to harass ourselves with doubt and blame.

It is a similar situation when we are given a word from God and are sure of it, but the events indicated do not come to pass. Others may be involved, and *they* may not know or may not do the will of God. And God may not override them. Our world is the crucible of soul making, in which we can still remain always certain of inevitable triumph, "more than conquerors." The will of God made plain to *us* is sometimes not fulfilled because of the choices of *other* people. We must not because of that lose confidence in God's guiding words.

Greater Than a Word from God

There is something even greater than always knowing what is the right thing to do and always being directed by the present hand of God. Paul brought this out very clearly in 1 Corinthians 13. In this passage he writes of knowledge, prophecy and many other great things that we might find desirable. But he says that all of these are only partial and incomplete goods. The three greatest things—truly inseparable from each other, when properly understood—are faith, hope and love.

Even in the hour of darkness these three—faith, hope and love—remained with Christ. They will remain with us. The great height of our development as disciples of Christ is not that we should always be hearing God's voice but that we should have been trained under the hand of God—which includes hearing God as he speaks and guides—in such a way that we are able to stand at our appointed times and places in faith, hope and love *even without a word from God:* "and having done everything, to stand firm" (Eph 6:13).

I can be assured at a certain point in my progression toward spiritual maturity simply that "the one who sent me is with me; he has not left me alone" (Jn 8:29). It should be the hope and *plan* of every disciple of Christ to come, by gracious assistance, to this place of rest in God's companionship and service. We will then, as Brother Lawrence advises, "not always scrupulously confine ourselves to certain rules, or particular forms of devotion, but act with a general confidence in God, with love and humility."[7] We will simply "stand fast . . . in the liberty wherewith Christ hath made us free" (Gal 5:1 KJV). The liberty is not an opportunity to indulge the flesh; it should be instead the arena within which we "serve one another in love" (Gal 5:13 NIV), precisely because "the one who sent me is with me." The branch thus abides in the vine. The branch and the vine share a common life and together produce abundant fruit for God (Jn 15:1-8).

But Never Beyond Risk

It is absolutely essential to the nature of our personal development toward maturity that we venture and be placed at risk, for *only risk produces character.* This truth is intensified when it comes to our walk with God. In this matter I find myself disagreeing with certain very wise people, such as A. T. Pierson, who regard God's guidance as *precluding* risk:

> One great law for all who would be truly led by God's pillar of cloud and fire, is to take no step at the bidding of self-will or without the clear moving of the heavenly guide. Though the direction be new and the way seem beset with difficulty, there is never any risk provided we are only led of God. Each new advance needs separate and special authority from Him, and yesterday's guidance is not sufficient for today.[8]

This is a beautiful and helpful statement, *except* for what it seems to be saying about risk. In this respect it is not a completely accurate account of what it means to live with God's words in our lives. The immaturity of many Christians today is due to their adopting the attitude toward risk expressed in this statement as the *whole* truth about hearing from God.

Having adopted this attitude, we then try to *use* our ability to hear God as a device for securing a life without risk. When it does not work—as it certainly will not—we begin attacking ourselves, someone else or even God for being a failure. Such a response partly explains why God remains humanity's greatest disappointment. Who does not have a grievance against him? In truth, we need not seek risk, but we will never be without it, at least in this world. Nor should we try to be.

With Guidance and Beyond . . . Life and Rest

The key concept underlying all the themes I have raised in this book is this: *Hearing God's word will never make sense except when it is set within a larger life of a certain kind.*

To try to locate divine communication within human existence alienated from God is to return to idolatry, where God is there for our *use.* To try to solve all our life's problems by getting a word from the Lord is to hide from life and from the dignity of the role God intended us to have in creation. As John Boykin remarks, "God does not exist to solve our problems."[9] *We* exist to stand up with God and count for something in his world.

We must ultimately move *beyond* the question of hearing God and into a life greater than our own—that of the kingdom of God. Our concern for discerning God's voice must be overwhelmed by and lost in our worship and adoration of him and in our delight with his creation and his provision for our whole life. Our aim in such a life is to identify all that we are and all that we do with God's purposes in creating us and our world. Thus we learn how to do all things to the glory of God (1 Cor 10:31; Col 3:17). That is, we come in all things to think and act so that his goodness, greatness and beauty will be as obvious as possible—not just to ourselves, but to all those around us.

God's speaking will always be an essential part of this, to the extent and in the manner God deems suitable. It will come without threat to the full participation of the redeemed self, as a unique individual, in the work of God. For those who come to this point, their life will be *theirs*—irreducibly, preciously so—and yet also God's; and through them will flow God's life, which is also theirs. This is the life *beyond,* and yet *inclusive of,* his guiding word. It is the life that has its beginning in the additional birth and its culmination in the everlasting, glorious society of heaven.

With this life in view John Wesley answered an intelligent and serious man who said to him, "I hear that you preach to a great number of people every night and morning. Pray what would you do with them? Whither would you lead them? What religion do you preach? What is it good for?" Honest and searching questions which no minister should allow out of his mind. Wesley replied,

> I do preach to as many as desire to hear, every night and morning. You ask, what I would do with them: I would make them virtuous and happy, easy in themselves and useful to others. Whither would I lead them? To heaven; to God the Judge, the lover of all, and to Jesus the mediator of the New Covenant. What religion do I preach? The religion of love; the law of kindness brought to light by the gospel. What is this good for? To make all who receive it enjoy God and themselves: to make them all like God; lovers of all; contented in their lives; and crying out at their death, in calm assurance, "O grave, where is thy victory! Thanks be unto God, who giveth me the victory, through my Lord Jesus Christ."[10]

While I was teaching at a ministers' conference, one minister asked me what was the *human* issue, irrespective of church life or religion, that Jesus came to address. This is the question facing the Christian church today. My answer was this: Jesus came to respond to the universal human need to know *how to live well*. He came to show us how through reliance on him we can best live in the universe as it really is. That is why he said, "I came that they may have life, and have it abundantly" (Jn 10:10). His supremacy lies in the greatness of the life he gives to us. Putting Jesus Christ into a worldwide competition with all known alternatives is the only way we can give our faith a chance to prove his power over the whole of life.

A Formula for Living with God's Voice

Within such a life as Wesley described to his inquisitor, God's word is to be reliably and safely sought and found—free of mystification, gimmickry, hysteria, self-righteousness, self-exaltation, self-obsession and dogmatism. On the presupposition of such a life we can lay down something close to a formula for *living with* God's guiding voice.

Note, however, that it is *not* a formula for *getting God to speak to us* on matters that may concern us. Any such "formula" is ruled out by the very nature of God and of our relationship with him. This much should be clear by now. It is instead a formula for *living with* God's voice, for hearing his word in a life surrendered and brought to maturity by him.

The first two steps in the formula may be described as foundational, since they provide the basis for hearing God's individual word to us but do not exclusively and specifically concern it as the rest do.

Foundational steps.

1. We have entered into the additional life by the additional birth, and so far as it lies within our understanding and conscious will, we plan and make provision to do what we know to be morally right and what we know to be explicitly commanded by God. This commitment includes the intention to *find out* what may be morally right or commanded by God and hence to grow in our knowledge.

2. We seek the fullness of the new life in Christ at the impulse of the Spirit of God in service to the good wherever it may appear, venturing beyond our merely natural powers in reliance on God's upholding power. Thus we move from faith to more faith (Rom 1:17) as we find him faithful. Above all we venture in the proclamation of the gospel of Jesus Christ and his kingdom as presented in the New Testament Gospels.

Steps to hearing God.

3. We meditate constantly on God's principles for life as set forth in the Scriptures, always striving to penetrate more deeply into their meaning and into their application for our own lives.

> Happy are those
>> who do not follow the advice of the wicked,
> or take the path that sinners tread,
>> or sit in the seat of scoffers;
> but their delight is in the law of the LORD,
>> and on his law they meditate day and night.
> They are like trees
>> planted by streams of water,
> which yield their fruit in its season,

and their leaves do not wither.
In all that they do, they prosper. (Ps 1:1-3)

4. We are alert and attentive to what is happening in our life, in our mind and in our heart. For here is where God's communications come and identify themselves, whatever the external occasion may be. It was said of the prodigal son that he came *to himself* (Lk 15:17) and then he found the truth and repentance that saved him from his plight.

When God came to Adam after he had sinned, he did not ask "Adam, where is God?" but "Adam, where are you?" (Gen 3:9). We must purposefully, humbly and intelligently cultivate the ability to listen and see what is happening in our own souls and to recognize therein the movements of God.

5. We pray and speak to God constantly and specifically about the matters that concern us. This is essential to our part of the conversation with God. You would not continue to speak to someone who did not talk to you; and you could not carry on a coherent conversation with someone who spoke to you only rarely and on odd occasions. In general the same is true of God.

Nothing is too insignificant or too hopeless to bring before God. Share all things with God by lifting them to him in prayer, and ask for his guidance even—or perhaps especially—in those things that you think you already understand.

6. Using a regular plan, such as the one described in pages 199-201, *listen*, carefully and deliberately, for God. When God does speak to you, pay attention and receive it with thanks. It is a good habit to write such things down, at least until you become so adept at the conversational relationship that you no longer need to. If he gives you an insight into truth, meditate on it until you have thoroughly assimilated it. If the word he has given concerns action, carry it out in a suitable manner. God does not speak to us to amuse or entertain us but to make some real difference in our lives.

7. In those cases where God does *not* speak to you on the matter concerned, take the following steps:

a. Ask God to inform you, in whatever way he chooses, if some hindrance is within you. Be quiet and listen in the inner forum of your mind for any indication that you are blocking his word. But do not endlessly pursue this. In prayer set a specific length of time for the inquiry about hindrances: normally no more than three days. Believe that if a problem exists, God will make it clear to you. Share the robust confidence of Abraham Lincoln, who said, "I am satisfied that, when the Almighty wants me to do, or not to do, a particular thing, he finds a way of letting me know it."

b. Take counsel from at least two people whose relationship with God you respect, preferably those who are *not* your buddies. This may be done in a group setting if it does not concern an inherently private matter.

c. If you find a cause for why God's word could not come, correct it. Mercilessly. Whatever it is. Just do it.

d. If you cannot find such a cause, then act on *what seems best to you* after considering the itemized details of each alternative. If certain alternatives seem equally desirable, then select one as you wish. This will rarely be necessary, but your confidence, remember, is in the Lord who goes with you, who is with his trusting children even if they blunder and flounder. In this instance you may not know God in his specific word to you, but you *will* know him in his faithfulness. "His mercies never come to an end; they are new every morning: great is your faithfulness" (Lam 3:22-23). These words were written by the prophet Jeremiah in a time of utter failure, when the guiding hand of God was totally hidden from Israel and his punishing hand was raised against them.

If we proceed in this way, we will come to know God's voice as a familiar personal fact, which we can both comfortably live with and effectively introduce others to. We will know what to do when God speaks, but we will also know what to do when he does not speak. We will know how to find and remove any hindrance if there is one and how to move firmly but restfully onward in loving peacefulness when there is none. We will know that God is inviting us to move forward to greater maturity, relying on his faithfulness alone. We will know, in short, how to live in our world within a conversational relationship with our Father who is always there for us.

Some Topics for Reflection

1. What is your response to the idea that hard study and thinking about basic issues of faith is *commanded* by God as the way of loving him with our mind?

2. What do you take to be the three most important points to understand about hearing God?

3. What would be some signs that whatever I may say, I really do not want to hear God and give his word a place in my life?

4. What is the difference, if any, between *not planning* to hear God's voice and *planning not* to hear God's voice?

5. What do you think it is like to listen for God to communicate with us, and what are some practical tips that will help us to do it successfully?

6. What is the effect of too much guidance on a personality? How are receiving directions from God and deciding on your own interrelated?

7. How can we be in God's perfect will with respect to matters where he has given us no specific word?

8. Is it right to expect that a person who hears God word will be beyond risk in life? Is it desirable to live without risk? What is the *ultimate* safety that we have in God?

9. What more is there to life in Christ than hearing God's voice?

Epilogue

The Way of the Burning Heart

Blessed are those who have not seen
and yet have come to believe.
JOHN 20:29

Were not our hearts burning within us while he was talking to us
on the road, while he was opening the scriptures to us?
LUKE 24:32

I HAVE TRIED TO CLARIFY WHAT HEARING GOD AMOUNTS TO AND TO make a life in which one hears God's voice, in the Way of Jesus, accessible to anyone who would enter it. I have aimed to give a biblical and experiential understanding of the theory and practice of that life. Now as we come to the end of the book, I am still painfully aware of *the one great barrier* that might hinder some people's efforts to make such a life their own. That barrier is what Henry Churchill King many years ago called "the seeming unreality of the spiritual life."[1] We could equally well speak of it as "the overwhelming presence of the visible world."

The visible world daily bludgeons us with its things and events. They pinch and pull and hammer away at our bodies. Few people arise in the morning as hungry for God as they are for cornflakes or toast and eggs. But instead of shouting and shoving, the *spiritual* world whispers at us ever so gently. And it appears both at the edges and in the middle of events and things in the so-called real world of the visible.

God's spiritual invasions into human life seem by their very gentleness almost to invite us to explain them away, even while soberly reminding us that to be obsessed and ruled by the visible is death but that to give one's self over to the spiritual is life and peace (Rom 8:6).

We are hindered in our progress toward becoming spiritually competent people by how easily we can explain away the movements of God toward us. They go meekly, without much protest. Of course his day will come, but for now he cooperates with the desires and inclinations that make up our character, as we are gradually becoming the kind of people we will forever be. That should send a chill down our spine.

God wants to be wanted, to be wanted enough that we are *ready,* predisposed, to find him present with us. And if, by contrast, we are ready and set to find ways of explaining away his gentle overtures, he will rarely respond with fire from heaven. More likely he will simply leave us alone; and we shall have the satisfaction of thinking ourselves not to be gullible.

The test of character posed by the gentleness of God's approach to us is especially dangerous for those formed by the ideas that dominate our modern world. We live in a culture that has, for centuries now, cultivated the idea that the *skeptical* person is always smarter than one who believes. You can be almost as stupid as a cabbage, as long as you *doubt.* The fashion of the age has identified mental sharpness with a pose, not with genuine intellectual method and character. Only a very hardy individualist or social rebel—or one desperate for another life—therefore stands any chance of discovering the substantiality of the spiritual life today. Today it is the skeptics who are the social conformists, though because of powerful intellectual propaganda they continue to enjoy thinking of themselves as wildly individualistic and unbearably bright.

Partly as a result of this social force toward skepticism, which remains very powerful even when we step into Christian congregations and colleges for ministers, very few people ever develop competence in their prayer life. This is chiefly because they are *prepared* to explain away as coincidences the answers that come to the prayers that they do make. Often they see this as a sign of how intelligent they are. ("Ha! *I* am not so easily fooled as all that!") And in their pride they close off the entrance to a life of increasingly confident and powerful prayer. They grow no further, for they have proven to their own satisfaction that prayer is not answered.

Nearly all areas of life in which we could become spiritually competent (hearing God and receiving divine guidance among them) confront us with the same type of challenge. They all require of us *a choice to be a spiritual person, to live a spiritual life.* We are required to "bet our life" that the visible world, while real, is not reality itself.

We cannot make spirituality "work" without having a significant degree of confidence in and commitment to the truth that the visible world is always under the hand of the unseen God. Our own spiritual substance and competence grows as we put what faith we have into practice and as we thereby learn to distinguish and count on the characteristic differences that begin to emerge as evidence of God's presence in our life. This is how, through the gospel of Christ, God's righteousness—what it is about him that makes him absolutely good, "really okay"—is revealed from faith to faith (Rom 1:17).

The greatest of divides between human beings and human cultures is between those who regard the visible world as being of primary importance—possibly alone real or at least the touchstone of reality—and those who do not. Today we live in a culture that overwhelmingly gives primary, if not exclusive, importance to the visible. This stance is incorporated in the power structures that permeate our world and is disseminated by the education system and government.[2]

But neither God nor the human mind and heart are visible. It is so with all truly personal reality. "No one has ever seen the Father," Jesus reminds us. And while you know more about your own mind and heart than you could ever say, little to none of it was learned though sensory perception. God and the self accordingly meet in the *invisible* world because they *are* invisible *by nature.* They are not parts of the visible world, though both are related to it.

The second of the Ten Commandments tries to help us find God by forbidding us to think of him in visual terms (Ex 20:4). It forbids the use of *images* as representations of the divine being. The entire weight of the history of Israel—and its extension through Jesus and his people—presses toward the understanding of God as personal, invisible reality. This God invades history to call human beings individually to *choose* whether they will live in covenant relation with him or whether they will put something else—something visible—in the place of ultimate importance.

This is the challenge that I face every day when I wake. It walks with me through the events of each day. Will I, like Moses, "endure as seeing him who is invisible"? Will I listen for God and then obey? For me this tension is what it means to live as one who is learning from Christ how to live in the kingdom of God. Right where I am, moment to moment, I sweat it out with my brother Paul: "My visible self may be perishing, but inwardly I am renewed day to day, . . . producing something far greater than my troubles, and eternal in its glory, while we disregard the seen and focus on the unseen" (2 Cor 4:16-18, paraphrase).

God is not insensitive to our problem of overcoming the power of the visible world. He invades the visible. The elaborate *visible* provisions dictated to Moses by God—the rituals and equipment of sacrifice, the tabernacle and so forth—provided a point of constant interaction *in* the visible world between the invisible God and the people he had selected to reconcile the world to himself. There was to be a continual sacrifice, morning and evening, at the door of the tent for meeting between God and the Israelites, "where I will meet with you, to speak to you there" (Ex 29:42). This is the form in which God chose to "dwell among the children of Israel, and . . . be their God" (Ex 29:45).

This speaking was not metaphorical, as the biblical records clearly indicate. There was an audible voice, usually with no visible presence. Although still physical in the manner of sounds, it was a step away from the visible toward the unseen and spiritual world (Deut 4:10-14). As for Moses himself, when he "went into the tent of meeting to speak with the LORD, he would hear the voice speaking to him from above the mercy seat that was on the ark of the covenant from between the two cherubim; thus it spoke to him" (Num 7:89).

We have seen that the audible voice unaccompanied by visible presence continued well into the events of the New Testament. No doubt it can occur today as well, since God is still "alive and well on planet Earth." But the tendency of life in Christ is progressively toward the inward word to the receptive heart The aim is to move entirely into the hidden realm of spiritual reality, where God desires to be worshiped (Jn 4:24).

God's audible voice that comes from heaven also came in the presence of Jesus. But as he himself explained on one occasion where an audible voice came from heaven, "This voice has come for your sake, not for mine" (Jn 12:30). Jesus constantly presses us toward a life with our "Father who is in secret" (Mt 6:6), toward an eternal kind of life in the invisible and incorruptible realm of God.

After his resurrection Jesus appeared to his disciples in visible form only on a very few occasions over a period of forty days. His main task as their teacher during these days was to accustom them to hearing him without seeing him. Thus it was "through the Holy Spirit" that he gave instructions to his apostles during this period (Acts 1:2). He made himself visible to them just enough to give them confidence that it *was* he who was speaking in their hearts. This prepared them to continue their conversation with him after he no longer appeared to them visibly.

An instructive scene from these very important days of teaching is preserved in the last chapter of Luke's Gospel. Two of Jesus' heartbroken students were walking to Emmaus, a village about seven miles northwest of Jerusalem. He caught up with them in a visible form that they did not recognize, and he heard their sad story about what had happened to Jesus of Nazareth and about how, it seemed, all hope was now lost.

He responded by taking them through the Scriptures and showing them that what had happened to their Jesus was exactly what was to befall the Messiah that Israel hoped for. Then as they sat at supper with him, suddenly "their eyes were opened, and they recognized him; and he vanished from their sight" (Lk 24:31). But their recognition was much more than a visual recognition, and *that* was the whole point. They asked one another, "Were not our hearts burning within us while he was talking to us on the road, while he was opening the scriptures to us?" (Lk 24:32).

What were they saying to one another? They were recalling that his words had always affected their heart, their inward life, in a peculiar way. That had been going on for about three years, and no one else had that effect on them. So they were asking themselves, "Why did we not recognize him from the way his words were impacting us?" The familiar "Jesus heartburn" had no doubt been a subject of discussion among the disciples on many occasions.

Soon he would meet with them one final time as a visible presence. There in the beauty and silence of the Galilean mountains, he would explain to them that he had been given authority over everything in heaven and on the earth. Because of that they were now to go to every kind of people on earth and make them his students, to surround them with the reality of the Father, Son and Holy Spirit and to teach them how to do all the things he had commanded.

You can well imagine the small degree of enthusiasm with which these poor fellows rose to greet the assignment. But his final words to them were simply, "Look, I am with you every minute, until the job is done" (Mt 28:20, paraphrase). He is with us now, and he speaks with us and we with him. He speaks with us in our heart, which burns from the characteristic impact of his word. His presence with us is, of course, much greater than his words to us. But it is turned into *companionship* only by the actual *communications* we have between us and him, communications that are frequently confirmed by external events as life moves along.

This companionship with Jesus is the form that Christian spirituality, as practiced through the ages, takes. Spiritual people are not those who engage in certain spiritual practices; they are those who *draw their life from a conversational relationship with God.* They do not live their lives merely in terms of the human order in the visible world; they have "a life beyond."

Today, as God's trusting apprentices in the kingdom of the heavens, we live on the Emmaus road, so to speak, with an intermittently burning heart. His word pours into our heart, energizing and directing our life in a way that cannot be accounted for in natural terms. The presence of the physical world is, then, if I will have it so, no longer a *barrier* between me and God. My visible surroundings become, instead, God's gift to me, where I am privileged to see the rule of heaven realized through my friendship with Jesus. He makes it so in response to my expectation. There, in some joyous measure, creation is seen moving toward "the glorious liberty of the children of God"—all because my life counts for eternity as *I* live and walk with God.

Now is the shining fabric of our day
Torn open, flung apart, rent wide by love.
Never again the tight, enclosing sky,
The blue bowl or the star-illumined tent.
We are laid open to infinity,
For Easter love has burst His tomb and ours.
Now *nothing* shelters us from *God's desire*—
Not flesh, not sky, not stars, not even sin.
Now glory waits so He can enter in.
Now does the dance begin.[3]

Notes

Chapter 1: A Paradox About Hearing God

[1]John Calvin *Institutes of the Christian Religion* 1.7; and chapter five of William Law, *The Power of the Spirit,* ed. Dave Hunt (Fort Washington, Penn.: Christian Literature Crusade, 1971).

[2]George Fox, *The Journal of George Fox* (London: J. M. Dent & Sons, 1948), pp. 8-9.

[3]Wilhelm Hermann, *The Communion of the Christian with God,* 3d English ed. (London: Williams & Norgate, 1909), p. 14.

[4]John Baillie, *Our Knowledge of God* (New York: Charles Scribner's Sons, 1959), p. 132.

[5]C. Austin Miles, "In the Garden," hymn chorus.

[6]J. A. Sargent, "Astrology's Rising Star," *Christianity Today*, February 4, 1983, pp. 37-39.

[7]Russ Johnston, *How to Know the Will of God* (Colorado Springs: NavPress, 1971), p. 5.

[8]Frederick B. Meyer, *The Secret of Guidance* (Chicago: Moody Press, 1997), p. 12.

[9]E. Stanley Jones, "For Sunday of Week 41," *Victorious Living* (Nashville: Abingdon, 1938), p. 281.

Chapter 2: Guidelines for Hearing from God

[1]The Council of Chalcedon (A.D. 451) makes this use of the idea of virgin birth: "That Christ was really divine and really human; in his divinity co-eternal, and in all points similar to the Father; in his humanity, son of the Virgin Mary, *born like all others,* and like unto us men in all things except sin." From "Monophysites," in *Cyclopaedia of Biblical, Theological and Ecclesiastical Literature,* ed. McClintock and Strong (New York: Harper & Row, 1894), p. 509 (emphasis added).

[2]A. W. Tozer, *The Root of the Righteous* (Harrisburg, Penn.: Christian Publications, 1955), p. 34.

[3]A. T. Pierson, *George Mueller of Bristol and His Witness to a Prayer-Hearing God* (New York: Baker & Taylor, 1899), pp. 185-86.

Chapter 3: Never Alone

[1]"Never Alone," in *The Broadman Hymnal* (Nashville: Broadman, 1940).

[2]Hymn no. 315 in *The Hymnal* (Oxford: Oxford University Press, 1889).

[3]Thomas à Kempis, *The Imitation of Christ* (Chicago: Moody Press, 1958), pp. 106-7. A. W. Tozer sharply states the contemporary need in this connection: "What we need very badly these days is a company of Christians who are prepared to trust God as completely now as they know they must do at the last day. For each of us the time is coming when we shall have nothing but God. Health and wealth and friends and hiding places will be swept away and we shall have only God. To the man of pseudo faith that is a terrifying thought, but to real faith it is one of the most comforting thoughts the heart can entertain." From A. W. Tozer, *The Root of the Righteous* (Harrisburg, Penn.: Christian Publications, 1955), p. 54.

[4]Augustine *The City of God* 22.30.

[5]Westminster Shorter Catechism, first paragraph.

[6]A. P. Fitt, *The Shorter Life of D. L. Moody* (Chicago: Moody Press, 1900), p. 67.

[7]Ibid., p. 76.

[8]Brother Lawrence, *The Practice of the Presence of God* (Old Tappan, N.J.: Revell, 1958), pp. 37-38.

[9]Leslie Weatherhead, *The Transforming Friendship* (London: Epworth, 1962), pp. 155ff.

[10]An excellent supplementary discussion to the above is found in Jeremy Taylor, "General Manners of the Divine Presence," *The Rule and Exercise of Holy Living* (n.p., 1650), sec. 3, chap. 1.

[11]E. Stanley Jones, *A Song of Ascents* (Nashville: Abingdon, 1979), p. 191.

Chapter 4: Our Communicating Cosmos

[1]Catherine Marshall, *A Man Called Peter* (New York: Fawcett, 1962), p. 24.

[2]David Pytches, *Does God Speak Today?* (Minneapolis: Bethany House, 1989).

[3]Agnes Sanford, *Sealed Orders* (Plainfield, N.J.: Logos International, 1972), p. 98.

[4]E. Stanley Jones, *A Song of Ascents* (Nashville: Abingdon, 1979), p. 188.

[5]G. Campbell Morgan, *How to Live* (Chicago: Moody Press, n.d.), p. 78.

[6]Frank Laubach, *Letters by a Modern Mystic* (Syracuse, N.Y.: New Reader's Press, 1955), p. 14.

[7]Alfred, Lord Tennyson, "In Memoriam A. H. H.," 1850.

[8]Blaise Pascal, *Pensées* (Baltimore: Penguin, 1966), p. 88.

[9]A. H. Strong, *Christ in Creation* (Philadelphia: Griffith & Rowland, 1899), p. 3.

[10]James Jean, *The Mysterious Universe* (New York: E. P. Dutton, 1932), p. 27.

[11]Michael Talbot, *Mysticism and the New Physics* (New York: Bantam, 1981), from the introduction and chap. 1.

[12]William Temple, "The Divinity of Christ," in *Foundations*, ed. B. H. Streeter (London: Macmillan, 1920), pp. 258-59.

[13]For elaboration of this point please see chapter three of Dallas Willard, *The Divine Conspiracy* (San Francisco: HarperSanFrancisco, 1998).

[14]Francis Thompson, "The Kingdom of Heaven, God," 1913.

[15]Henri Nouwen, *Creative Ministry* (Garden City, N.Y.: Doubleday, 1978), pp. 12-13.

[16]David Otis Fuller, ed., *Spurgeon's Lectures to His Students* (Grand Rapids, Mich.: Zondervan, 1945), p. 187.

[17]St. Francis de Sales, *Introduction to the Devout Life*, trans. John K. Ryan (Garden City, N.Y.: Doubleday, 1957), p. 106.

[18]Ibid.

[19]Joyce Huggett, *Listening to God* (London: Hodder & Stoughton, 1986), p. 141.

[20]G. Wade Robinson, "Loved with Everlasting Love."

Chapter 5: The Still Small Voice & Its Rivals

[1]Letter number 117-2 in *Guideposts* (December 1982).

[2]Ibid.

[3]See the preface of Mortimer J. Adler, *The Angels and Us* (New York: Macmillan, 1982). See also Billy Graham, *Angels: God's Secret Agents*, rev. ed. (Waco, Tex.: Word, 1986) and A. C. Gaebelein, *What the Bible Says About Angels* (Grand Rapids, Mich.: Baker, 1987).

[4]Gustave Oehler, *Theology of the Old Testament* (Grand Rapids, Mich.: Zondervan, n.d.), p. 143.

[5]Ibid.

[6]Today we unfortunately do not have on hand an adequate, common vocabulary to discuss the movements of God within and upon the soul. We are now without a psychology of the spiritual life. Distinctions in the individual's experience of God that were once widely understood and used are now either unknown or wholly the object of scholarly curiosity. On vital distinctions to be drawn in experiences of voices and visions, Teresa of Ávila, for example, has this to say: "Some of them [voices] seem to come from without; others from the innermost depths of the soul; others from its higher part; while others, again, are so completely outside the soul that they can be heard with the ears, and seem to be uttered by a human voice." From chapter three of the Sixth Mansion in Teresa of Ávila, *The Interior Castle* (many editions). See also the remarkably analytical and sane discussion in Evelyn Underhill, "Voices and Visions," in *Mysticism,* 12th ed. (New York: New American Library, 1974).

[7]Samuel Shoemaker, *With the Holy Spirit and with Fire* (New York: Harper & Row, 1960), p. 27.

[8]Russ Johnston, *How to Know the Will of God* (Colorado Springs: NavPress, 1971), p. 13.

[9]Thomas Goodwin, *The Vanity of Thoughts and Let Patience Have Its Perfect Way* (Wilmington, Del.: Classic-a-Month Books, 1964), p. 4.

[10]Rosalind Rinker, *Prayer: Conversing with God* (Grand Rapids, Mich.: Zondervan, 1959), p. 17 (italics added).

[11]Ibid., p. 19.

[12]Leona Choy, *Andrew Murray: Apostle of Abiding Love* (Fort Washington, Penn.: Christian Literature Crusade, 1978), pp. 152ff.

[13]Ibid.

[14]Charles H. Spurgeon, *Morning by Morning* (London: Passmore & Alabaster, 1865), p. 191.

[15]E. Stanley Jones, *The Way* (Nashville: Abingdon/Cokesbury, 1946), p. 283.

[16]Bob Mumford, *Take Another Look at Guidance: A Study of How God Guides* (Plainfield, N.J.: Logos International, 1971), pp. 140-41.

[17]Ibid.

[18]Frances Ridley Havergal, sonnet.

Chapter 6: The Word of God & the Rule of God

[1]Plato *Theaetetus,* p. 190 (Stephanus edition).

[2]Augustine *On the Trinity* 4.10.

[3]William Penn, *The Peace of Europe, Etc.* (London: J. M. Dent, n.d.), p. 65.

[4]Mary W. Calkins, ed., *Berkeley: Essay, Principles and Dialogues with Selections from Other Writings* (New York: Charles Scribner's Sons, 1929), p. 370.

[5]Ibid., p. 373.

[6]David Otis Fuller, ed., *Spurgeon's Lectures to His Students* (Grand Rapids, Mich.: Zondervan, 1945), p. 182.

[7]Martin Buber, *I and Thou,* trans. Ronald G. Smith (New York: Collier, 1958), p. 83.

[8]Consider on this point the studies of physiologist Walter Cannon, referred to in *Psychology Today,* June 1983, 71-72.

[9]Mary Ann Lathbury, "Break Thou the Bread of Life," hymn, st. 1.

[10]Ibid., v. 3.

[11]Washington Gladden, "The Holy Scriptures."

Chapter 7: Redemption Through the Word of God

[1]Hannah Hurnard, *God's Transmitters* (Wheaton, Ill.: Tyndale House, 1981), p. 12.

[2]David Otis Fuller, ed., *Spurgeon's Lectures to His Students* (Grand Rapids, Mich.: Zondervan, 1945), p. 172.

[3]James S. Stewart, *A Man in Christ* (London: Hodder & Stoughton, 1935), pp. 192ff.

[4]Ibid., p. 193.

[5]William Law, *The Power of the Spirit,* ed. Dave Hunt (Fort Washington, Penn.: Christian Literature Crusade, 1971), p. 62.

[6]Thomas à Kempis, *The Imitation of Christ,* trans. Leo Shirley-Price (London: Penguin, 1952), p. 27.

[7]Madame Guyon, *Experiencing the Depth of Jesus Christ* (Goleta, Calif.: Christian Books, 1975), p. 16.

[8]On the *lectio divina* see, for example, Thomas Keating, *Intimacy with God* (New York: Crossroad, 1994).

[9]For an introduction to disciplines for the spiritual life, see especially Richard Foster, *Celebration of Discipline: The Path to Spiritual Growth* (San Francisco: HarperCollins, 1998).

Chapter 8: Recognizing the Voice of God

[1]It is possible to understand the teaching of the sufficiency of the anointing in various ways, but no biblical Christian can deny it. Since the flood tide of European mysticism in the thirteenth and fourteenth centuries (for a good introduction see Jeanne Ancelet-Hustache, *Master Eckhart and the Rhineland Mystics* [New York: Harper/Torchbooks, n.d.]), this teaching has been nowhere more strongly defended than by the Quakers or Friends; their best presentation is in propositions 1, 2 and 3 of Robert Barclay, *An Apology for the True Christian Divinity* (many editions).

I believe that on the whole a more correct view of the relationship between the Bible and the anointing is given by William Law, John Wesley and Andrew Murray. See Law, *The Power of the Spirit,* ed. Dave Hunt (Fort Washington, Penn.: Christian Literature Crusade, 1971); Law, *Serious Call to a Devout and Holy Life* (many editions); Murray, *The Spirit of Christ* (London: James Nisbet, 1899); John Wesley, "The Witness of the Spirit," in *Sermons on Several Occasions* (New York: Waugh & Mason, 1836), 1:91-92; and Wesley's various discourses on the Spirit

[2]Frederick B. Meyer, *The Secret of Guidance* (Chicago: Moody Press, 1997).

[3]In addition to ibid., see also chapter seven of Bob Mumford, *Take Another Look at Guidance: A Study of How God Guides* (Plainfield, N.J.: Logos International, 1971); and G. Campbell Morgan, *God's Perfect Will* (Grand Rapids, Mich.: Baker, 1978), pp. 155ff.

[4]Meyer, *Secret of Guidance,* p. 18.

[5]Beth Spring, "What the Bible Means," *Christianity Today,* December 17, 1982, pp. 45-48.

[6]Law, *Power of the Spirit,* p. 61.

[7]Professor Don Ihde of the State University of New York has published a very helpful guide to a deeper examination of the phenomenon of voice in Don Ihde, *Listening and Voice* (Athens, Ohio: Ohio University Press, 1976).

[8]E. Stanley Jones, *A Song of Ascents* (Nashville: Abingdon, 1979), p. 190.

[9]Wesley 'Witness of the Spirit," pp. 91-92.

[10]Adele Rogers St. John, *Guideposts,* December 1968, p. 8.

[11]Mumford, *Take Another Look,* pp. 85-86.

[12]Charles Stanley, *How to Listen to God* (Nashville: Thomas Nelson, 1985), p. 51.

[13]J. Edwin Orr, "What Made the Welsh Revival 'Extraordinary,' " *The Forerunner* 2, no. 8 (n.d.): 11.

[14]Isaac Watts, "Am I a Soldier of the Cross?"

[15]Meyer, *Secret of Guidance*, p. 31.

[16]John Bunyan, *Grace Abounding to the Chief of Sinners* (Grand Rapids, Mich.: Baker, 1981), pp. 46-47.

[17]I recommend reading Stanley, *How to Listen*, chaps. 1 and 2, with this section.

[18]The communal side of discerning God's voice is not studied in this book. See Richard Foster, *Celebration of Discipline: The Path to Spiritual Growth* (San Francisco: HarperCollins, 1998), pp. 150-62; see also section two of Danny E. Morris, *Yearning to Know God's Will* (Grand Rapids, Mich.: Zondervan, 1991). In general the same features that characterize the individual's process of hearing God apply also to the process individuals use in groups, but there is a greater certainty of the message when a spiritually qualified group is involved. Group guidance is deadly, however, when the group is dominated by legalism, ignorance or superstition.

Chapter 9: A Life More Than Guidance

[1]G. Campbell Morgan, *How to Live* (Chicago: Moody Press, n.d.), p. 76.

[2]James Dobson, "The Will of God," radio broadcast (December 3, 1982). See also the excellent chapter "Interpretations of Impressions" in Dobson, *Emotions: Can You Trust Them?* (Ventura, Calif.: Regal, 1981).

[3]Frederick B. Meyer, *The Secret of Guidance* (Chicago: Moody Press, 1997), p. 43.

[4]John Wood Oman, *Grace and Personality* (Cambridge: Cambridge University Press, 1931).

[5]W. R. Sorley, *The Moral Life* (Cambridge: Cambridge University Press, 1911), p. 138.

[6]Garry Friesen, *Decision Making and the Will of God* (Portland, Ore.: Multnomah Press, 1980), p. 145.

[7]Brother Lawrence, *The Practice of the Presence of God* (Old Tappan, N.J.: Revell, 1958), p. 51.

[8]A. T. Pierson, *George Mueller of Bristol* (New York: Baker & Taylor, 1899), p. 196.

[9]John Boykin, "Rethinking the Will of God," *The Door*, May-June 1992, p. 13.

[10]John Wesley, *Selections from the Writings of Reverend John Wesley,* ed. Herbert Welch (New York: Eaton & Mains, 1901), p. 138.

Epilogue

[1]Henry Churchill King, *The Seeming Unreality of the Spiritual Life* (New York: Macmillan, 1908).

[2]You will be tremendously strengthened in your understanding of this situation by a study of P. A. Sorokin, *The Crisis of Our Age* (New York, E. P. Dutton, 1941). See also my book *The Divine Conspiracy* (San Francisco: HarperSanFrancisco, 1998).

[3]Elizabeth Rooney, "The Opening." I have been unable to find a bibliographic reference for this poem or locate the author.